ENDORSEMENTS

The book *Total Turnaround* by Pastor Danette Crawford was a joy to read. I found the book to be down to earth, practical, and insightful. We all go through seasons when life can seem difficult to handle and this book reveals ways we can turn around situations for the better at any time. These twelve keys cover every aspect of our lives and reveal the biblical foundation for how we can achieve all that God intends in our lives. I would recommend *Total Turnaround* for anyone at any time in his or her daily walk.

PETE SUMRALL
President and CEO, LeSea Broadcasting (WHT)

Pastor Danette is a unique peg in the wheel of modern-day revival! Her anointing, charisma, and total comfort in front of a crowd or television camera have made her one of the most in-demand prophetic voices of our day. She thrills audiences with her grace, fun, and transparent, absolute love for JESUS! One minute you are laughing, and the next minute you are crying at the revelation she has brought you. Few ministers have that sincerity and gifting! The words of this book will release a total turnaround in you, if you listen! Thank you, Pastor Danette...I'm waiting for the next one already!

REV. DR. DAN WILLIS
Senior Pastor, Lighthouse Church of All Nations, Chicago, Illinois
Emmy-Nominated Television Host, "I'm Just Sayin," TCT Network

Pastor Danette Crawford's *Total Turnaround* will help you understand how much you need a turnaround in so many areas of your life, and you will find, as you make one turn, another turn pops up. This is a real-life scriptural and spiritual commentary that you will want to keep in your library for personal checkups and for ministry to others.

Robert D'Andrea
President and Founder, Christian Television Network (CTN)

I am a living witness that, through Jesus, true transformation is possible. *Total Turnaround* is a power-packed guide to transforming your life into one of purpose and fulfillment. If you are wondering how to go to the next level in God, here is a step-by-step guide. This book will empower you and encourage your faith. I urge you to read it and then take action!

WESS MORGAN
Recording Artist, Associate Pastor and Senior Worship Leader at Celebration of Life Church, Nashville, Tennessee

I've had the opportunity to interview Danette on my television show and have been impressed with her deep spiritual insights. It's obvious that God has blessed her with special ministry gifts. There is a time in all our lives when we need to reevaluate and make changes that help us have a more satisfying and productive spiritual life. *Total Turnaround* is an excellent guidebook to help us through that process and get us through to a better place.

JERRY ROSE
President and CEO, Total Living Network (TLN)

Regardless of all the rocky roads you've traveled, the detours you've taken, the dead ends you've encountered, or the wrecks you've made of your life, Danette Joy Crawford reveals the truth that God is always faithful to provide a turn-around for the way out! Encouraging, faith-building, and packed with truth from God's Word, *Total Turnaround* will bless your life.

BABBIE MASON
Award-winning Singer, Songwriter, Author, and TV Talk Show Host

This book provides not only encouragement and hope that change and victory are possible, but it also gives practical advice and spiritual wisdom to guide the reader toward transformation. I love this book because it addresses key areas such as health, finances, and especially the critical issue of self-image. The points for reflection at the end of each chapter make it easy to apply the teachings to practical life situations. Thanks, Danette, for your passion for God and your desire to help others. This book reflects both.

SHIRLEY ROSE
Author, Speaker, Host of "Aspiring Women" Television Program

What a timely book for the body of Christ! Not only does this book give a broad perspective of biblical and personal truths gained during the process of a turnaround, but it also provides the reader with a much needed expectation for breakthrough.

Using Danette's advice of silencing our buts, what ifs, doubts, rejections, and deceptions with focused thoughts of peace, joy, trust, expectation, and forgiveness, is only one of the revealed Master's keys to unlocking any turnaround in your life.

With the combined wisdom of scriptural referencing, personal experiences, and a heart to supply encouragement to the body of Christ, *Total Turnaround* is destined to be another success.

For those who have read Danette's other books, *Don't Quit in the Pit, Pathway to the Palace* and *God, You've Got Mail*, this newest help manual to overcoming is a winner.

REVEREND H. WADE TRUMP III
Jamestown Christian Fellowship
Williamsburg, Virginia

Yet again, Danette has astounded and enlightened us with more great biblical wisdom. The twelve keys are totally explained with many interesting examples. Follow her recommendations and turnaround is inevitable.

WILLIAM F. COX, JR. PH.D.
Professor and Director
School of Education, Regent University

TOTAL
TURNAROUND

DESTINY IMAGE BOOKS BY DANETTE CRAWFORD

God, You've Got Mail

TOTAL
TURNAROUND

*12 Keys to Breakthrough
in Every Area of Your Life*

DANETTE JOY CRAWFORD

DESTINY IMAGE® PUBLISHERS, INC.
P.O. Box 310, Shippensburg, PA 17257-0310

"Promoting Inspired Lives."

This book and all other Destiny Image, Revival Press, MercyPlace, Fresh Bread, Destiny Image Fiction, and Treasure House books are available at Christian bookstores and distributors worldwide.

For a U.S. bookstore nearest you, call 1-800-722-6774.
For more information on foreign distributors, call 717-532-3040.
Reach us on the Internet: www.destinyimage.com.

ISBN 13 TP: 978-0-7684-0408-1
ISBN 13 Ebook: 978-0-7684-0409-8

For Worldwide Distribution, Printed in the U.S.A.

1 2 3 4 5 6 7 8 / 18 17 16 15 14

DEDICATION

This book is dedicated to my brother, David. Thank you, David, for being an awesome "big brother." Your heart and life really gave new definition to that term. I will always love you and cherish the years that the Lord allowed you to be in my life. I know that you experienced the ultimate "total turnaround" the moment you entered heaven. I look forward to seeing you again one day when my work for the Lord on this earth is complete.

ACKNOWLEDGMENTS

First and foremost, I want to thank the Lord for His unfailing, unconditional love for me. Thank You, Lord, for saving my soul and allowing me the awesome privilege of ministering to Your people.

To my daughter, Destiny—thank you for filling my life with such joy. I can always count on you to keep me laughing, to keep me running, and to keep me "styling."

To my family and friends—thank you for believing in me and for encouraging me along the way as I seek to fulfill God's calling on my life and as I walk in obedience to write every book the Lord has put in me.

To the most awesome staff and intercessors anyone could ever have— the Joy Ministries team—thank you for standing with me through prayer, long hours of work, and mountain-moving faith. Thank you for your passion for the Lord, your desire to see souls saved, and your heart to see lives changed. We truly are a team, and without you Joy Ministries would not be what it is today. Krystle, thank you for paying the price, no matter how high the cost, to assist me in all that God has called me to do.

To my most precious partners—without your generous gifts of time, prayer, and financial support, Joy Ministries could not do everything it is doing today. Thank you! Together, we are transforming lives, healing hearts, and winning souls.

To my amazing editors—you are the best! I'm blessed to have editors and proofreaders who flow with me in the Holy Spirit and don't take away from the message God has put in me to get out through print.

Finally, to Ronda and the entire team at Destiny Image—thank you for your heart to minister to people through printed material. Thank you for believing in me and for being such a great team to work with. I'm excited to partner together to change lives!

CONTENTS

FOREWORD

I am honored that my friend, Danette Crawford, asked me, a Christian singer and evangelist, to write the Foreword to this powerful book. Danette is an anointed minister, a well-rounded Christian, and a dedicated mother to her daughter, Destiny. She writes from her heart with passion and from personal experience. Her books are a compilation of who she is in Christ and a reflection of what God has called her to teach and preach.

Danette has a superior gift to hear and discern the Spirit of the Lord. I have been blessed to be the beneficiary of this gift. I was invited a few years ago to do a concert at one of Danette's ministry events. After the event, I sat at Danette's kitchen table where she prophesied that I would go back on tour and she saw my career expanding. Shortly thereafter I was diagnosed with multiple myeloma cancer. This challenge suppressed my vision for Danette's prophetic words. I thank God that circumstances did not cause her to doubt. With her support and prayers, I am making a total turnaround in my life. The tour she saw in the Spirit manifested in the natural.

Danette may not be there in person to prophesy over your life. However, her same anointing, encouragement, and instruction is found in this book. Let it be your guide. The message in *Total Turnaround* is that God is no respecter of persons when it comes to giving you the triumph over life's obstacles. You are not alone or helpless. There is hope for you and me. This book is your blueprint for change and total victory! If you are at a crossroads in your life, struggling with indecision, not sure what can be done to change your circumstances; if you are discouraged or feel helpless, you must read *Total Turnaround*. Change is just a chapter away.

CARMAN LICCIARDELLO

IT'S TURNAROUND TIME!

Jonah was running away (sailing, actually) from a missionary assignment when he was caught in a storm, tossed overboard, swallowed by a fish, and convicted of his cowardice. He went on to obey the Lord's instructions and preached to the people of Nineveh, who repented of their waywardness and averted God's vengeance. His spiritual life, and the spiritual life of the Ninevites, underwent a total turnaround!

Ruth was a young widow gleaning barley in the fields in order to provide for her mother-in-law, Naomi, when her wealthy kinsman Boaz took note of her devotion, showered her with favor, and made her his wife, so that she wanted for nothing. Her financial situation underwent a total turnaround!

Esther was a humble young woman who joined the king's harem and ended up replacing the reigning queen because of her all-around beauty, inside and out. Her circumstances underwent a total turnaround!

Bartimaeus was a blind beggar who believed that Jesus would heal his condition—and He did. His health underwent a total turnaround!

Paul, back when he was still answering to "Saul," was on his way to Damascus to arrest as many Christians as he could when the Lord showed up in a blinding light (literally; Paul couldn't see for three days), knocked

Paul to the ground, and spoke to him in such a way that he was converted immediately. His mind-set underwent a total turnaround!

From that day forward, Paul devoted all of his effort and energy—and, later, gave his very life—to convert as many people as he could to the very faith he'd spent years fighting to uproot. Talk about a dramatic turnaround! The most vocal detractor of Jesus Christ became His most passionate advocate. He traveled extensively, preaching the Word with boldness and bringing multitudes into the fold of faith. And he authored the bulk of the New Testament—timeless teachings that attract and instruct believers today. Thus, a turnaround in the life of one man produced countless turnarounds in the lives of people all around the world.

If you think about it, *turnaround* is really the theme of the whole Bible. It tells the story of God bringing turnaround in the lives of individual characters—such as Jonah, Ruth, Esther, and Elijah—and the bigger story of the turnaround He wrought for humanity, making it possible for us to be forgiven, justified, and free from sin, in order to enjoy an eternity with Him in heaven. Jesus underwent the biggest turnaround of all—dying and then resurrecting to reign forevermore—and, because of His turnaround, we can count on ours as well. He brings turnaround from slavery to sin to salvation in Christ; turnaround from an eternal destination of hell to one in heaven; turnaround from loss and defeat to prosperity and victory.

Sadly, there are lots of people struggling to see the same turnaround in their lives that these Bible characters experienced. Too many Christians are suffering and stuck in a place of lack, defeat, discouragement, and disease. If you're among them, I have great news—it's turnaround time!

When God works a turnaround in your life, He does so in order that you might, in turn, work turnaround in the lives of those around you: in your family, your neighborhood, your community, your city, your nation, and the entire world. So, buckle your seat belt—God's about to turn this car around and set you on the fast track to blessings. But you'd better be prepared to make a lot of stops along the way, so that you can "unload" those blessings into the lives of others.

In which area of your life do you need total turnaround? You can probably name more than just one area. Your obedience to simply do whatever the Lord tells you to do is an important key to your turnaround.

You have the key to your turnaround—it's in your possession. And, by reading this book, you are well on your way to your God-ordained destiny. Expect your turnaround today!

Chapter 1

TRUTHS ABOUT TOTAL TURNAROUND

God is the God of total turnaround! When He turns a situation around or changes your circumstances, He does a complete job—180 degrees, if necessary. When God does something, He does it right—He always does an A-plus job. God doesn't do shabby work. But there are some principles that apply, regardless of the type of turnaround you're awaiting. Once you get these truths established in your mind, you'll have a better idea of what to expect when you're expecting a total turnaround, whether it's in the area of your relationships, your health, your finances, or another area.

TURNAROUND OPERATES ON GOD'S TIMETABLE

The Lord wants to totally turn your situation and circumstances around, but you shouldn't be surprised if His timetable doesn't correspond with your preferred schedule. Sometimes the turnaround that you wish would take only days requires years instead. Always remember, God's timing is perfect! Before your situational turnaround is manifested in the natural realm, God works in your heart, your attitude, your faith, and the overall development of your Christian character. His priority is to prompt transformation in those areas before—and as a prerequisite of—the turnaround you're awaiting. Your heavenly Father loves you so much that He's more concerned about turning your character around than He is about turning your situation around.

It's all part of the divine setups He plans for our lives. The truth is, God could turn your situation around overnight, but sometimes it's more important for you to undergo a turnaround in your character, your faith, or your heart attitude. And those types of turnarounds never happen instantaneously. It's a process.

The book of Exodus tells how God heard the cries of the children of Israel while they were enslaved in Egypt, and He turned their situation around. But it didn't happen overnight. He delivered the children of Israel, brought them out of their bondage, and led them into their Promised Land, but He didn't take them there by the shortest route. That's because He knew that the shortest route was not the best route for them—and God always has our best interests in mind. He knew that if the Israelites traveled the shortest, quickest route—if they fast-tracked their way to the Promised Land—they would have missed some crucial steps in character development. Plus, they might have faced battles that would have over-whelmed them to the point of discouragement and defeat. They might have turned around and retreated right back into the bondage they had been delivered from in the first place.

We are great at detecting when a turnaround is needed in our situations and circumstances, but we are not quite so skilled at determining the route and process by which that turnaround should come.

DON'T DISCOUNT YOUR SAY IN THE SCHEDULE

When the time comes that God has ordained for total turnaround to take place, He brings it to pass, regardless of what anyone else may think, want, or try to do to oppose it. In the case of the Israelites, Pharaoh wasn't very smart; time and again, he tried to stand in the way of the omnipotent, all-powerful God, who declared that it was turnaround time! When God says it's time for your turnaround, no person, no circumstance, no demon in hell—nothing—can stop it!

God sent plague after plague upon the Egyptians, from frogs to gnats to flies to worse, in order to compel Pharaoh to let His people go. If Pharaoh had been smart, he would have gotten with the program during the first plague. But he assumed—mistakenly—that he could prevent the turnaround God had declared. Pharaoh even chose to keep the plague upon his people for longer than was necessary. Then, as he became disgusted with the situation posed by the various plagues, he would consent to let the Israelites go, only to change his mind and renege on his decision.

For example, during the first plague, when the land was covered with frogs, we read:

> *Moses said to Pharaoh, "I leave to you the honor of setting the time for me to pray for you and your officials and your people that you and your houses may be rid of the frogs, except for those that remain in the Nile." "Tomorrow," Pharaoh said. Moses replied, "It will be as you say, so that you may know there is no one like the Lord our God." (Exodus 8:9-10)*

Pharaoh was given the honor of setting the time, but he chose to spend one more night with the frogs—how stupid can a person get? In many cases, we are given the choice to set the time for our turnaround, but we make poor choices that only prolong the plague on our lives! Never choose to spend another night with the bondage or the plague that is upon you. Choose deliverance, as quickly as possible!

Although God is the one who ultimately schedules our turnaround, the choices we make, for good or for ill, often come to bear on the time-table. When we walk in obedience and make the right decisions, we often expedite the process. It's our choice—will we make a decision to bring about immediate turnaround, or will we spend another night with the frogs? To me, it's a no-brainer!

Don't live with the plague longer than you have to. Make today the day of turnaround!

UNDERSTAND THAT GOD'S TIMING IS PERFECT

Long before the Israelites were taken into captivity in Egypt, God had said to their ancestor Abraham,

> ...*Know for certain that your descendants will be strangers in a country not their own, and they will be enslaved and mistreated four hundred years. But I will punish the nation they serve as slaves, and afterward they will come out with great possessions....In the fourth generation your descendants will come back here, for the sin of the Amorites has not yet reached its full measure.* (Genesis 15:13-14, 16)

Wouldn't you know it, *"The length of time the Israelite people lived in Egypt was 430 years. At the end of 430 years, to the very day, all the Lord's divisions left Egypt"* (Exodus 12:40-41). You can't tell me that this wasn't planned. God knew the day—the very hour—from the beginning of time! When it was God's time, to the very day, the children of Israel received their total turnaround!

While you're waiting for your turnaround, don't ever doubt that God's timing for your miracle is anything less than perfect! God can do whatever He wants, whenever He wants, and there are always plenty of reasons for His timing that are way above the ability of our natural minds to comprehend. *"For my thoughts are not your thoughts, neither are your ways my ways,' declares the Lord. 'As the heavens are higher than the earth, so are my ways higher than your ways and my thoughts than your thoughts'"* (Isaiah 55:8-9).

You might think that God should have brought your turnaround ten years ago. You might have thought that God would bring about your miracle a completely different way than He did. Well, join the club! None of us can figure God out, but I have learned to enjoy the journey while trusting that my heavenly Daddy has got me covered! I've learned the hard way that

I can't make God move even one minute before the time He has appointed to do so. I've also learned that if everything went according to my "perfect" plan, I'd probably spend night after night with the frogs because of my own poor choices and misguided decisions. So, as for me, I'm getting rid of all frogs as soon as possible—and I'm leaning on God's understanding, not mine. He alone will decide the day and details of its execution!

DON'T DESPAIR WHEN YOUR TURNAROUND TARRIES

During that long period, the king of Egypt died. The Israel-ites groaned in their slavery and cried out, and their cry for help because of their slavery went up to God. God heard their groaning and he remembered his covenant with Abraham, with Isaac and with Jacob. So God looked on the Israelites and was concerned about them. (Exodus 2:23-25)

The children of Israel cried out to God in the midst of their desperate situation. They were in the bondage of slavery in Egypt, and they needed the hand of God to move on their behalf. It was their cries to God that got the ball rolling. If you are caught in a challenging situation today, don't cry out to this person or that person; cry out to God in prayer! He is the only one who can truly turn your entire situation around. And He loves you so much that He wants to turn your situation around even more than you want Him to.

God hears your cry, and He is concerned about you. Just because things don't turn around overnight doesn't mean that He hasn't heard your prayers, nor does it mean that He is not concerned about you. God does His best work behind the scenes, during the "night seasons" of our lives.

We will talk about these "night seasons" in greater depth before long. For now, just know that God is working behind the scenes on your behalf. But, since He is working "total" turnaround, it doesn't happen overnight. He loves you and cares about you so much that He is going to turn it around, not just partially, but totally! Remember, God is the miracle

Maker! He's skilled at turning things around for His children, and He has a proven track record, to boot. Your own miraculous turnaround is nothing for Him. So, be patient while you wait with expectation for your total turnaround!

TURNAROUND IS PART OF A PROCESS

We don't have to understand or even agree with God's plan and process in order for a turnaround to take place. When we fully comprehend that we don't have to fully comprehend God's ways and plans, we can rest in our trust in the Lord.

Don't Expect to Understand Every Step

The Bible exhorts us: *"Trust in the Lord with all your heart and lean not on your own understanding; in all your ways acknowledge him, and he will make your paths straight"* (Proverbs 3:5-6). God has promised to make your paths straight, but He didn't say that you would always approve of or even understand those paths. When we try to lean on our own understanding, we can get discouraged, frustrated, and prone to quit. But when we acknowledge God as our heavenly Father who loves us unconditionally, who is all-knowing and all-wise, then we can trust that His path is the best route to take, that His plan of action for bringing about total turnaround in our situations is the best!

Moses certainly had reason to doubt God's plans, especially when God told him, *"When you return to Egypt, see that you perform before Pharaoh all the wonders I have given you the power to do. **But I will harden his heart so that he will not let the people go**"* (Exodus 4:21; the emphasis is mine). God told Moses right up front that his path was not going to be without major trials! He never misled Moses by allowing him to believe this was going to be a quick and easy turnaround. We all like quick and easy, but the truth is that "quick and easy" does not always equate to "best." And "quick and easy" often doesn't bring glory to God as much as "slow and hard," when it's guided by the hand of God.

For example, in my experience, if you pay a debt for someone, that person often turns around and falls right back into debt. But, if that person is required to work hard and pay off his or her own debt, taking responsibility for it, then it becomes less likely that he or she will fall into debt again, because of the effort of paying the price to see a turnaround.

I don't know why God brought about the turnaround for the children of Israel the way He did; I only know that He wanted to get all the glory for the situation—and He did! He did a complete work, He brought them total turnaround, and they never went back! That's good enough for me!

Every time Moses doubted, every time the children of Israel doubted, God answered with the same statement: "I am the Lord."

> [God said to Moses,] *"Therefore, say to the Israelites: 'I am the Lord, and I will bring you out from under the yoke of the Egyptians. I will free you from being slaves to them, and I will redeem you with an outstretched arm and with mighty acts of judgment. I will take you as my own people, and I will be your God. Then you will know that I am the Lord your God, who brought you out from under the yoke of the Egyptians. And I will bring you to the land I swore with uplifted hand to give to Abraham, to Isaac and to Jacob. I will give it to you as a possession. I am the Lord.'"* (Exodus 6:6-8)

Every time they said "What if?" God said, "I will!" Every time they said, "But, God," God said, "I am!" Every time you and I speak in doubt and unbelief, God says the same thing: "I am, and I will!"

Trust that God's Got the Details Covered

Moses was the man. Not perfect, not totally excited about it, but he was the man God chose to deliver the children of Israel. God had supernaturally spared Moses' life on multiple occasions (Exodus 1:15–2:15). He'd had His hand on Moses from the very beginning, and He did a total turnaround for Moses as part of His plans to prepare Moses to be the vessel to bring total turnaround in the lives of many, many other people.

God always has a plan—again, it's almost always different from what we imagined it would be!

> *There the angel of the Lord appeared to [Moses] in flames of fire from within a bush. Moses saw that though the bush was on fire it did not burn up. So Moses thought, "I will go over and see this strange sight—why the bush does not burn up." When the Lord saw that he had gone over to look, God called to him from within the bush, "Moses! Moses!" And Moses said, "Here I am." "Do not come any closer," God said. "Take off your sandals, for the place where you are standing is holy ground." Then he said, "I am the God of your father, the God of Abraham, the God of Isaac and the God of Jacob." At this, Moses hid his face, because he was afraid to look at God. The Lord said, "I have indeed seen the misery of my people in Egypt. I have heard them crying out because of their slave drivers, and I am concerned about their suffering. So I have come down to rescue them from the hand of the Egyptians and to bring them up out of that land into a good and spacious land, a land flowing with milk and honey—the home of the Canaanites, Hittites, Amorites, Perizzites, Hivites and Jebusites. And now the cry of the Israelites has reached me, and I have seen the way the Egyptians are oppressing them. So now, go. I am sending you to Pharaoh to bring my people the Israelites out of Egypt."*
> (Exodus 3:2-10)

God had a detailed plan of action, and He had prepared every person, every heart, and every detail. It was a fail-proof plan. It was a blueprint for the total turnaround of the children of Israel and their situation. When God was announcing this plan of action, when God was putting things in place, the children of Israel could not yet see anything different about their situation in the natural realm. But God was at work, bringing about their total turnaround!

In the midst of your cries to the Lord for your turnaround, you must know that God will work everything together for your good as you love and trust in Him (Romans 8:28). In the future, God will use you to bring total turnaround in the lives of many others faced with similar situations. The compassion that the Lord has worked in you through your situation will, in turn, be used as you reach out in compassion to others in the future. This truth brings perspective and purpose to any perceived "delay" in the manifestation of your turnaround.

In the midst of the devastating situations I have experienced—from rejection to divorce to financial hardship and more—I had to trust that God had the details covered! I have a heart for single moms and fatherless children because I know their pain—I've experienced it firsthand, and I have compassion for them. I know the pain of the widow because my former husband died. My ministry, Joy Ministries, organizes over twenty-five different outreaches, many of which reach widows, single moms, and fatherless children. What Satan meant for evil in my life, God has used for His good and His glory, just as He did for Joseph (Genesis 50:20). And He will do the same for you—just stay focused on Him as He takes you to the other side of your total turnaround.

God had the details covered for the children of Israel, and yet they doubted Him time and time again. God saw the detailed plan of deliverance for the children of Israel, but they had to walk by faith and trust in Him alone. They didn't know how their deliverance was even possible—all they knew was that they needed a total turnaround.

Maybe today all you know is that you need a total turnaround. When you continue to walk by faith and trust in God while you are crying out to Him, know that He's got the details covered!

Silence Your "Buts" and "What Ifs"

The first thing Moses said when God called him to deliver the Israelites out of slavery was, "But, God...." *"But Moses said to God, 'Who am I that I should go to Pharaoh and bring the Israelites out of Egypt?'"* (Exodus 3:11). God is always bigger than anyone's "but"! God was bigger than Moses' "but," and He's bigger than our "but" today. When God has determined the plan of action to bring about a total turnaround, no "but" or "what if?" can stand in the way.

However, it took Moses awhile to figure this out. He continued to question God, saying, *"What if they do not believe me or listen to me and say, 'The Lord did not appear to you'?"* (Exodus 4:1). Moses was focused on the wrong thing—the "what if?" Yet God had an answer for every "but" and "what if?" Moses voiced. We need to turn our "what if?" around: What if we just went for it and did what God has told us to do? What if we were to simply walk in obedience and allow God to step in and use us for the biggest turnaround our nation has ever seen? What if God wants to use us to display His miraculous power and His miracle-working hand? What if?

When we realize that our obedience to God is all that remains to be done to secure a total turnaround, we will forget about saying "but" and "what if?" We'll forget our doubts and disbelief. When you think about it, every "but" and "what if?" stems from doubt and unbelief. Moses doubted his abilities to lead the Israelites out of bondage, even going so far as to ask God to please send someone else instead! (See Exodus 4:13.) His excuses were frustrating to the Lord (Exodus 4:14), but God still carried out His plan to deliver the Israelites through Moses.

Watch Your Words

God could have taken the children of Israel into the Promised Land in eleven days, but they didn't cooperate, to say the least! Yet, throughout their journey, God showed Himself powerful and faithful to them time and time again, even as they continued to grumble and complain against Him and His chosen leader, Moses. A major reason for the delay was the negative heart attitudes they harbored and the doubt-filled words they spoke.

Our words and our hearts are closely connected. The Bible says, *"Out of the abundance of the heart* [the] *mouth speaks"* (Luke 6:45c NKJV), and *"The tongue has the power of life and death"* (Proverbs 18:21a). In other words, whatever is in your heart will eventually come out of your mouth, and what comes out of your mouth predicts your future course. In the case of the Israelites, their grumbling became a major setback in their progress toward the Promised Land.

> *In the desert the whole community grumbled against Moses and Aaron. The Israelites said to them, "If only we had died by the Lord's hand in Egypt! There we sat around pots of meat and ate all the food we wanted, but you have brought us out into this desert to starve this entire assembly to death."* (Exodus 16:2-3)

First off, the Israelites had prioritized the comforts of their flesh—food and drink to satisfy their hunger and thirst—over the deliverance God had brought about for them. God had freed them from the bondage of slavery in Egypt so that they could worship Him, and almost immediately they began to "worship" food instead! When we choose the comforts and desires of our flesh over our freedom to worship and our freedom from the bondages out of which God has brought us, there's a problem!

The more the Israelites grumbled and complained, the bigger their problems became. Our words play an important role in the process of total turnaround. If you want to see your total turnaround manifested, then watch your words! Again, we speak either life or death, depending on the attitude of our heart. This is why we are instructed in Proverbs 4:23, *"Above all else, guard your heart, for it is the wellspring of life."* If your heart is not right—if you are harboring anger, bitterness, and offense—your mouth will give voice to those negative attitudes, thus speaking words of death, not life. Don't allow your heart to be a wellspring of death! Fan the flame of faith in your heart and speak only words that affirm your belief in God and your trust in His promises. Speak life! Proclaim turnaround! Start speaking the Word of God over yourself and all that pertains to you, and faith will arise within your spirit.

To speak the Word of God, you need to read it first! Joshua 1:8 says, *"Do not let this Book of the Law depart from your mouth; meditate on it day and night, so that you may be careful to do everything written in it. Then you will be prosperous and successful."* Father has given us the instruction; now it's up to us to carry it out. He has clearly told us how to be prosperous and successful. Joshua 1:8 says that we are not to *"let"* God's Word depart from our mouths. This implies that it's up to us. If we get lazy, or if we "let" the words of the enemy fill our mouths, we have made a bad choice. No one can choose for us. We must choose daily to speak the Word of God with our mouth.

Remember the power that Father God said He has given you? A lot of that power is right there under your nose—literally! The power of life and death is in your tongue. Speak the Word of God daily over you and over your circumstances. Don't speak what the devil says—speak what the Word says!

Joshua 1:8 also commands us, *"Be careful to do everything written in it* [God's Word]." So, we must speak the Word, think the Word, and do the Word. Our words, thoughts, and actions must be in agreement with the Word of God. The more we speak the Word and meditate on it, the easier and more natural it becomes to "do" the Word—to live it out. When we live a lifestyle of speaking the Word, thinking the Word, and doing the Word, we will be prosperous and successful in every area of life. And that's when God can bring about the total turnaround that He wants for our lives.

Don't be like the children of Israel, speaking death with words uttered out of a heart filled with anger, resentment, and bitterness. Trust that God has a great plan for your life and speak faith all the way to your own Promised Land! Your words are a secret key to your total turnaround!

Follow His Lead

I said several years ago that I would never use a GPS. Well, I have learned two things since then: Number one, never say never! And, number two, I don't like fast-changing electronic gadgets, but once I try one of them, I never want to go back. Dr. Marilyn Hickey was the first person to convince me to try text messaging on my phone—and she's in her eighties! She wanted to communicate with me via text messaging; meanwhile, my phone didn't even offer that option. For years I'd thought that texting was ridiculous. I'm a verbal person; I'm a talker and a communicator. In the body of Christ, I'm the mouth. But then I tried texting—only because I thought that if Dr. Hickey was doing it—someone old enough to be my mother—then I needed to get with the program. Once I tried it, I loved it, and I have never gone back.

Understandably, I was hesitant to use a GPS. And my first experience was hardly encouraging! I was in Chicago to plan for a large ministry outreach. The woman traveling with me was determined to use her GPS, and because she was driving, I agreed. (Of course, I had a map and my MapQuest directions in hand as I navigated from the passenger seat.) It wasn't long before we got lost—on Wacker Street, of all places! For the record, that street name is very appropriate—it's very wacky!

Her GPS kept saying, "Recalculating, recalculating, recalculating," and just about drove me crazy. I was ready to toss the whole thing out the window!

I finally demanded that she stop at the firehouse we had passed at least fifteen times as we were circling around the city (in the middle of a snow-storm, I might add). I thought to myself, *The people at the fire department know this city; surely they can help us deal with this Wacker Street situation.*

When I entered the station and explained our situation to the fire chief, he showed me a map of the city they had hanging on the wall. It was at that moment that I saw a visual of Wacker Street—and realized that it was shaped in a square. Without advance notice, the street would take a sharp left, only to make another sharp left less than a mile later. No wonder we and our GPS were totally confused!

We finally found our destination, and it was on that day that I dismissed the idea of ever using a GPS again! Fast-forward to several years later: I got lost driving back to my hotel from a TV studio where I had just filmed two interviews. It was late, it was dark, we were lost, and we were desperate! So I pulled out my new iPhone. I remembered how excited my teenage daughter, Destiny, had been when she'd learned that my new phone had a GPS, and I'd seen her playing around with it one day. She had been quite emphatic that it was easy to use, but I still refused—until I was desperate. I got out that GPS and finally found out how easy it really is! All I had to do was follow the bubble. When I went off course, the bubble showed it. When I got back on track, the bubble flashed to confirm it. All I had to do was type in the destination and follow the bubble. Needless to say, I have been following the bubble ever since!

In the midst of our desperate situations and trying circumstances, God wants us to use our "Holy Ghost GPS" and follow His lead to the destination He has for us. His GPS may not lead us on the path or the route we had in mind, but His GPS will always get us there safely.

TURNAROUND INVOLVES TIMES OF TRANSITION

Crossing over always involves a period of transition, or a place between seasons or stages. When a woman is about to give birth, she goes through a time of transition. When that baby is transitioning, it can be very painful! Yet, without transition, the baby can't be born—the next season or stage can never occur.

Times of transition can be painful, and they often cause people to question whether the Lord has forgotten about them. If you are in transition in your life today, be encouraged—God hasn't forgotten about you. This, too, shall pass! The season of transition is only a time in between where you were and where you are going!

The Transition Process Rarely Makes Perfect Sense

The children of Israel were in transition when they needed to cross over the Red Sea. It didn't make a lot of sense to them, and that wasn't the route they would have chosen, but their God-inspired GPS took them that route!

> When Pharaoh let the people go, God did not lead them on the road through the Philistine country, though that was shorter. For God said, "If they face war, they might change their minds and return to Egypt." So God led the people around by the desert road toward the Red Sea. The Israelites went up out of Egypt armed for battle. (Exodus 13:17-18)

Remember, just follow the bubble—the Holy Ghost, who guides your spiritual GPS system. God's not interested in the shortest route for you; He's interested in the successful route! He wants you to go all the way and arrive at the destination that He has programmed in His "GPS" for your life.

He guided the Israelites in a unique way: *"By day the Lord went ahead of them in a pillar of cloud to guide them on their way and by night in a pillar of fire to give them light, so that they could travel by day or night"* (Exodus 13:21). When we are following the leading of the Holy Spirit, we are advancing toward our new season and new place in God, even if we are in a night season. The children of Israel made progress toward their Promised Land—their place of total turnaround—during the night season as well as during the day. The only requirement was that they practice obedience by following the Lord's leading. God made that leading very obvious with the pillar of cloud by day and the pillar of fire by night. That was their God-given "GPS system," and it never failed—it led them all the way through the transition of wilderness to the place of turnaround in the Promised Land.

Pharaoh may have changed his mind and altered his game plan, but God wasn't thrown off guard—His divine plan was still fully carried out.

The only ones who were surprised were the children of Israel! They hardly could have expected to traverse the Red Sea when Moses parted the waters. (See Exodus 14:20-22.) If they had known all of the details in advance, they probably would have stayed put and never chosen to step into the season of transition that was required for them to cross over to the new level. When the going got rough, they were pretty panicked!

> *The Egyptians—all Pharaoh's horses and chariots, horsemen and troops—pursued the Israelites and overtook them as they camped by the sea....As Pharaoh approached, the Israelites looked up, and there were the Egyptians, marching after them. They were terrified and cried out to the Lord.* (Exodus 14:9-10)

First off, you should never expect to transition into a new season or climb to a higher level without the enemy marching out after you. Yes, God is all-powerful and, yes, you and God are the winning team. However, you shouldn't be so naïve to think that your crossover will occur without a spiritual battle. It doesn't work that way. The important thing is to avoid focusing on the battle or worrying about the outcome because the battle is God's to fight, not ours (1 Samuel 17:47). And God always gets the victory! We live in the midst of a spiritual battle. This is war, so stand up and fight! Don't shrink back; you are about to cross over! You must take up your position and stand firm!

The Path to Turnaround Depends on Faith

The Israelites were pretty grouchy during their transition time. They began speaking doubt and unbelief. They grumbled against their leader, Moses, and launched verbal attacks on him.

> [The Israelites] *said to Moses, "Was it because there were no graves in Egypt that you brought us to the desert to die? What have you done to us by bringing us out of Egypt? Didn't we say to you in Egypt, 'Leave us alone; let us serve the Egyptians'? It*

would have been better for us to serve the Egyptians than to die in the desert!" (Exodus 14:11-12)

But it wasn't their leader who was the problem—it was their hearts! The children of Israel were filled with doubt and skepticism, and their mouths gave voice to their defeatist attitudes, which are poison on the path to turnaround.

Moses was quick to urge them to have faith.

Moses answered the people, "Do not be afraid. Stand firm and you will see the deliverance the Lord will bring you today. The Egyptians you see today you will never see again. The Lord will fight for you; you need only to be still." (Exodus 14:13-14)

Fear hinders everything when God wants to advance you. Stand firm! Don't allow the spirit of fear to come into your life, even the slightest little bit. God wanted to bring their deliverance about that day! God even said, *"The Egyptians you see today you will never see again."*

Today is the day for your total turnaround! The bondage that you have been in with your situations and circumstances you will never again have to see or deal with. Embrace the word of the Lord. Receive the promise of God for you. Then, let the Lord do the fighting for you. Remember, this battle is not yours—it's the Lord's. Don't wear yourself out trying to do it on your own. You need only to be still in your spirit and march forward in obedience to God during this season of transition.

Pruning Is Part of Every Transition Period

Although it was God's time to bring the Israelites out of Egypt, it was not yet His time to take them all the way into the Promised Land. A time of transition was necessary—a period during which God would prune them and prepare them to inherit the next level of His blessings. While we eagerly anticipate the completion of our total turnaround, we must remember that the process itself, transitions and all, is meant to prune us of any sinful, self-destructive habits and negative behaviors. It's meant to prune the flesh, ridding us of doubt and unbelief, while cultivating godly character within us. Jesus said, *"I am the true vine, and my Father is the gardener. He cuts off every branch in me that bears no fruit, while every branch that does bear fruit he prunes so that it will be even more fruitful"* (John 15:1-2). If we want to see the fruit of our turnaround, we must be patient during the pruning process!

The children of Israel needed a good deal of pruning before they were ready to enter the Promised Land. To be exact, 39 years and 354 days' worth of pruning! The Bible records that their journey through the wilderness could have been made in eleven days. Instead, they wandered around for forty years! I guess that's what it took for them to be pruned and prepared. One might have expected them to learn a little faster after having spent 430 years in Egypt. But I guess we all have a little "slow learner" in us.

On a trip to Israel several years ago, I drove on a bus through the area called the wilderness and arrived in the area known as the Promised Land. I was shocked how short the distance was. If I remember correctly, we made it there in an hour and a half. Now, it doesn't take a mathematician or a rocket scientist to figure this one out—they really missed the boat! They wasted time—something we all do if we aren't careful.

We don't have time to waste. We need to make every day count for the kingdom of God. If we engage in habits and practices that waste time, we risk dying in the wilderness. If we choose not to answer when the King calls, we can lose our position, like Vashti did (Esther 1:10-20), and God may raise up someone more qualified to fulfill our position in the kingdom.

Total Turnaround Is Designed to Get God the Glory

In delivering the Israelites from bondage in Egypt, the Lord orchestrated everything in such a way that it would bring Him all the glory. When the Egyptians saw the hand of God at work on behalf of the Israelites, they knew that He was the Lord. God gained glory through Pharaoh, his chariots, and his horsemen—the very things that caused the Israelites to be thrown into what I call "meltdown mode."

When the enemy throws you into "meltdown mode," it means that you have been attempting to fight a battle that isn't yours. When you acknowledge that the battle belongs to the Lord, your thoughts and attitudes are protected from "meltdown mode" moments.

The fact that the Israelites had slipped into meltdown mode made God's next move that much more amazing.

> *Then Moses stretched out his hand over the sea, and all that night the Lord drove the sea back with a strong east wind and turned it into dry land. The waters were divided, and the Israelites went through the sea on dry ground, with a wall of water on their right and on their left. The Egyptians pursued them, and all Pharaoh's horses and chariots and horsemen followed them into the sea.* (Exodus 14:21-23)

Yet again, God turned things around for the children of Israel—He turned the sea into dry land! Now, that's a turnaround! It was in the night season that the Lord drove the sea back. It was in the night season that the Lord turned things around. God often does His best behind-the-scenes work in our lives during the "night seasons" we experience.

No one likes the dark seasons of life, but I want to encourage you—even then, God is causing you to cross through the waters on dry land to your destiny on the other shore.

> *During the last watch of the night the Lord looked down from the pillar of fire and cloud at the Egyptian army and threw it into confusion. He made the wheels of their chariots come off so that they had difficulty driving. And the Egyptians said, "Let's get away from the Israelites! The Lord is fighting for them against Egypt."* (Exodus 14:24-25)

When God is on your side, that fact is obvious to everyone, including the enemy! Don't shrink back when you see the schemes of the enemy working against you. Look to God and stand up as you watch Him fight for you! The Egyptian army retreated when they recognized the hand of God, and your enemy will do the same. You aren't the one who's supposed to retreat! The enemy will shrink back in fear when he sees the hand of God fighting on your behalf.

At Daybreak, You Are Already on the Other Side

Then the Lord said to Moses, "Stretch out your hand over the sea so that the waters may flow back over the Egyptians and their chariots and horsemen." Moses stretched out his hand over the sea, and at daybreak the sea went back to its place. The Egyptians were fleeing toward it, and the Lord swept them into the sea. The water flowed back and covered the chariots and horsemen—the entire army of Pharaoh that had followed the Israelites into the sea. Not one of them survived. (Exodus 14:26-28)

After the night season, daybreak came, and the children of Israel had already crossed over to safety! At daybreak, they were already on the other side of the Red Sea. You may see nothing but darkness and challenges from the enemy right now, but wait till daybreak—you will wake up and realize that you have already made it to the other side! It's during the night seasons in our lives that God causes us to cross over, supernaturally.

I want to encourage you today—it's just about daybreak! Every new day begins with yesterday's darkness. At 12:01 a.m., the new day has already begun. Nothing looks different. It still looks dark. But we know it's a new day because the clock tells us it is.

Every new day in the Lord begins with yesterday's darkness, but we know in the spirit that it's a brand-new day! Just hang on for a few more hours and you'll see the sun rise. At daybreak, it's obvious to everyone that it's a brand-new day!

Welcome to the new day! Welcome to the new season! Welcome to the new level! Remember, transition is only a season. Seasons come and seasons go. Transition is only a time of preparation for you to enter your new season. Enjoy the next level.

Trust in God's timing and technique for your turnaround.

POINTS TO PONDER

1. While you wait for your turnaround, why is it crucial to understand that God's timing is perfect?

2. In the life of Moses, we can see that God had a blueprint for the turnaround of the children of Israel. How does the fact that God has a detailed plan of action already prepared for you provide you with encouragement?

3. Our words and our hearts are so closely connected. Why is this so important in regard to total turnaround?

4. Turnaround always involves a period of transition. Explain why this is necessary and what is meant by "transitioning."

Meditate on these Scriptures, speak them aloud, and commit them to memory:

> *Trust in the Lord with all your heart and lean not on your own understanding; in all your ways acknowledge him, and he will make your paths straight.* (Proverbs 3:5-6)

> *And we all know that in all things God works for the good of those who love him, who have been called according to his purpose.* (Romans 8:28)

> *The tongue has the power of life and death, and those who love it will eat its fruit.* (Proverbs 18:21)

> *Above all else, guard your heart, for it is the wellspring of life.* (Proverbs 4:23)

Chapter 2

TOTAL TURNAROUND IN YOUR PRAYER LIFE

In Jeremiah 7:13, the Lord declares, *"I spoke to you again and again, but you did not listen; I called you, but you did not answer."* Before we experience any type of turnaround, we need to hear from God. He is the one with the master plan, and any turnaround we try to bring about on our own, without His guidance, will be a big flop. And the way in which we hear from God, besides by the reading of His Word, is by consulting Him through times of prayer. If we don't have a dynamic prayer life, we'll remain ignorant to His wonderful plans for our lives.

God wants you to experience His highest level in your prayer life. I've learned that you go from level to level in the Lord and in the things of God. His Word says He wants to take His people *"from glory to glory"* (2 Corinthians 3:18 NKJV). No matter where you are in your prayer life today, I want to challenge you to ascend to a higher level—to a more intimate relationship with your heavenly Father. God continually woos you and me to a higher, more intimate place in Him. As He woos us, we must respond by reaching for that place. And as we reach for that greater place of intimacy in prayer, He will grant it. *"Come near to God and he will come near to you"* (James 4:8a).

If you have been distracted from your place of prayer, today is the day for your turnaround. As you experience a total turnaround in your prayer life, that powerful place of intimacy with the Father will serve as your means to total turnaround in every other area of your life. Prayer is another secret to total turnaround in every area of your life.

SEEING, REACHING, ATTAINING

God-given vision is necessary if we are to know what to strive for. And we have to see something in order for us to reach for it. For example, unless we see ourselves graduating from college or earning our master's degree, chances are we never will. Unless we see ourselves paying off our mortgage, we probably won't. Unless we envision ourselves starting a business, founding a ministry, finishing a marathon—whatever our dream may be—we'll never see its realization. We have to envision it first for it to become a reality in our lives.

After seeing our goal, we need to reach for it. If our goal is to graduate from college, then we must see ourselves holding the diploma and wearing the cap and gown; next, we need to take a step of faith and send in our application to the college or university of our choice. We must continue walking by faith when we're accepted and we schedule our first semester of classes. And we keep on walking by faith through the challenges we face, from term papers to final exams, until commencement day dawns. That's reaching!

Know What to Reach For

The Lord has great plans for us. *"For I know the plans I have for you,' declares the Lord, 'plans to prosper you and not to harm you, plans to give you hope and a future'"* (Jeremiah 29:11). And He wants to see us fulfill those plans! Father will speak to us through divine nudges that tell us what steps to take or show us what we should reach for. But we can't receive His instructions just anywhere—we need to be in a place of prayer! Setting aside a special time to commune with God every day makes us receptive to the leading of His Holy Spirit.

Hearing from our heavenly Father, whether it's through an impression in our spirit or instructions on our heart, causes faith to rise up within us, prompting us to reach for the very things He has promised us. You heard me right—I said "reach." It's rare to have our blessings simply drop in our lap. In most cases, God's plans for us will require some effort on our part. That's why we must keep our faith alive— to ensure that we'll go all the way in our quest to fulfill the will of the Father.

After we hear the initial word, we must respond in obedience, continually pressing forward to obtain the goals that Father God has given us. Like the apostle Paul, we *press on toward the goal to win the prize for which God has called* [us] *heavenward in Christ Jesus"* (Philippians 3:14). Many start out on the right path, yet few cross the finish line. The Bible is filled with examples of individuals who pressed on to pursue their God-given goals. One of those people was Abraham, formerly known as Abram. Let's see how he received and then acted on a God-given vision.

Keep Your Eyes on the Prize

The Lord had said to Abram, "Leave your country, your people and your father's household and go to the land I will show you. I will make you into a great nation and I will bless you; I will make your name great, and you will be a blessing. I will bless those who bless you, and whoever curses you I will curse; and all peoples on earth will be blessed through you." So Abram left, as the Lord had told him; and Lot went with him. Abram was seventy-five years old when he set out from Haran. He took his wife Sarai, his nephew Lot, all the possessions they had accumulated and the people they had acquired in Haran, and they set out for the land of Canaan, and they arrived there. (Genesis 12:1-5)

Abram set out to fulfill the vision God had given him, and he arrived there. Prompt obedience grounded in faith and expectation caused Abram to reach for the place that the Lord had ordained for him. Because his obedience was grounded in faith and expectation, Abram arrived at the place he set out for.

Similarly, as we reach through prayer for the place God has shown us, we can receive the details of His plans for our lives. And then, when we respond to His instructions by acting in faith, we will enjoy the fruit of our obedience.

One definition of *reach* is "to stretch." Yes, reaching for a higher place will stretch you! It will definitely get you out of your comfort zone. Think of Abram—he had to pack up everything and ship out to reach the land God had for him. Yes, it will take effort and labor to arrive at the place you are reaching for, but as you reach for that place, Father will carry you across the finish line if necessary.

Again, your sight first takes place in the Spirit before it manifests in the natural. You must first see it in the Spirit; then you can see it come to pass in the natural. God will show you in the Spirit, and then you need to reach for it in the natural. But you won't know what you are reaching for, much less attain it, unless you hear from God in prayer!

God wants us to be caught up in His presence and in His plan for our days and our lives as a whole. When we are really caught up in prayer, we lose track of time. But, when we are really caught up in time, we lose track of prayer.

Make prayer a priority and let the Lord woo you into His presence daily. You won't be disappointed!

COME UNTO ME

Father wants us to come unto Him, not only when we need a major turnaround, not only to pour our hearts out to Him, but also so that we may experience His presence and feel His love on a daily basis. His presence carries us through every turnaround and sustains us during the times in between.

The glory of the Lord is hidden in His presence. As we get into the presence of the Lord through fasting, prayer, worship, and the study of His Word—the Bible—we tap into the realm of His glory. And there's nothing like the presence and the glory of the Lord. Nothing!

All we really need is the presence and the glory of the Lord. In His presence is rest. In His presence is joy. In His presence is peace. In His presence is protection. As you come unto Him, you can experience all of the benefits that await you in His presence.

Rest for the Weary

Jesus said, *"Come to me, all you who are weary and burdened, and I will give you rest"* (Matthew 11:28). Weary can mean "tired; worn out; without…patience, tolerance, zeal, etc." Well, that just about covers every one of us, doesn't it? Tired. Worn out. Without patience. No tolerance or zeal. Wow—that sounds like much of the body of Christ! If we don't come to Him on a regular basis, if we neglect to spend time with Him in prayer, we can expect to be weary.

Even the greatest warriors in the Bible needed to rest and come before the Lord in prayer before, during, and after each battle. Take David, for example. He was a man of prayer, to the extent that God called him *"a man after my own heart"* (Acts 13:22). And the Bible says of him, *"The Lord gave David victory everywhere he went"* (1 Chronicles 18:6b). When we try to fight the good fight of faith without the backing of a powerful prayer life, we can expect to be weary and burdened. But, when we come unto the Lord in prayer, He promises to give us the much-needed rest required for us to be refreshed enough to face the next day's battles.

People today are looking for rest in many different forms. This constant pursuit motivates much of the things people do—as the song says, "Everybody's Working for the Weekend." Many people put in extra hours saving up for their "dream vacation," believing that it will finally bring the rest they so desperately need. There's nothing wrong with taking a nice vacation, but let me tell you—in most cases, you feel the need for a "stay-cation" to recover from your vacation. At the end of even the most relaxing of trips, I often wish for one more week to stay at home and recover! The truth is that rest cannot be found on a remote island, at a day spa, or on a cruise ship. Real rest is found only in the presence of the Lord.

In Exodus 33:14, God said to His people, *"My Presence will go with you, and I will give you rest."* When His presence is with us, His rest comes along with it. It's a package deal—a free bonus! We "pray" the price for His presence, and we get His rest, to boot. It's a great package offer!

The great news is, we never need to be away from God's presence. It doesn't have to be a temporary "place" we visit from time to time. Psalm 91:1 says, *"He who dwells in the shelter of the Most High will rest in the shadow of the Almighty."* Dwell is actually defined as "to make one's home; reside; live." That's so powerful! God's shelter is always open. It's a place of permanent existence! There is always room in the shelter of the Most High God, and we are always welcome there. Come and dwell; come and live; come and take up residence today in the shelter of the Most High God. His rest is waiting there for us!

Another unique feature of God's rest is that it refreshes every aspect of ourselves. Most people, when they're planning a vacation with the goal of R&R (rest and recuperation), will book a seaside condo or someplace else where they can rest their bodies and their minds. Sleeping, lounging, and similar "activities" are what they spend their time doing (or not doing). But what about the soul? A break from the rigors of daily living offers little by way of refreshment for the soul.

Not so in the presence of God! Forget a travel brochure; the psalmist summed it up pretty well: *"My soul finds rest in God alone; my salvation comes from him. He alone is my rock and my salvation; he is my fortress, I will never be shaken"* (Psalm 62:1-2). The soul comprises the natural mind, including the will and the emotions. It cannot find rest outside of God. Only in the presence of the Lord can we experience true rest and renewal in our minds and emotions.

The key to enjoying the rest of God's presence is a right relationship with Him. If we keep our hearts pure, confessing our sins to God and repenting of them on a daily basis, we can enter into His holy presence and find true refreshing and rest. *"Repent, then, and turn to God, so that your sins may be wiped out, that times of refreshing may come from the Lord"* (Acts 3:19).

Maybe today you are tired and weary due to a sin in your life that has separated you from the presence of the Lord. Sin really weighs you down! The writer of Hebrews compared sin to a heavy burden that wears you down and holds you back when he said, *"Let us throw off everything that hinders and the sin that so easily entangles"* (Hebrews 12:1b). Maybe you have sought refreshment in everything the world has to offer, yet nothing has worked. I want to encourage you today to accept Jesus Christ, God's one and only Son, into your life as your Lord and Savior. Salvation is the first step to entering His presence and experiencing His rest! Isaiah 30:15 says, *"In repentance and rest is your salvation."*

Even as Paul exhorted us to free ourselves from the burden of sin, he acknowledged that it's something all of us struggle with: *"For all have sinned and fall short of the glory of God"* (Romans 3:23). But that isn't the end of the story! In Romans 10:9-10, Paul goes on to tell us that if we confess our sins and accept Christ as the Lord and Savior of our lives, we will be born again. Then and only then will we experience true times of refreshing and rest in our lives—after our sins have been washed away by the blood of Jesus.

If this describes you today, I want to encourage you to pray this prayer and accept Christ as your Lord and Savior, right now!

> *Dear God, I confess that I am a sinner. But I believe that Your Son, Jesus Christ, paid the price for my sins by dying on the cross and rising again from the grave to pay the penalty I was due. Forgive me and accept me as Your child. I am Yours, today and forevermore. In Jesus' name, amen.*

Congratulations! You just made the most important decision of your life—the decision to accept Christ as Lord and Savior. Welcome to the family of God! All of the benefits that belong to His children are yours, including Isaiah 32:18: *"My people will live in peaceful dwelling places, in secure homes, in undisturbed places of rest."* What a promise! And there are plenty more where that came from. They're spread throughout the pages of the Bible, which is His Word to us. His promises are yours to enjoy, now and for eternity!

Zeal for the Indifferent

The psalmist wrote, *"Zeal for your house consumes me"* (Psalm 69:9a). Are you zealous for the Lord? Do you have a consuming zeal for the things of God? If not, put the brakes on. Stop and assess the reason for this lack of zeal in your life. The apostle Paul exhorts, *"Never be lacking in zeal, but keep your spiritual fervor, serving the Lord"* (Romans 12:11). "Never" means "never," in Greek, Hebrew, and English. You must keep your zeal and fervor!

One definition of fervor is "intense heat." We must be like the prophet Jeremiah, who said that God's Word *"is in my heart like a fire, a fire shut up in my bones"* (Jeremiah 20:9). Let's keep the fire of God alive in our hearts! One of the theme songs at our ministry's annual women's conference is "Fire in the House." Don't let your fire go out! Keep the fire of the Holy Ghost burning in your house. I'm singing it right now as I write: "Fire, fire, fire in the house." Glory to God!

Let's fan the flame of our zeal for the Lord. How? By worshipping Him, meditating on His Word, and spending time just basking in His presence. When we feed our spiritual fervor with daily prayer, we can easily maintain a bonfire in our souls.

Peace for the Panicked

One thing that we all could use a little more of is peace! Fear is the archenemy of peace. When the spirit of fear is allowed to creep into our hearts and minds, we are quick to lose our peace.

Jesus said, *"Peace I leave with you; my peace I give you. I do not give to you as the world gives. Do not let your hearts be troubled and do not be afraid"* (John 14:27). The Lord has commanded us not to let our hearts be troubled, nor to be afraid. Fear and worry are not part of the covenant benefits that the Lord Jesus left for us! *"For God has not given us a spirit of fear..."* (2 Timothy 1:7 NKJV). Rather, He left the Spirit of peace—the Holy Spirit, also called the Comforter (John 14:16 KJV)—for us as He ascended to sit at the right hand of the Father (John 14:16-28).

Father's peace is found in His presence. Psalm 34:14 says, *"Turn from evil and do good; seek peace and pursue it."* As you seek the Lord, you are also seeking peace—peace in your heart and mind; peace that overflows into your daily life and your relationships. Not only must you seek peace, but you must also pursue it. Seeking is one thing; pursuing takes the search to a whole different level. Pursuing means that you won't quit or give up easily. You will pay the price to run after peace in His presence, no matter what it takes. It may inconvenience you. Your pursuit of peace in His presence may take longer during the stormy seasons of life. But the wait is worth it. Pursue peace, and don't quit until you arrive at that place of perfect peace.

The prophet Isaiah spoke of this place of perfect peace. Addressing God, he said, *"You will keep in perfect peace him whose mind is steadfast* ["whose mind is stayed on You" NKJV], *because he trusts in you"* (Isaiah 26:3). If we keep our minds "stayed" on the Lord—rather than "stayed" on the situations, circumstances, or storms of our lives—we will remain in perfect peace, no matter how rocky the situations of life become. When we trust in the Lord with all of our hearts (Proverbs 3:5-6), we can maintain the perfect peace that's found in His presence. But if we allow our minds to wander, letting them be weighed down with concerns and worries and petty matters, then our peace will fly right out the window. It won't be steadfast. It will fluctuate—up and then down; left and then right. We will be tossed to and fro in our minds. As a result, we will feel as if our life is falling to "pieces" instead of enjoying true "peace"—the peace of God, which passes all understanding.

To pursue peace, we must guard our minds so that they won't wander down the paths of worry, concern, obsession, or worse. Then *the peace of God, which transcends all understanding, will guard your hearts and your minds in Christ Jesus"* (Philippians 4:7). The perfect peace of God will guard our hearts and our minds against the lies and destructive schemes of the enemy. It's one of our countless covenant benefits.

Don't pay a price that was already covered by the blood of Christ! The price of losing your peace is a costly one. Child of God, you have covenant benefits—cash in on them!

Joy for the Downcast

"You have made known to me the path of life; you will fill me with joy in your presence, with eternal pleasures at your right hand" (Psalm 16:11). Yes, in God's presence is fullness of joy. We need a full tank of joy to maintain victory in our daily life. It's often after our greatest victories that we need rest, peace, and joy the most. Take the prophet Elijah, for example. He experienced great victory on Mount Carmel (1 Kings 18:16-38). God showed up like never before, and the people called on the name of the Lord, saying, *"The Lord—he is God!"* (1 Kings 18:39). Yet, after this, his greatest victory, Elijah lost his joy—and understandably so—when he found out that Jezebel was trying to kill him. Yep, a death threat will do it! No wonder Elijah lost his joy.

Elijah was afraid and ran for his life. When he came to Beersheba in Judah, he left his servant there, while he himself went a day's journey into the desert. He came to a broom tree, sat down under it and prayed that he might die. "I have had enough, Lord," he said. "Take my life; I am no better than my ancestors." (1 Kings 19:3-4)

"I have had enough, Lord"—it would be funny if it wasn't so serious. Have you ever cried out to God along those lines? Have you ever felt hopeless to the point of wishing to die? Earlier today, perhaps? Maybe even right now? If you feel that you have had enough, begin to shout praise to God. You need to stir up your joy because you can't afford to quit. You have come this far by faith, and God will see you through to the very end. Quitting is not an option, and neither is dying, so get up out of your mess, press into the presence of the Lord, and know that this, too, shall pass!

Then [Elijah] *lay down under the tree and fell asleep. All at once an angel touched him and said, "Get up and eat." He looked around, and there by his head was a cake of bread baked over hot coals, and a jar of water. He ate and drank and then lay down again. The angel of the Lord came back a second time and touched him and said, "Get up and eat, for the journey is too much for you." So he got up and ate and drank. Strengthened by that food, he traveled forty days and forty nights until he reached Horeb, the mountain of God. There he went into a cave and spent the night....* (1 Kings 19:5-9)

A good night's sleep goes a long way, doesn't it? Things always look better and brighter when you are well rested—not just physically, from sleep, but also in your soul and spirit, with the rest that comes from being in the presence of the Lord. Maybe you have experienced great victories, yet you are overwhelmed by a bad report or the situation you find yourself in today. Be encouraged—and get some rest! Enter into the presence of God and find His joy, which will be your strength to endure this challenging season.

The Bible says, *"The joy of the Lord is your strength"* (Nehemiah 8:10). Without strength, you will easily throw in the towel and quit. You will be tempted to surrender in your quest to fulfill God's will for your life if you don't have any strength. So don't rely on your own strength—rely on the strength that comes from the joy of the Lord! God's abundant joy is waiting for you in His presence.

Rejoicing for Those Who Lament

"Rejoice in the Lord always. I will say it again: Rejoice!" (Philippians 4:4). We don't have to be rejoicing because of our situations and circumstances, but we must keep rejoicing even in the midst of them. Again, it is the strength of God that enables us to do this. As the apostle Paul explained,

> *...I have learned to be content whatever the circumstances. I know what it is to be in need, and I know what it is to have plenty. I have learned the secret of being content in any and every situation, whether well fed or hungry, whether living in plenty or in want. I can do everything through him who gives me strength.* (Philippians 4:11-13)

You have much to be thankful about. You have a lot to shout about! You may not have ideal circumstances at the moment, but, just remember, this situation is temporary! As you shout and rejoice, you will be strengthened for the journey.

Proverbs 10:28 says, *"The prospect of the righteous is joy, but the hopes of the wicked come to nothing."* You can expect joy to result from doing the "right" thing. When you respond in righteousness, you tap into the powerful strength of the Father, and the result will be a joy that transcends your circumstances. So keep on doing the right thing, even in the midst of the storm. When you do the righteous thing or the "right thing," you can tap into the Father's joy.

I want you to assess the level of your joy. When is the last time you really sat back and had a good belly laugh? Have you taken time lately with friends or family to sit around and just laugh?

In Galatians 4:15, Paul asked his listeners, *"What has happened to all your joy?"* He was concerned for the Galatians. Among other things, they had lost their joy. Ask yourself today, "What has happened to all your joy?" You need to guard your joy and not allow anything or anyone to steal your God-given source of strength.

The joy of the Lord is our only reliable source of strength. Anything else from which we might attempt to draw strength—our money, our education, our own intelligence, our physical endurance—will ultimately fail us. But the joy of the Lord will never let us down! We can have joy in the midst of all kinds of challenges, whether emotional, relational, mental, physical, or financial. As we learn to find joy in the midst of our circumstances, we can maintain the strength we need to come out of every storm a victor! God's joy really is our greatest source of strength.

PRAYER: A KEY TO EVERY TYPE OF TURNAROUND

Turnaround in your prayer life paves the way for turnaround in every situation. Prayer is the most powerful form of communication, and it really does change things—dramatically!

As proof, consider Paul and Silas, who prayed their way to a jailbreak. They had just been thrown in prison, when...

> *About midnight Paul and Silas were praying and singing hymns to God, and the other prisoners were listening to them. Suddenly there was such a violent earthquake that the foundations of the prison were shaken. At once all the prison doors flew open and everybody's chains came loose.* (Acts 16:25-26)

In spite of their circumstances, Paul and Silas continued to pray and shout praises to God—two methods of maintaining their joy. And prayer paved the way for their total turnaround! Now, even though the cell door had been opened and their shackles unlocked, Paul and Silas didn't leave. They were honorable men, and their witness ended up resulting in the salvation of their prison guard and his family. (See verses 27-34.) Ultimately they were released from prison by the authority of the local magistrate. The point is, their freedom still came about as a result of their joy-filled prayers in the midst of difficult circumstances.

Don't allow your circumstances to turn your life upside down today. Instead, be determined to see a total turnaround in your circumstances as you stand in faith by the power of prayer!

Suddenly, you will experience your turnaround, as Paul and Silas did—if you refuse to quit and give up. Total turnaround is coming your way—just stand in prayer and keep on standing!

Develop a dynamic prayer life.

POINTS TO PONDER

1. How does prayer enable you to see, reach, and attain all that God has for you?

2. When we are really caught up in prayer, we lose track of time, but when we are really caught up in time, we lose track of prayer. How have you found this to be true in your own life? What steps will you take to make prayer a priority?

3. List four benefits of being in God's presence that are promised in His Word.

4. What promise do we have in God's Word to assure us that when we reach for a greater place of intimacy in prayer, He will grant it?

Meditate on these Scriptures, speak them aloud, and commit them to memory:

"For I know the plans that I have for you," declares the Lord, "plans to prosper you and not to harm you, plans to give you hope and a future." (Jeremiah 29:11)

He who dwells in the shelter of the Most High will rest in the shadow of the Almighty. (Psalm 91:1)

You have made known to me the path of life; you will fill me with joy in your presence, with eternal pleasures at your right hand. (Psalm 16:11)

Come near to God and he will come near to you.... (James 4:8)

Chapter 3

TOTAL TURNAROUND IN YOUR SPIRITUAL STATE

God wants to prompt a spiritual turnaround in you, and then He wants to bring a total spiritual turnaround—in your family, your neighborhood, your church, your community, your city—through you, just as He did through the apostle Paul. The truth is, you and I can't take someone else to a place we haven't reached ourselves. A church worship leader cannot lead the congregation to a place in the spirit unless he has already reached it. A pastor can lead the people only as far as he himself has gone. That's why it is so important for you to continually reach for the next level in the Lord. There are always greater levels and higher heights in the Lord, and you must continually press your way into His presence, for then and only then will you reach the next level.

If you have never accepted Jesus Christ as the Lord and Savior of your life, today can be the day that you do so. *"Now is the day of salvation"* (2 Corinthians 6:2)! Make today your day of salvation. It's the most important turnaround you could ever undergo, and it's guaranteed to you, if you'll only accept it.

If you have already come to salvation but have lapsed in your commitment to the Lord, repent and get back on track—today! Fine-tune your focus on the Lord and on finding His will for your life. For then and only then will you be completely, truly satisfied, in times of turnaround as well as in times of relative consistency.

Turnaround in Your Heart

In the book of Esther, we read of Esther replacing Vashti as queen. Queen Vashti had already been promoted. She had already stepped into the "palace position" that God had for her. Yet she needed a turnaround in her heart. Somewhere along the line, her focus was broken. Somewhere along the line, it became all about her rather than about the reason the Lord had elevated her to that position.

If we aren't careful, we can lose our focus on why the Lord has granted us promotion and placed us in our palace positions—the place of our God-given assignments. That's what happened to Vashti, and we should never think that we are immune to such distracted focus. Too many times we see talented individuals start out with a motivation to glorify God with their gifts, only to sell out to the world for fortune and fame. Too many times we see pastors and other ministry leaders obtain a place of notoriety and promotion, only to get their eyes off of the Lord and focused instead on their personal gain.

Vashti's broken focus cost her everything. The position she had already obtained was taken out from under her because she refused to receive the spiritual heart turnaround she so desperately needed. Esther 1:12 says, *"But when the attendants delivered the king's command, Queen Vashti refused to come. Then the king became furious and burned with anger."* No one is free to break the king's laws! Vashti lost sight of why she was in her palace position and did not maintain the standard that the king required. When the king called Vashti, she refused to answer; as a result, she lost her position.

There is always someone else waiting to take our place. If we don't listen to the King of kings and answer when He calls, and if we fail to uphold

His standards, we may forfeit it all. None of our God-given appointments is guaranteed for life! We may have qualified for a position, but our hearts must keep us continually qualified daily if we want our assignment from the Lord to be a lifelong appointment. We must have a lifelong commitment to the King, and we must continually be committed to keeping His standards, if we want our position to last.

> *This very day the Persian and Median women of the nobility who have heard about the queen's conduct will respond to all the king's nobles in the same way. There will be no end of disrespect and discord. Therefore, if it pleases the king, let him issue a royal decree and let it be written in the laws of Persia and Media, which cannot be repealed, that Vashti is never again to enter the presence of King Xerxes. Also let the king give her royal position to someone else who is better than she. Then when the king's edict is proclaimed throughout all his vast realm, all the women will respect their husbands, from the least to the greatest.* (Esther 1:18-20)

The King is looking for those who will set the standard and be effective role models. Vashti's decision to defy the king's command affected not only her but all of those in the land—all who were under her position of authority. The point is, we must always answer when the King of kings calls our name. We must always do what He has commanded us to do. No excuse is acceptable!

Vashti didn't temporarily lose her position; she lost it permanently. When the door was closed due to her disobedience, the door was closed forever. Esther 1:19 says, *"Vashti is never again to enter the presence of King Xerxes."* She was never allowed back in her position. Instead, the king gave her position to one who was greater than she. An ordinary young woman with an obedient heart was chosen for the position. That young person was Esther—the *"someone else...better than"* Vashti.

DON'T FORFEIT YOUR GOD-ORDAINED POSITION

God always has someone else "waiting in the wings" who would love to take our place if we make bad choices. God *will* get His work done. He will see His purposes fulfilled. He always has plenty of applicants longing for positions as His "palace personnel" who will get His work done and build up His kingdom. If someone disqualifies him or herself, there is another hungry heart longing to be used as a vessel of God's glory.

> *Then the king's personal attendants proposed, "Let a search be made for beautiful young virgins for the king. Let the king appoint commissioners in every province of his realm to bring all these beautiful girls into the harem at the citadel of Susa. Let them be placed under the care of Hegai, the king's eunuch, who is in charge of the women; and let beauty treatments be given to them. Then let the girl who pleases the king be queen instead of Vashti." This advice appealed to the king, and he followed it.* (Esther 2:2-4)

Esther's heart of purity and obedience attracted the king. Spiritual beauty attracts the King. The inward beauty of a pure heart and spirit causes one to shine with beauty on the outside. Yes, inward purity causes outward beauty in ever-increasing radiance.

> *Now the king was attracted to Esther more than to any of the other women, and she won his favor and approval more than any of the other virgins. So he set a royal crown on her head and made her queen instead of Vashti.* (Esther 2:17)

Again, obedience attracts the King. The presence of the Lord and the anointing attract His favor. Emotional health on the inside causes physical health on the outside, just as inward beauty in the spirit causes outward beauty to radiate.

REALIGNMENT: AN IMPORTANT STEP IN SPIRITUAL TURNAROUND

Like Vashti, Jonah needed a realignment. God tried to send him to preach to the Ninevites, and he went running in the opposite direction. But the difference between Jonah and Vashti was that Jonah received the realignment he desperately needed. After a few course corrections from the King of kings, he turned around and headed to the place where God was sending him.

I'm sure there were little things that led up to Vashti's grand finale of disobedience. I'm sure the Lord had dealt with her along the way. The Holy Spirit will nudge us when our hearts begin to drift away from our commitment to the King. I'm sure it was a gradual fading away of her heart of commitment to the king—Vashti didn't lose her allegiance overnight. Yet she never received the realignment she needed.

Jonah, on the other hand, submitted to the realignment process. Yes, God strongly encouraged him—with whale breath, seaweed, and salt water! But we must give credit where credit is due—Jonah finally received his realignment.

Submit to the Process, Regardless of Your Feelings

> The word of the Lord came to Jonah son of Amittai: "Go to the great city of Nineveh and preach against it, because its wickedness has come up before me." But Jonah ran away from the Lord and headed for Tarshish. He went down to Joppa, where he found a ship bound for that port. After paying the fare, he went aboard and sailed for Tarshish to flee from the Lord. (Jonah 1:1-3)

Jonah had a mind of his own. He didn't "feel like" going where God told him to go. He didn't "feel like" doing what God told him to do. So he figured he would just ignore God and follow his own agenda instead. God's plan didn't appeal. Well, FYI—you can never run away from God, and your plan will never be better than God's.

I have learned over the years that the things the Lord tells me to do that I really, really don't want to do end up being my greatest blessings. The places where the Lord tells me He wants me to go, even though I really, really don't want to, always end up being the locations where I receive the greatest overflow of blessings. This is just further proof that God's plan is always far better than ours, for His ways are far greater (Isaiah 55:8-9).

Submit to the Process—You Can't Afford Not To!

Because God's ways and thoughts are much higher and better than ours, disobedience always costs us a lot more than we could ever imagine. Jonah thought he was paying a cheap price, a cheap "*fare*" (Jonah 1:3), to go in his own direction. However, the price of disobedience was so high, it almost cost him his life.

> Then the Lord sent a great wind on the sea, and such a violent storm arose that the ship threatened to break up. All the sailors were afraid and each cried out to his own god. And they threw the cargo into the sea to lighten the ship. But Jonah had gone below deck, where he lay down and fell into a deep sleep. The captain went to him and said, "How can you sleep? Get up and call on your god! Maybe he will take notice of us, and we will not perish." Then the sailors said to each other, "Come, let us cast lots to find out who is responsible for this calamity." They cast lots and the lot fell on Jonah. (Jonah 1:4-7)

Sometimes God allows storms to arise in our lives. He loves us so much that He may allow a storm to arise if it will give us the realignment we so desperately need. Every storm is meant to serve as a wake-up call—it wakes us up and causes us to call on our God!

Submit and Own Up to the Area Where You Need Realignment

When all indications pointed to Jonah, he did not shift blame but accepted responsibility. That was an important first step in the right direction. When folks with addictions stop blaming those around them and finally take responsibility for their own actions, they take that all-important first step in the right direction.

> *This terrified them and they asked, "What have you done?" (They knew he was running away from the Lord, because he had already told them so.) The sea was getting rougher and rougher. So they asked him, "What should we do to you to make the sea calm down for us?" "Pick me up and throw me into the sea," he replied, "and it will become calm. I know that it is my fault that this great storm has come upon you."* (Jonah 1:10-12)

Everyone else on the ship was in the middle of Jonah's storm. In the same way, the people in your life—the others on your "boat"—are subject to the storms that arise when you have been walking in disobedience and leading a sinful lifestyle. But, when you get back on the boat of obedience through a realignment, the storm will subside and things will return to normal for everyone else around you.

When you make the choice to get out of the place where you aren't supposed to be, God will supernaturally give you a route out! The only place Jonah could think of for them to send him was overboard and into the ocean. That makes me respect him even more for owning up to his responsibility and choosing to get realigned. The only place for him to "exit stage left" was to go overboard! When he finally decided to take responsibility for his disobedience, he was determined to pay the price—whatever that ended up being. I'm not sure that you or I would have chosen that course. Being thrown into the ocean is a scary thing when the seas are calm—imagine being tossed into the waves in the midst of a raging storm! But Jonah did the right thing.

God loved Jonah so much that He provided a way out. It wasn't a Marriott or a Hilton hotel, but it was shelter from the storm.

Then they took Jonah and threw him overboard, and the raging sea grew calm. At this the men greatly feared the Lord, and they offered a sacrifice to the Lord and made vows to him. But the Lord provided a great fish to swallow Jonah, and Jonah was inside the fish three days and three nights. (Jonah 1:15-17)

God always works everything for our good and His glory, even when we've made a mess of things. He always gets the glory when we decide to get back on track. In Jonah's situation, the hand of God was displayed powerfully, and the nonbelievers who witnessed it began to call on Jonah's God.

Pray in Repentance for Realignment

As for Jonah, he spent the next three nights checked in at a "whale" of a hotel. And he had a whale of a prayer meeting—one unlike any he had ever had before!

From inside the fish Jonah prayed to the Lord his God. He said: "In my distress I called to the Lord, and he answered me. From the depths of the grave I called for help, and you listened to my cry. You hurled me into the deep, into the very heart of the seas, and the currents swirled about me, all your waves and breakers swept over me. I said, 'I have been banished from your sight; yet I will look again toward your holy temple.' The engulfing waters threatened me, the deep surrounded me; seaweed was wrapped around my head. To the roots of the mountains I sank down; the earth beneath barred me in forever. But you brought my life up from the pit, O Lord my God. When my life was ebbing away, I remembered you, Lord, and my prayer rose to you, to your holy temple. Those who cling to worthless idols forfeit the grace that could be theirs. But I, with a song of thanksgiving, will sacrifice to you. What I have vowed I will make good.

Salvation comes from the Lord." And the Lord commanded the fish, and it vomited Jonah onto dry land. (Jonah 2:1-10)

If you skimmed those verses or skipped over them, I want you to go back and read them carefully. I included all of them for a reason. There are many important truths hidden in these verses, and the Lord wants you to glean them all.

Jonah truly repented. He thanked the Lord for sparing his life. Jonah renewed his commitment to the Lord, and he truly received his realignment. This was a turning point for Jonah. He experienced a total turnaround. The Lord forgave him for his disobedience and placed him back on His original track for his life.

God is ready to do the same for you. When you truly repent, when you truly allow the Lord to give you a realignment, He will supernaturally restore you to the place where you were intended to be. It's at that time and that place of your original appointment that you will experience true peace, pure joy, and complete fulfillment. It's at your place of appointment that you will bear fruit. And it's at that place and assignment that God will use you to bring turnaround in the lives of others, just as Jonah did for the people of Nineveh.

ORDINARY PEOPLE BRINGING EXTRAORDINARY TURNAROUNDS

When the Lord spoke to Jonah a second time, he followed the Lord's instructions, and the fruit of his obedience was great. The city of Nineveh repented, and God cancelled the punishment He had threatened— that's huge!

God used Jonah to bring about total turnaround in the city. And God wants to use you and me to bring total turnaround into the lives of others. But He can't use us until we've submitted to the turnarounds He wants to work in our own hearts and lives.

Esther was just an ordinary young girl who maintained a heart for God. Her faithful obedience kept her on the right path. When we accept the Lord the first time, it's just much easier and most fruitful to never require another turnaround in our lives. If, like Jonah, we veer off track, we'd better get turned back around. But it's even better and more fruitful just to keep the original turnaround from the Lord that we received the first time through salvation.

The Lord wants you to be fine-tuned in your focus so He can bring spiritual turnaround in the lives of those you come into contact with on a daily basis. There are people all around you who need a spiritual turnaround. As you are fine-tuned in your focus, God will use you to jump-start their turnaround!

Fine-tune your focus on following God obediently.

POINTS TO PONDER

1. What is the most important turnaround that one can ever make? Have you experienced this for yourself?

2. Broken focus caused Queen Vashti to lose her position in the palace. What are some things that have broken your focus and kept you from obediently following God?

3. Why is realignment an important step in spiritual turnaround? And what is the all-important "first step in the right direction" to be realigned, as seen in the life of Jonah?

4. God can't use you and me until we have submitted to the turnarounds He wants to work in our hearts and lives. What is He waiting for you to submit to? Are you ready to do so today?

Meditate on these Scriptures, speak them aloud, and commit them to memory:

Repent, then and turn to God, so that your sins may be wiped out, that times of refreshing may come from the Lord. (Acts 3:19)

Blessed is the man who listens to me, watching daily at my doors, waiting at my doorway. (Proverbs 8:34)

Do not conform any longer to the pattern of this world, but be transformed by the renewing of your mind. Then you will be able to test and approve what God's will is—his good, pleasing and perfect will. (Romans 12:2)

Therefore we do not lose heart. Though outwardly we are wasting away, yet inwardly we are being renewed day by day. For our light and momentary troubles are achieving for us an eternal glory that far outweighs them all. (2 Corinthians 4:16-17)

Chapter 4

TOTAL TURNAROUND IN YOUR MIND-SET

The mind is often the number one place where the enemy tries to bring a showdown in spiritual warfare. If Satan manages to establish a stronghold in your mind, he gains a strategic position from which he will launch an offensive over your entire existence. When he has control of your mind-set, he can affect—and infect—your thinking, your words, and, ultimately, your actions. His goal is to infiltrate your ways of thinking and to implant a mind-set of fear, doubt, and unbelief.

Maybe this is the mind-set you're operating with today. Maybe your outlook is mostly negative. Maybe you find yourself consumed by fear and crippled by self-doubt. That's not the way God's children are supposed to live! And if that describes you, today is the day God wants to bring a total turnaround in your mind-set. He wants to transform your mind so that rather than being *ruled by* fear, doubt, and unbelief, you *rule* with God over the enemy and his schemes with a mind that's governed by bold trust in God's promises, guided by expectation of their fulfillment, and grounded in faith.

What is your role in this radical transformation? The first step is to get a clear picture of your mind-set by assessing where you've been setting your mind.

WHERE HAVE YOU SET YOUR MIND?

The apostle Paul gives us the following exhortation in Colossians 3:2-3: *"Set your minds on things above, not on earthly things. For you died, and your life is now hidden with Christ in God."*

Whatever you set your mind on becomes your mind-set. It determines the lens through which you perceive the world, and it influences how you interpret and act upon your impressions. All of your thoughts, words, choices, and decisions stem from your mind-set, which, in turn, motivates your actions.

Therefore, we must be extremely careful where we set our minds. People set their minds on all manner of things, and it's very easy to set one's mind on the wrong thing.

Set Your Mind with Ownership

From the start you and I see that the responsibility for setting our minds lies with us. You and I are the ones who decide where to set our minds. No one can set your mind somewhere for you. I can set your water glass down on the counter, I can set your books on a shelf across the room for you, I can set your car keys on the table, but I can't set your mind anywhere. You alone have the power to set your mind, and you alone decide where to set it.

Some people have set their minds back to a time ten years prior, when certain words were spoken over them, allowing their mind-set to stem from those words. Others have set their minds back to a time fifteen or twenty years ago, when someone did something to them that now informs the way they perceive reality and interact with the world around them. Some people operate with a mind-set that is based on a major disappointment or a perceived failure from their past. Where is your mind-set today?

The apostle Paul tells us to set our minds on things above—on those things with eternal significance, most notably the Word of truth. When we set our minds on the Word of God, both written and in the flesh (Jesus Christ), our minds will remain set on things above, not on things below. Whatever others have said or done to wound us, let's not set our minds on those things. A mind that's set on past hurts and pains usually develops a "victim" mind-set, always feeling offended and slighted. Don't be a slave to a misinformed mind-set!

Have you ever heard someone say, "I feel like I'm losing my mind"? Well, when someone sets his or her mind on a situation or circumstance by continually meditating on it, that feeling is only natural—the mind that is set on anything other than the Word of truth is, in essence, lost to the lies of the enemy and the mire of dwelling on unpleasant circumstances.

Set Your Mind with Urgency

After telling us to set our minds on things above, the apostle Paul says, *"But now you must rid yourselves of all such things as these: anger, rage, malice, slander, and filthy language from your lips"* (Colossians 3:8). The key word is *"now."* Don't wait to rid yourself of these things—you can't afford to delay! If you wait to rid yourselves of ungodly heart attitudes and actions, you open the door for the enemy to develop a stronghold of bitterness and unforgiveness in your mind.

It's important for us to humble ourselves before the Lord on a daily basis—many times a day—and ask Him to reveal any junk we've been harboring in our hearts and minds. The Holy Spirit is always ready and willing to reveal to us any junk that may be trying to pollute the river of our souls. The longer we hang on to an offense, the more deeply embedded it becomes, to the point where it takes over as our mind-set if we don't eliminate it in time.

"Now you must rid yourselves...." Again, no one else can do it for you. It requires action on your part. And the first course of action is to be willing to rid yourself of ungodly habits and ways of thinking, through the power

of the Holy Spirit. When you willingly repent before the Lord, the Holy Spirit is right there to help you carry out the will of the Father for you—that is, to forgive others and release them, thereby freeing yourself from bondage to bitterness and resentment.

Set Your Mind Obediently

"Now you must rid yourselves...." The truth is, you don't have a choice. There's no way around it. If you want to please the Lord, if you want to be in right standing with the Father, and if you want to enjoy all of the blessings and benefits of a relationship with Him, then you must rid yourself of ungodly emotions and heart attitudes. To rid is defined as "to...clear, relieve, or disencumber, as of something undesirable...to save or deliver, as from danger, difficulty, etc.; rescue." You rid yourself of the negative "muck" in your mind-set, by setting your mind on Jesus Christ and the Word of God, through repentance, prayer, and worship. *"Finally, brothers, whatever is true, whatever is noble, whatever is right, whatever is pure, whatever is lovely, whatever is admirable—if anything is excellent or praiseworthy—think about such things"* (Philippians 4:8).

A mind that is set in the right place operates with a mind-set of trust, faith, hope, and expectation.

THE MIND-SET OF TRUST

A vital aspect of our mind-set is trust in God. When we "set" our minds on the fact that we can trust God, remembering all of the times He has proven Himself trustworthy in the past, it frees us to yield to His leading and to obey His commands, even when they seem extremely illogical to our natural minds. When we trust in the Lord with all of our hearts, rather than leaning on our own understanding (Proverbs 3:5-6), we can rest in the knowledge that He is all-knowing, all-powerful, and all-wise. His wisdom exceeds the capacities of our natural minds, and that fact—coupled with the knowledge that He has our best interests at heart—should be reason enough to trust Him with every ounce of our being.

Your heavenly Father desires that all of His children experience the peace that comes when you trust Him completely. When you yield to His desire to turn your mind-set around, you can have the same mind-set of trust that the prophet Elijah possessed. Even in the face of adversity and lack, Elijah trusted God, and his mind-set made all the difference—not only for himself but also for those to whom he ministered, as you are about to see.

Trust Leads to Obedience

> *Now Elijah the Tishbite, from Tishbe in Gilead, said to Ahab, "As the Lord, the God of Israel, lives, whom I serve, there will be neither dew nor rain in the next few years except at my word." Then the word of the Lord came to Elijah: "Leave here, turn eastward and hide in the Kerith Ravine, east of the Jordan. You will drink from the brook, and I have ordered the ravens to feed you there."* (1 Kings 17:1-4)

Without a mind-set of trust, Elijah never would have carried out the Lord's command. I can imagine that many of us, myself included, would have thought, *That can't be what God wants me to do. I must be missing it! God would never expect me to rely on a brook and a bunch of ravens for my sustenance. That makes no sense.* Yet, as we have established, God's commands are often illogical. They rarely align with our expectations. That's why a mind-set of trust is so important! Without it, we would rarely, if ever, walk in obedience to the Lord.

God was sending Elijah as His representative to deliver a divine word to a widow and her son. Because of King Ahab's worship of pagan gods—including Baal, the god of the rainclouds—the land was in crisis. God sent a drought as judgment on a nation that had turned to idolatry, as well as to prove that Baal was powerless to bring rain.

Yet, in the midst of His judgment on the land, God made special provision for His faithful servant Elijah. But Elijah needed to trust in God, or he never would have received his miraculous sustenance. It was Elijah's mind-set of trust in God that enabled him to walk in obedience and thereby receive the Lord's provision. Obedience to God always brings success!

But disobedience brings curses. Jeremiah 17:5 says, *"Cursed is the one who trusts in man, who depends on flesh for his strength and whose heart turns away from the Lord."* When we start walking in disobedience, we have literally turned away from the Lord. And when we turn from Him and trust in man, instead, we risk bringing a curse upon whatever we are doing. But, when we have the right mind-set—when we operate from a place of trust in the Lord—we open the door to abundant blessings. Blessings always await us on the other side of obedience.

Jeremiah 17:7 says, *"Blessed is the man who trusts in the Lord, whose confidence is in him."* Elijah's confidence was in the Lord! I think it was a setup from God that a brook and some ravens, rather than a man or woman, were Elijah's first place of provision. God was "sealing the deal," making sure that Elijah's mind-set would stay where it should—trusting in God and God alone! There was no man involved in this act of provision— nobody owned the brook or the ravens. Elijah's provision came directly from the hand of God!

Trust Leads to Love

In Jeremiah 31:3, the Lord says to us, *"I have loved you with an ever-lasting love; I have drawn you with loving-kindness."* When we love the Lord God with all of our hearts, and when we understand the unconditional love He has for us, we can't help but trust Him in all circumstances. Our love for Him can be the type that the apostle Paul describes in First Corinthians 13:7—love that *"always protects, always trusts, always hopes, always perseveres."* God's love for us is everlasting and unfailing. Who wouldn't want to trust Someone who loves like that? Someone whose commands are for our good; Someone who *"guides [us] in paths of righteousness for his name's sake"* (Psalm 23:3); Someone who *"in all things...works for the good of those who love him, who have been called according to his purpose"* (Romans 8:28). We can trust God for everything!

God provided for the multitudes on the mountainside, as we saw in the story of Jesus feeding the five thousand (Matthew 14:13-21; Mark 6:30-44; Luke 9:10-17; John 6:1-15). And He provided for a single faithful man at the riverside. God's blessings are for everyone who operates with a mind-set of trust in Him.

Elijah reaped his blessings when he followed the Lord's instructions.

> *So he did what the Lord had told him. He went to the Kerith Ravine, east of the Jordan, and stayed there. The ravens brought him bread and meat in the morning and bread and meat in the evening, and he drank from the brook.* (1 Kings 17:5-6)

Wow—it happened just the way the Lord had said it would! All that was required of Elijah was the right mind-set—the mind-set of trust—to set the promises of God in motion.

THE MIND-SET OF FAITH

The second phase of Elijah's journey of obedience required him to have a mind-set of faith. It was his faith that brought about a turnaround in his situation, as well as in the life of the widow he encountered who was utterly lacking faith.

> *Some time later the brook dried up because there had been no rain in the land. Then the word of the Lord came to him: "Go at once to Zarephath of Sidon and stay there. I have commanded a widow in that place to supply you with food."* (1 Kings 17:7-9)

Even when the brook dried up and Elijah's needs were no longer being met, he didn't switch from a mind-set of faith to one of doubt.

I feel quite confident that most of us would have been tempted to act out of our flesh and switch to a mind-set of doubt. Our words, or at least our thoughts, would have probably sounded something like this: "I can't believe this, God! You sent me here, and now my source of provision has dried up. You must not love me anymore. Maybe I didn't hear You correctly after all. If I was really supposed to be here, this brook never would have dried up! What have I done to deserve this, Lord?" And on and on we probably would have gone!

But not Elijah. He had a mind-set of faith. The reason that the brook dried up was because the Lord wanted to get Elijah to his next assignment—a widow woman in need of a dramatic turnaround in her mind-set. Doubt had consumed her to the point where she was ready to die. But God had other plans for her, and they involved Elijah and his mind-set of faith.

Faith Is Contagious

You may not have realized it, but your mind-set affects others around you. And others around you can affect your mind-set as well. It's almost contagious. It says in the Word of God that you become like those you hang around (1 Corinthians 15:33).

One purpose of Jesus' hanging out with the disciples was so that they might become like Him—so that His character would rub off on them. In the same way, our presence—our actions, attitudes, and words—profoundly affect those around us.

Faith Propels Us Forward

Elijah knew that what God had done before, He would do again. Phase one took Elijah to the brook; phase two took him to the widow. Both phases required the right mind-set—one of trust and faith. Most people shy away from stepping into a new season. As a general rule, we don't like change! But if we're resistant to change, we miss out on the blessings God has planted in future seasons, on the other side of our obedience to His assignments.

Elijah remembered that God's provision is always at His place of positioning. So, Elijah fully understood that he had better be in the right position to receive his God-given provision.

> *So he went to Zarephath. When he came to the town gate, a widow was there gathering sticks. He called to her and asked, "Would you bring me a little water in a jar so I may have a drink?" As she was going to get it, he called, "And bring me, please, a piece of bread."* (1 Kings 17:10-11)

Elijah did just what the Lord had told him to do: he *went*. Failure to obey will rob us of God's blessings, but stepping out in obedience always sets those blessings in motion. Where obedience abounds, so do the blessings of God!

Elijah had the confidence to ask because he obeyed instructions. He wasn't shy about it. He didn't beat around the bush; he just boldly presented his need. He was acting out of the mind-set of faith.

Remember, *"Faith comes by hearing, and hearing by the word of God"* (Romans 10:17 NKJV). Elijah heard the voice of the Lord, and it increased his mind-set of faith! If we don't take time to get a word from God—if we act out of our flesh before we hear a word in our spirit from the Lord—our actions are likely to be ruled by fear rather than faith. Fear always limits God, but faith always causes us to embrace the limitless possibilities that He has for us.

Faith Frees Us from Limited Thinking

The battle for your mind-set starts at ground zero—your mind itself! If your mind is not grounded in faith, or if your faith is weak, your thinking will be limited as well, setting limits on what God can do in you, for you, and through you.

We set limits with our words, but God removes the limits with His Word. We set limits with our thoughts, but God removes all limits with His thoughts, which are high above our thoughts (Isaiah 55:8-9).

A mind-set of faith knows, first and foremost, that God's thoughts and ways blow ours out of the water! Therefore, nothing shocks us, rocks our boat, or throws us into "meltdown mode"! That's a great place to be, but, it is easier said than done. It isn't easy to maintain a mind-set of faith in the midst of a storm, but it is possible. Remember, we don't need "easy"; we just need possible! And *with God all things are possible* (Matthew 19:26). I believe that truth with all my heart, but I still have to remind myself of it on a regular basis.

Limitless thinking starts with limitless faith. And limitless faith begins with having a mind grounded on God's Word, which is truth (John 1:17).

Philippians 4:8 shows us a key to living with a sound mind. It says, *"Finally, brothers, whatever is true, whatever is noble, whatever is right, whatever is pure, whatever is lovely, whatever is admirable—if anything is excellent or praiseworthy—think about such things."* Our greatest battles always begin in our minds. As we renew our minds daily to the truth of God's Word, we can maintain a sound mind—a mind-set of faith—in the midst of every challenge life throws our way. God's Word is the answer key to every test in life, and the good news is, it isn't considered cheating to use it!

Faith Comes from Feeding Daily on God's Word

Joshua 1:8 instructs us, *"Do not let this Book of the Law depart from your mouth; meditate on it day and night, so that you may be careful to do everything written in it. Then you will be prosperous and successful."*

The words *"Do not let"* indicate that we have a choice in the matter. It means that it's up to us. If we get lazy, or if we "let" the words of the enemy fill our mouths, we have made a bad choice. No one can choose for us. You and I must choose daily to speak the Word of God with our mouth. Just as no one else can "set" our mind for you or me, no one else can carry out this instruction for us. We must do it ourselves, as God empowers us. And He will empower you and me because He wants us to do it!

You must choose not to let the Word of God depart from your mouth. And when the Word of God is continually in your mouth, that means it's also in your thoughts—you are renewing your mind by His truth (Romans 12:2), so that it becomes worry free and filled with peace, not fear and doubt. *"For God has not given us a spirit of fear, but of power and of love and of a sound mind"* (2 Timothy 1:7 NKJV). A sound mind is not plagued with thoughts of fear, doubt, and unbelief. Rather, it is filled with faith.

Father has given us the instruction; now it's up to us to carry it out. He has clearly told us how to be *"prosperous and successful."* He has clearly told us that His desire is for us to have a sound mind. *The power of life and death is in our tongue* (Proverbs 18:21). So, let's speak the Word of God daily over ourselves and over our circumstances.

Don't speak what the devil says—speak what the Word says! The more you speak the Word, the stronger your mind-set of faith becomes because faith always comes by hearing the Word. When you are the one speaking the Word, the same principle applies!

Not only are you supposed to speak the Word, but you are also supposed to think the Word and do the Word daily. Joshua 1:8 says, *"Meditate on [the Word] day and night."* In other words, you are to think about the truth—God's Word. Let your mind be filled with the Word. Then the verse goes on to specify the reason for doing this: *"So that you may be careful to do everything written in it."* That means, "Do the Word." So, you need to speak the Word, think the Word, and do the Word.

Say it out loud right now: "I need to speak the Word, think the Word, and do the Word. Daily, I need to speak the Word, think the Word, and do the Word!" If you do those three things, fear and doubt will flee from you. James 4:7 says, *"Resist the devil, and he will flee from you."* One way you resist the devil is by speaking, thinking, and doing the Word of God. Resist the devil's mind-set and walk boldly in the same mind-set of faith that Elijah had.

The Mind-set of Faith Motivates Turnaround in Others

Elijah's mind-set of bold faith caused his path to cross with the widow woman. Elijah did just what the Lord had told him to do. When he asked the widow woman for his provision, he asked boldly, in faith. Yet, she responded out of her own mind-set.

> *"As surely as the Lord your God lives," she replied, "I don't have any bread—only a handful of flour in a jar and a little oil in a jug. I am gathering a few sticks to take home and make a meal for myself and my son, that we may eat it—and die."* (1 Kings 17:12)

Talk about limited thinking! When you feel as if your only option is to throw in the towel, it's a pretty good indicator that you need a turnaround in your mind-set! If you feel hopeless and devoid of faith, you need a new mind-set because the one you are operating out of is not from the Lord, who is the "God of hope":

> *May the God of hope fill you with all joy and peace as you trust in him, so that you may overflow with hope by the power of the Holy Spirit.* (Romans 15:13)

God wants you to be filled to overflowing with His hope! After all, He is the God of hope. And He wants you to overflow with hope, that you might share it with others and "infect" their mind-sets with the same faith. That's why God sent Elijah to the widow woman for the second phase of his assignment. She needed what he had (hope) more than he needed what she had (food).

She told him, *"I don't have any bread—only a handful of flour in a jar and a little oil in a jug"* (1 Kings 17:12b). She thought she didn't have what was needed. What she didn't realize was she did have everything that was needed; it just wasn't in its final form.

Many times we have what we need, but we miss it because of our mind-set, if it isn't grounded in trust and faith in God. Over the years, as my ministry has grown, I have needed to add a number of staff members to fill certain roles. In the hiring process, there were times when I would meet with a prospect and then later say to God, "Is this really the staff member You are bringing me?" Some of the individuals who got the job were actually the last people I would have hired, had the decision been up to me. But, time and time again, the Lord would say to me, "They aren't in final form." In other words, they had everything they needed—all of the necessary "raw ingredients" of character—they just weren't completely "baked." Their qualifications needed to be refined in the "oven" of experience, with me mentoring them, teaching them, and pouring into them from my own life.

In the same way, the widow woman in First Kings 17 had everything she needed; she merely lacked the proper mind-set and, therefore, didn't realize how well-equipped she really was. So, God sent Elijah to adjust her mind-set and mentor her to adopting his mind-set of faith.

> *Elijah said to her, "Don't be afraid. Go home and do as you have said. But first make a small cake of bread for me from what you have and bring it to me, and then make something for yourself and your son. For this is what the Lord, the God of Israel, says: 'The jar of flour will not be used up and the jug of oil will not run dry until the day the Lord gives rain on the land.'"* (1 Kings 17:13-14)

Elijah challenged the widow to obey the Lord's instructions. If she followed through in obedience, her provision would never run out. But if she chose not to take the step of faith and obey, her mind-set would be the death of her. Ultimately, she was encouraged by Elijah's mind-set of faith, and she responded in obedience. As a result, she stepped into abundant provision. She had more than enough—for herself, her family, and even Elijah. She ended up being his source of provision after all!

She went away and did as Elijah had told her. So there was food every day for Elijah and for the woman and her family. For the jar of flour was not used up and the jug of oil did not run dry, in keeping with the word of the Lord spoken by Elijah. (1 Kings 17:15-16)

GUARD YOUR FAITH-FILLED FRAME OF MIND

God always keeps His Word! When we have received instructions from the Lord, we must allow the Holy Spirit to guard our minds and to keep us in peace, so that we may fulfill those instructions without wavering in our faith. This is a lesson that the widow woman needed to learn. After seeing God supernaturally supply her with food and oil, she nevertheless doubted His provision in another area of her life: the health and well-being of her son.

Some time later the son of the woman who owned the house became ill. He grew worse and worse, and finally stopped breathing. She said to Elijah, "What do you have against me, man of God? Did you come to remind me of my sin and kill my son?" "Give me your son," Elijah replied. He took him from her arms, carried him to the upper room where he was staying, and laid him on his bed. Then he cried out to the Lord, "O Lord my God, have you brought tragedy also upon this widow I am staying with, by causing her son to die?" Then he stretched himself out on the boy three times and cried to the Lord, "O Lord my God, let this boy's life return to him!" The Lord heard Elijah's cry, and the boy's life returned to him, and he lived. Elijah picked up the child and carried him down from the room into the house. He gave him to his mother and said, "Look, your son is alive!" (1 Kings 17:17-23)

Yet again, Elijah responded with his mind-set of faith. Although the widow wavered and lost her mind-set of faith, Elijah once again assisted her with her needed turnaround. And, once again, she received it!

> *Then the woman said to Elijah, "Now I know that you are a man of God and that the word of the Lord from your mouth is the truth." (1 Kings 17:24)*

The Word again brought about the mind-set of faith. We must keep our mind-set of faith and trust in the Lord. We must guard our minds and our mind-sets daily. The widow received her turnaround, but then she lost it temporarily when she began to look in the natural. Let's not make the same mistake!

The widow woman's loss of faith was not too different from that of Peter when he stepped out of the boat and walked on the water toward Jesus.

> *During the fourth watch of the night Jesus went out to them, walking on the lake. When the disciples saw him walking on the lake, they were terrified. "It's a ghost," they said, and cried out in fear. But Jesus immediately said to them: "Take courage! It is I. Don't be afraid." "Lord, if it's you," Peter replied, "tell me to come to you on the water." "Come," he said. Then Peter got down out of the boat, walked on the water and came toward Jesus. But when he saw the wind, he was afraid and, beginning to sink, cried out, "Lord, save me!" Immediately Jesus reached out his hand and caught him. "You of little faith," he said, "why did you doubt?" (Matthew 14:25-31)*

Peter was doing just great until he focused on the wind, which represents the natural world and the "facts" it presents us with. His faith was upholding him on the surface of the water, until his natural senses took over and told him that he would surely sink. See how easily self-doubt becomes a self-fulfilling prophecy? We need to keep from backsliding into doubt and disbelief. And we do this, again, by keeping our minds stayed on God!

The prophet Isaiah made this point when he said to the Lord, *"You will guard him and keep him in perfect and constant peace whose mind [both its inclination and its character] is stayed on You, because he commits himself to You, leans on You, and hopes confidently in You"* (Isaiah 26:3 AMP).

After you receive your instructions from the Lord, you can't allow your mind to wander! Father will keep you in perfect and constant peace as long as your mind stays on Him, maintaining a mind-set of faith. So, park your mind in peace and put on the emergency brake, so that you do not shift into reverse!

THE MIND-SET OF HOPE

Let's "shift gears" from the prophet Elijah to David, whom God called *"a man after my own heart"* (Acts 13:22). David wasn't perfect, but he found favor with God; as king, he led Israel with a standard of excellence. We should be encouraged by the knowledge that God doesn't require perfection of us; He simply longs for us to have a heart that yearns for Him, as David's did.

Out of his excellent heart grew the right mind-set. David had the very mind-set of turnaround! David had his mind set on the promises of God, so he had the mind-set of faith and of hope—in short, he had the mind-set of victory.

When others were overwhelmed and hopeless, David's hopeful mind-set turned the entire situation around. He possessed an attitude that said, "God is able." And it was because of his proper mind-set that David was selected as the replacement for King Saul.

King Saul lost the crown and gave up his throne due to a wrong mind-set. We read in First Samuel 15:24, *"Then Saul said to Samuel, 'I have sinned. I violated the Lord's command and your instructions. I was afraid of the people and so I gave in to them.'"* The mind-set of fear can disqualify you from receiving the Lord's best. Saul's mind-set of fearful timidity cost him everything, while David's mind-set of confident hope ushered him into greatness.

> *So Samuel took the horn of oil and anointed him in the presence of his brothers, and from that day on the Spirit of the Lord came upon David in power.... (1 Samuel 16:13)*

David was a gifted musician and a mighty warrior. With these gifts, he would eventually become famous in Israel and end up leading the nation into great spiritual and political victories! The Lord's anointing was upon David, and everyone knew it. When you are anointed, others know it. When you aren't anointed, or when you have lost your anointing, as Saul did, others know it as well.

Word began to get out about David, and when the need arose for someone to play the harp, David's name came up.

> *One of the servants answered, "I have seen a son of Jesse of Bethlehem who knows how to play the harp. He is a brave man and a warrior. He speaks well and is a fine-looking man. And the Lord is with him." (1 Samuel 16:18)*

David was a great man with great gifts, but the fact that the Lord was with him and that he was anointed from the Lord—that outweighed everything! Your anointing is your greatest asset. That's why it is so important for you and me to guard our anointing by guarding our hearts and keeping a heart of obedience.

When you try to do things in your own strength, when you try to do things with a wrong mind-set, you can easily get overwhelmed. You can actually bring defeat on yourself as a result of a wrong mind-set.

> *A champion named Goliath, who was from Gath, came out of the Philistine camp. He was over nine feet tall. He had a bronze helmet on his head and wore a coat of scale armor of bronze weighing five thousand shekels; on his legs he wore bronze*

greaves, and a bronze javelin was slung on his back. His spear shaft was like a weaver's rod, and its iron point weighed six hundred shekels. His shield bearer went ahead of him. Goliath stood and shouted to the ranks of Israel, "Why do you come out and line up for battle? Am I not a Philistine, and are you not the servants of Saul? Choose a man and have him come down to me. If he is able to fight and kill me, we will become your subjects; but if I overcome him and kill him, you will become our subjects and serve us." Then the Philistine said, "This day I defy the ranks of Israel! Give me a man and let us fight each other." On hearing the Philistine's words, Saul and all the Israelites were dismayed and terrified. (1 Samuel 17:4-11)

The enemy had succeeded in creating a mind-set of fear in the Israelite army. The soldiers were dismayed. They were terrified. They had no hope! It doesn't matter how big the giant is that you're facing; when you have a mind-set of hope, you are fearless in the face of every enemy.

That was "little" David—fearless due to his mind-set of hope. The "big boys"—well, let's just say they needed a major overhaul in their mind-set!

David left his things with the keeper of supplies, ran to the battle lines and greeted his brothers. As he was talking with them, Goliath, the Philistine champion from Gath, stepped out from his lines and shouted his usual defiance, and David heard it. When the Israelites saw the man, they all ran from him in great fear. (1 Samuel 17:22-24)

The other brothers, the "big boys," were the ones chosen to go into battle with King Saul against the Philistines. Little David was left to tend a few little sheep on the backside of the desert. It was that hidden place, the seemingly insignificant position, that became the launching pad for David to be the greatest king Israel ever had. David had a servant's heart. He would tend the sheep faithfully, day after day, week after week, month after month. Then, as needed, he would take food to the front lines to feed the "big boys."

Usually, those who are dubbed the "big boys" according to human standards are the "spiritual squirts" in God's eyes. They may have looked big and intimidating, physically speaking, but their great fear exposed how small and limited they really were, especially in their mind-set.

> *David asked the men standing near him, "What will be done for the man who kills this Philistine and removes this disgrace from Israel? Who is this uncircumcised Philistine that he should defy the armies of the living God?"* (1 Samuel 17:26)

David had the right mind-set. He basically said, "Who is this dude who thinks he can come against the King of kings and the Lord of lords? Who is this disgraceful guy presuming to challenge God's people?" Because of his confident hope, David was not intimidated by the seeming "giant" of a problem in front of him.

Everyone laughed at David. The giant Goliath laughed at David, but so did his own brothers. His brothers actually made false accusations against David, which was a dead giveaway of their envy. It's true that false accusations are a reliable indicator of envy.

David's mind-set of hope was expressed in his comment to Israel's leader, Saul. David said to him, *"Let no one lose heart on account of this Philistine; your servant will go and fight him"* (1 Samuel 17:32). David's mind was set on how powerful his God was. His mind was set on the fact that God was more than able to handle this giant. And his mind was set on the hope he had in his God.

> *David said to the Philistine, "You come against me with sword and spear and javelin, but I come against you in the name of the Lord Almighty, the God of the armies of Israel, whom you have defied. This day the Lord will hand you over to me, and I'll strike you down and cut off your head. Today I will give the*

carcasses of the Philistine army to the birds of the air and the beasts of the earth, and the whole world will know that there is a God in Israel. All those gathered here will know that it is not by sword or spear that the Lord saves; for the battle is the Lord's, and he will give all of you into our hands." (1 Samuel 17:45-47)

Well, all right, then! David was telling it like it was! His passionate determination and bold confidence in the Lord were both fueled by his mind-set of hope.

If you don't have the right mind-set, it's important for you to experience a turnaround today! The wrong mind-set can cause you to lose the battle at hand, while the right mind-set can cause you to win the battle with relative ease.

David developed the right mind-set on the backside of the desert while tending sheep. David developed the right mind-set while he served the Lord and while he served those in authority over him. Then, at the appointed time—at the time the Lord had ordained for David—he triumphed with ease.

As the Philistine moved closer to attack him, David ran quickly toward the battle line to meet him. Reaching into his bag and taking out a stone, he slung it and struck the Philistine on the forehead. The stone sank into his forehead, and he fell face-down on the ground. So David triumphed over the Philistine with a sling and a stone; without a sword in his hand he struck down the Philistine and killed him. (1 Samuel 17:48-50)

David's mind-set brought about a total turnaround, not only for him, but also for the entire nation of Israel. Your mind-set can cause turnaround in the lives of all of those around you—even your entire nation! But you must keep a mind-set of hope. Keep believing that God can do anything. Nothing is too difficult or too big for Him. Allow Him to bring a turnaround to your mind-set today!

After David had slain Goliath, we read that *"when the Philistines saw that their hero was dead, they turned and ran. Then the men of Israel and Judah surged forward with a shout…"* (1 Samuel 17:51-52).

A mind-set of hope will cause the enemy to run away in fear. Stand your ground! Because David stood his ground, Israel not only won the battle at hand—an "impossible" victory—but they also "surged forward." God wants you to surge forward today. But there is often a "purge" before the "surge" in your life. The Lord purges, or prunes His people, to get you and me ready for the surge—a harvest of abundant fruit.

Maybe you have been going through a season of "purging." Maybe you need a "purging" of your current mind-set. Well, stay encouraged—the greater the purge, the greater the surge that lies before you!

Israel surged forward with a shout. Don't wait any longer—give a shout of victory right now! A shout of victory testifies to your mind-set of hope, stemming from faith and founded on trust. Keep your mind set on the promises of God and expect Him to give you the victory.

THE MIND-SET OF EXPECTATION

David expected God to give him the victory on the battlefield against Goliath. And He did! Let's revisit the prophet Elijah. He expected God to fulfill His promises, and it was that mind-set that ensured his success. Elijah's hope gave him a sense of expectation that God would do all that He had promised. Then, when Elijah went to Mount Carmel for the show-down, he expected God to show up and show off! And that expectation was fulfilled.

What are you expecting today? Your expectation, or your lack thereof, reflects your mind-set. If you find yourself continually disappointed and unfulfilled, it's probably due to a lack of expectation. You will never birth something you aren't expecting! I was expecting my daughter for nine months before I gave birth to her. If you aren't expecting anything, you will never birth anything, either. But whatever you are expecting is eventually what you will birth, so make sure you are expecting "God things." Make sure you are expecting the promises of God and not the lies of the enemy.

Jesus said, *"Ask and it will be given to you; seek and you will find; knock and the door will be opened to you. For everyone who asks receives; he who seeks finds; and to him who knocks, the door will be opened"* (Matthew 7:7-8). Expectation causes us to ask, seek, and find greater and greater blessings in God. As we remain persistent, determined, and tenacious, we can set our minds on the promises of God and reap an abundant harvest of all that He has for us.

Matthew 11:12 says, *"From the days of John the Baptist until now, the kingdom of heaven has been forcefully advancing, and forceful men lay hold of it."* We don't possess the land by sitting back and twiddling our thumbs. We don't advance by lying in bed eating donuts and watching cartoons. We advance by force, and that takes some elbow grease! We will have to stay in the Word to maintain a right mind-set. We will have to get up out of the bed and pray regularly to maintain our expectancy of the promises of God.

Only forceful men and women will lay hold of all that God has for them—those who are forceful in taking a stand against the kingdom of darkness and advancing in the kingdom of God. Before we possess anything, we have to take a step of faith. To forcefully advance, it takes faith—one step at a time.

Again, the Lord says to us, *"For I know the plans I have for you…plans to prosper you and not to harm you, plans to give you hope and a future"* (Jeremiah 29:11). Father knows the awesome plan that He has for your life, and He wants you to know His plans for you as well. He wants you to be "expecting" all that He has for you. When you are clued in on the plan, you can expect your blessings. Your future is filled with hope, prosperity, and great blessings. And it's the right mind-set that opens the door for you to step into these future blessings.

At the time of sacrifice, the prophet Elijah stepped forward and prayed: "O Lord, God of Abraham, Isaac and Israel, let it be known today that you are God in Israel and that I am your servant and have done all these things at your command. Answer me, O Lord, answer me, so these people will know that you, O Lord, are God, and that you are turning their hearts back again." Then the fire of the Lord fell and burned up the sacrifice, the wood, the stones and the soil, and also licked up the water in the trench. When all the people saw this, they fell prostrate and cried, "The Lord—he is God! The Lord—he is God!" (1 Kings 18:36-39)

These people had a total turnaround in their mind-set. Elijah's mind-set of expectation led the way for their much-needed turnaround. They were never the same again. They began to expect the Lord to show up; they began to expect the promises of the Lord to be fulfilled.

Expectation is a key to having a total turnaround in your mind-set. Expectation is a law. Expectation comes from faith, and faith, as we've said, comes by hearing the Word of the Lord (Romans 10:17). We need to study, meditate on, speak, and pray the Word of God like never before, for only then will we maintain a mind-set of trust, faith, hope, and expectation—the mind-set that will usher us into victory in every area.

Cultivate the mind-set of trust, faith, hope, and expectation.

POINTS TO PONDER

1. Why is our mind often the number one place in which Satan tries to establish a stronghold?

2. Why is having a mind-set of trust so important, and what will it lead to in our lives?

3. What three things will a mind-set of faith do for us? Have you experienced any of these?

4. What did David's mind-set of hope and expectation accomplish for him in First Samuel 17?

Meditate on these Scriptures, speak them aloud, and commit them to memory:

> *Set your minds on things above, not on earthly things. For you died, and your life is now hidden with Christ in God. (Colossians 3:2-3)*

> *Finally, brothers, whatever is true, whatever is noble, whatever is right, whatever is pure, whatever is lovely, whatever is admirable—if anything is excellent or praiseworthy—think about such things. (Philippians 4:8)*

> *Do not let this Book of the Law depart from your mouth; meditate on it day and night, so that you may be careful to do everything written in it. Then you will be prosperous and successful. (Joshua 1:8)*

> *Ask and it will be given to you; seek and you will find; knock and the door will be opened to you. For everyone who asks receives; he who seeks finds; and to him who knocks, the door will be opened. (Matthew 7:7-8)*

Chapter 5

TOTAL TURNAROUND IN YOUR EMOTIONS

Fear, anxiety, and depression—that's the devil's recipe for his destructive attempt on the body of Christ. But you and I are not unaware of the enemy's schemes (2 Corinthians 2:11). If the enemy has been trying to "cook up" disaster in your life through these three ingredients, it's time for you to have a total turnaround in your emotions!

In the dictionary, *anxiety* is defined as "a state of being uneasy, apprehensive, or worried about what may happen." The key word here is *may!* The enemy tries to get you to worry about what "may" happen. His job is to try and put doubt in your mind about God and His ability to handle your situation. Fear and depression seep into the lives of God's precious people because they are worried about what "may" happen—as if worrying ever prevented bad things from happening. *"Who of you by worrying can add a single hour to his life?"* (Luke 12:25).

In reality, the devil is the one who is uneasy, apprehensive, and worried about what might happen if you grab ahold of the "rope of hope"—God's Word—and start standing on the Word of truth. The enemy has a lot to be anxious about! He has been trying to remind you of your past in order to hold you back from running after God simply because he knows what his future has in store: his loss and God's victory! When the devil reminds you of your past, you need to start reminding him of his future. His future is dark, while yours is bright—bright with eternal life!

FREEDOM FROM ANXIETY AND DEPRESSION

When it comes down to it, anxiety is an indicator of a lack of trust in God. Meanwhile, of all people, God is the one we can trust! When we trust God, we are not uneasy, apprehensive, or worried about what may happen. When we trust in the Lord and in God's Word, we already know the outcome because His Word tells us what it is.

When unexpected pits arise on your pathway to the palace position God has called you to, don't freak out. Don't give in to fear, and don't allow yourself to be anxious. Those pit stops haven't shaken God, changed His plan for your life, or caught Him off guard. They are simply opportunities for you to grow and mature on your path to the palace. Think about it—if you were never in a situation in which you desperately needed a total turnaround that God alone could pull off, you would never be able to encourage others through the pits they encounter!

Trust Is the Key

As you simply trust God in all things in spite of everything, you will mature in character, grow in faith, and progress in your overall walk with the Lord.

Proverbs 3:5-6 says it so well: *"Trust in the Lord with all your heart, and lean not on your own understanding; in all your ways acknowledge Him, and He shall direct your paths"* (NKJV). We can't afford to lean on our own understanding. When we try to figure things out ourselves, we can get into fear, anxiety, and depression. But when we trust God and know that He is always in control and working things out for our good, we can have peace.

My brother died at the age of fifty-one. When he passed away, the Lord reminded me of a prayer that I had prayed many times: "Lord, save everyone in my family. No matter what it takes, I want everyone in my family to go to heaven." At the time of my big brother's death, the Lord whispered into my heart, "Wouldn't you rather him go to heaven at the age of fifty-one than to live to be eighty-one and go to hell?" I'm not sure of exactly all that God meant by that, but I do know that my answer was yes, and I know that God was telling me to trust Him—to trust that He had a plan and that He didn't need my help to run the universe.

Even in our times of grief, we don't need to be anxious or fall into depression. God is a loving Father who works all things together for our good (Romans 8:28), and His plan accounts for every heartache and sorrow we'll ever face. When we trust Him, we protect our hearts against the ravages of depression.

Uproot Your Fears and Fend Off Depression

Depression and fear are closely connected. When fear is permitted to hang around, after a while it turns to depression. You may have never recognized that fear is the root of your problem. Fear is the root of many other issues, too, and when it goes undetected, depression often sets in. Ask the Holy Spirit to show you if an underlying spirit of fear has caused you to get into a deep pit of despair. If so, you dig your way out of the pit by speaking, thinking, and doing the Word of truth.

For you to penetrate the next level in God, you must be free from the spirit of fear. Disappointments and times of discouragement can serve as an open door for fear. Rejection, abuse, and harmful words also can serve as an open door for fear. No matter what door was opened or how, that spirit of fear must leave you, in the name of Jesus. The root of fear serves as a breeding ground for depression. But, when the spirit of fear is uprooted, depression must go.

I believe that, today, Father is turning things around for you. Say out loud, "It's turnaround time. Fear will no longer steal my power. Fear will no longer steal my love. And fear will no longer steal my sound mind!" Be encouraged—the best is yet to come.

Embrace the New Season

When the seasons of life undergo a significant change, we need to release the old in order to embrace the new. This is a process, yet we must seek to move forward, step by step, a little bit every day. If we aren't aware of the enemy's schemes, we can fall for the lies he sends our way—lies that make us susceptible to depression in the midst of significant life changes. In these times, it's crucial to remember that the joy of the Lord is our strength (Nehemiah 8:10)!

Never let the enemy steal your joy, even in the midst of grief. You can grieve. You must grieve, or you will surely get stuck in that season. But you should grow forward in the midst of grief, so that you may step into the new season without getting stuck in depression.

Consider Counseling

Sometimes, as the seasons of life shift and change, it's wise to seek Christian counseling. I'm all for godly counseling that's based on the Word of God. I have a master's degree in counseling, and I myself have sought counseling during the challenging seasons of life, including when my husband left me with a newborn baby. When you go to counseling, you are investing in yourself. Don't say, "I can't afford it." I didn't have any insurance; I didn't even have diapers or baby food, at times; yet I knew that for my sake, and for the sake of my little baby, I needed to go to counseling. God always made a way! Be determined to go, and God will make a way for you, too.

Don't allow any excuses to prevent you from getting the counseling you need! The enemy wants you to get stuck in your grief and your pain; he wants to throw you into a pit of despair and depression. But you are smarter and stronger than that!

Surrender to the Lord's Perfect Plan

When we find ourselves at the close of a season, waiting on the threshold of a new season that's about to begin, we must look to the Lord every day, awaiting His guidance. We don't have to know the plan for the next ten years, ten months, or even ten days. I know that this is challenging for those who consider themselves "control freaks," but that's why they need a turnaround in their mind-set and emotions! A turnaround may be what it takes for them to realize that God is in control and that they must only trust Him to reveal what's next, one day, one hour, or one minute at a time. This type of turnaround will teach us to be content knowing just one thing: whatever comes next, it's all good!

Remember Jeremiah 29:11: *"For I know the plans I have for you,' declares the Lord, 'plans to prosper you and not to harm you, plans to give you hope and a future.'"* That's all good! It doesn't promise that God's plans will be easy; it promises that they will be good. Sometimes, when we are in the midst of a transition from an old season into a new season—whether it's due to a death, a divorce, a job loss, or even a positive event, such as a birth, a wedding, or a promotion—we may feel insecure and anxious as we wonder what's next. In these times, we must remember that each new day begins with yesterday's darkness.

Every night at 12:01 a.m., just past midnight, a new day has begun. It doesn't look new. It doesn't feel new. And it doesn't look good—it looks dark. But we know it's a new day because the clock tells us it is. When God allows situations and circumstances to usher in a new day, we must hang on to the confident hope that the sun will rise again. The Light will shine into our darkness again and illumine the path we should take. The Son will shine, and we'll live to see a beautiful new day. Our joyful hope will not have been in vain.

NOT "NOW WHAT?" BUT "WHAT NOW?"

In the midst of seasonal shifts, some people get stuck in the "Now what?" syndrome. The "Now what?" syndrome is the place where people get depressed. It's the place where people find themselves saying, "Now what, God? What am I going to have to deal with next? I've already been through so much. I've had such a rough, unfair ride in life. What more could I possibly go through now, God?" The "Now what?" syndrome is a dangerous and depressing place to be. In the "Now what?" syndrome, we tend to expect the next painful season to start at any time. We have a spirit of anticipation, but it's the anxious kind that counts on the worst scenario imaginable occurring.

Those who get stuck in the "Now what?" syndrome forget all about God's promise in Jeremiah 29:11—or, if they remember it, they believe that the word good was a misnomer and that God's plans for them are bad, not good. They expect to feel worse and worse as the days go by. Most of the time, when folks have what I call the "Now what?" syndrome, they are blinded to their symptoms. Sometimes, they even convince others around them to join in their depressing pity party. Someday, they'll awaken to the fact that their true friends were those who refused to let them stay parked in their pity party of depression, saying, "Now what, God?"

When we refuse to get stuck in the "Now what?" syndrome, we can pick ourselves up by the power of the Holy Spirit and say, "What now, God? What do You want me to do today? I know by faith that You have good things ahead for me!" When we begin to say "What now?" for each day, one day at a time, we can move forward and not allow the spirit of depression to get a stronghold in our lives.

TAKE IT ONE DAY AT A TIME

I called my sister-in-law a few days ago to check in and see how she was dealing with the death of her husband, my brother. She said, "I'm just taking it one day at a time." She is strong in her faith, and she is fully relying on God to bring her through her grief, one day at a time. As you do the same, you can experience a total turnaround and be free from fear, anxiety, and depression. Remember to draw strength from the joy of the

Lord. Step away from your gloomy situation long enough to laugh—you'll be glad you did!

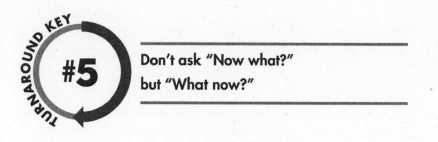

POINTS TO PONDER

1. Anxiety is an indicator of a lack of trust in God. Think of a time when you felt anxious. In what area were you withholding trust from God?

2. Uprooting your fears will help you fend off depression. How do you uproot fear?

3. Are you facing a season of change in your life? Do you know what to release from the old season in order to embrace the new season?

4. Refusing to get stuck in the "Now what?" syndrome enables us to say, "What now, God?" How will this affect our emotions for the better, and what will it enable us to do?

Meditate on these Scriptures, speak them aloud, and commit them to memory:

> *Who of you by worrying can add a single hour to his life? Since you cannot do this very little thing, why do you worry about the rest? (Luke 12:25-26)*

> *Do not be anxious about anything, but in everything, by prayer and petition, with thanksgiving, present your requests to God.*

And the peace of God, which transcends all understanding, will guard your hearts and your minds in Christ Jesus. (Philippians 4:6-7)

Cast all your anxiety on him because he cares for you. (1 Peter 5:7)

Peace I leave with you; my peace I give you. I do not give to you as the world gives. Do not let your hearts be troubled and do not be afraid. (John 14:27)

Chapter 6

TOTAL TURNAROUND IN YOUR SELF-IMAGE

Many people misinterpret the Scripture that says, *"Do not think of yourself more highly than you ought, but rather think of yourself with sober judgment"* (Romans 12:3), taking it to mean that they should embrace low self-esteem and not develop a positive self-image. They couldn't be more wrong! Our heavenly Father wants each of His children to appreciate his or her worth. One reason is that our self-esteem affects our confidence, and our confidence affects our boldness—and we need Holy-Ghost boldness to be effective witnesses for the Lord and to fulfill His call on our lives. Confidence also affects our emotional health; if we lack self-confidence, if all we see are our weaknesses, we're prone to wallow in despair.

If God wants us to walk with healthy self-confidence, it follows that the devil wants the opposite—he desires to steal our confidence, and his go-to tactic is to kill our self-esteem.

UPROOTING REJECTION

God created all of us with various needs, and one of those needs is our need to be valued or to feel loved, significant, and secure. When we experience rejection, whether it is real or perceived, we don't feel valued. A definition of *value* is "to think highly of; esteem." Without Christ, when we experience rejection, we can internalize others' opinions of us—whether those opinions are real or perceived. We are then left vulnerable to carnal defense mechanisms in our attempt to ease the pain or turn the situation around.

From childhood, the enemy tried to kill my self-esteem through his lies and the fears that were attached to those lies. The enemy will sometimes build strongholds in your life at an early age, even if the evidence does not manifest until much later in life. Maybe you grew up bold and confident, only to battle low self-esteem and negative self-image in adulthood due to situations and circumstances that crushed your confidence.

For men, in particular, losing a job, being forced to forfeit a position of authority, being overlooked repeatedly for a particular promotion, and experiencing other similar scenarios can deal a devastating blow to their self-esteem. Maybe you never made it into the college that you had always hoped to get in. Or, maybe you made it into that college, but you never made it to graduation. Whatever the stronghold, whatever the lie, whatever the circumstance, and whenever it took place, the truth—God's Word—is the only thing that can set you free from the bondage of lies from the enemy, lies that were part of his plan to keep you from boldly and confidently fulfilling the call of God on your life.

Learn to Recognize Perception Deception

The devil wants us to be susceptible to rejection, but the Lord wants us to be rejection-proof. Society today rejects us if we don't look a certain way, act a certain way, earn a certain income, and so forth. Society tries to teach our children at an early age to reject those who don't have name-brand clothes, who look different, or who speak with an accent. As we live a Christian life in these last days, we need to be rejection proofed more than ever so we can walk boldly with the Lord before an increasingly ungodly society.

As you know who you are in Christ, as you know the unconditional love God has for you, and as you acknowledge God's acceptance of you, you'll become rejection-proof. You have to know it in your heart and in your spirit—not just in your mind as head knowledge. This only comes by regular study and meditation on God's Word and from spending time in His presence through prayer and worship.

Someone who is "proofed" is impervious to or incapable of being penetrated, affected, influenced, and so forth. When we are rejection-proof because of God and His Word, rejection can't penetrate our hearts and spirits. We are not affected or influenced by rejection, whether it's legitimate or merely perceived. When we are rejection-proof, we are protected from, resistant to, and unaffected by the negative thoughts, words, and actions of others.

Again, there are two types of rejection: actual rejection and perceived rejection. Both of them hurt very much if we aren't "rejection-proof." The Lord taught me several years ago about perception deception. John 8:44 says that the devil *was a murderer from the beginning, not holding to the truth, for there is no truth in him. When he lies, he speaks his native language, for he is a liar and the father of lies."* There is no truth in the devil, and he is the father of all lies! The enemy loves to cause you to feel rejected, and if he can't cause actual rejection to come your way, he'll attempt to mess with your perception. I call it "perception deception." He'll deceive you into thinking that people are rejecting you.

Maybe you walk into a room and no one speaks to you. Or maybe you walk in on a group of people and you get the sense that they have been talking about you. The devil has a heyday trying to get you to feel rejected. He starts waging a war in your mind with thoughts straight from the pit of hell. His attempt is to get you to perceive rejection that isn't even there. He's deceiving you by perception deception—don't fall for it! Don't be susceptible to perception deception but make yourself rejection-proof. Renew your mind to the truth and keep on keeping on!

Know Who You Are in Christ

Unfortunately, I developed a stronghold of rejection in my life many years before I learned who I was in Christ. I was not yet familiar with Isaiah 41:9-10, which says, *"...'You are my servant'; I have chosen you and have not rejected you. So do not fear, for I am with you; do not be dismayed, for I am your God. I will strengthen you and help you; I will uphold you with my righteous right hand."* God has not rejected us, so we must not fear. Without the confidence that comes from knowing who we are in Christ—the infinite value He places on us—we are subject to fear as a result of experiencing rejection, whether real or perceived. The enemy began a cycle of stealing, killing, and destroying in my life when I was only a child. He worked hard to develop strategic strongholds to keep me from fulfilling God's purpose for my life. I am happy to say that his attempts were futile, but only because of the power of God!

A key to total turnaround in your self-esteem and confidence is the Word of God. As you know and meditate on the Word of truth, your identity and security can come from knowing—really knowing—who you are in Christ.

Remember the Real Enemy

As we go about our daily lives, we must know where the battles are coming from and we must identify the real enemy. If we don't identify the real enemy—Satan—we begin fighting with people around us. Our battle is not with our family members, with our coworkers, or our fellow church members. Although the enemy tries to use other people to rub us the wrong way from time to time, other people aren't our real opponent—the devil is.

Ephesians 6:12 says, *"For our struggle is not against flesh and blood, but against the rulers, against the authorities, against the powers of this dark world and against the spiritual forces of evil in the heavenly realms."* Well, there you go! That eliminates all those people who you thought were the source of your problem. They are all flesh and blood, so they are eliminated from the enemy list. Your struggle is not against them—get real. The struggle you are fighting is much greater than that. Your struggle is against rulers, against authorities, against the powers of this dark world, and against spiritual forces of evil in the heavenly realms. You don't have to be an army general to know that, in order to win a battle, you must fight against the real enemy. If not, you will be defeated. You will have your attention on someone else while the real enemy sneaks up behind you and blows you out of the water. You'll be destroyed before you even know what hit you.

Use the Right Weapons

As the stronghold of rejection strengthened in my life, and as my fears increased, I developed carnal attempts to deal with the pain. I was not yet familiar with Second Corinthians 10:3-5:

> *For though we live in the world, we do not wage war as the world does. The weapons we fight with are not the weapons of the world. On the contrary, they have divine power to demolish strongholds. We demolish arguments and every pretension that sets itself up against the knowledge of God, and we take captive every thought to make it obedient to Christ.*

Strongholds are arguments and pretensions that Satan presents to us that are against the Word of God. Satan pretends they are truth—and he makes a very convincing argument. Remember, he is the master of deception! The devil sets up "pretensions." He pretends things are true in order to get you to buy the lie. His argument is no one loves you. His pretension is you can't survive without that drug or without the acceptance and love from that special someone. Yes, you can! That's a lie from the pit. Satan has put up an argument, and you have bought the lie.

It's time to take up the weapons Christ has given us to wage a successful fight and demolish every stronghold of the enemy. As we recognize the real enemy and fight with the weapons that we have been instructed to fight with, we will be victorious every single time. Second Corinthians 10:4a says, *"The weapons we fight with are not the weapons of the world."* What are the *"weapons of the world"?* The world's weapons are anger, bitterness, hatred, jealously, backbiting, and other negative practices the Bible commands us not to observe. Although *"we live in the world, we do not wage war as the world does"* (2 Corinthians 10:3). Our battle tactics and weapons are quite different. The Word of God, or the sword of the Spirit (Ephesians 6:17), and the fruits of the Spirit—love, joy, peace, patience, kindness, goodness, faithfulness, gentleness, and self-control (Galatians 5:22-23)—have divine power to demolish every stronghold. But, when we fight and wage war as the world does, we use carnal weapons. Some of the carnal weapons that I used to fight the stronghold of rejection were anger, hatred, and unforgiveness, all of them aimed directly at those who had hurt me.

Whatever stronghold you are fighting against—whether it's rejection or anything else—that stronghold is a pretension that has set itself up against the knowledge of God. In other words, you may feel rejected. Well, that is an argument and pretension that the devil set up against what God says about you. Father says you are loved and accepted by Him. Don't fall for the devil's lie any longer. Get out your weapons of divine power, draw your sword, and demolish the strongholds in your life and in the lives of those around you!

Drown Out the Disparaging Words

It wasn't long before the feelings of rejection I experienced in early childhood turned into self-rejection, which was a huge open door for many insecurities. I hated the way I looked, and I became very insecure about most areas of my life. I felt unworthy of looking nice, so I would dress the part. If anyone complimented me, I would feel extremely uncomfortable and would immediately try to divert the attention away from myself. I was plagued with words that I would hear, over and over, in my head—words spoken innocently by well-meaning people that still fell on my ears, with devastating results.

But, with Christ, we can take those feelings of rejection to the foot of the cross. Does it happen overnight? No. It's a process. We must simply begin to renew our minds to the Word of God and allow the Holy Spirit to change our thinking, thereby making us "rejection-proof." As we learn to get our identity and our security from what God's Word says about us, rather than from what other people say about us, we can become bold and confident in the Lord.

The Bible says that out of the abundance of the heart, the mouth speaks (Matthew 12:34; Luke 6:45). Based on this Scripture, the Lord taught me that when someone says something negative about me, against me, or to me, those words don't reflect who I am; those words actually reflect the character of the speaker! The words spoken by others come out of their hearts, and so, even if they're talking about me, they're exposing their own hearts—their comments have nothing to do with me!

When someone rejects you, know that his words or actions don't define who you are. Most of the time, it actually defines who he is. If there's someone in your life who continually speaks negatively to you and about you, most likely his words are actually a reflection of who he is—a miserable, hurt, angry person. Those who don't like themselves tend to feel a little better about themselves when they constantly put others down. Whatever the case, their words and actions don't define your value or who you are. God's Word defines who you are: His child, fearfully and wonderfully made in His image (Psalm 139:14).

Rejection is often an attempt to control and manipulate your actions, choices, or behaviors. The person rejecting you may not even be aware of the fact that his underlying motive is to control you with rejection. Only when you do what he wants, when and how he wants it done, will he give you his "stamp" of approval and withdraw his rejection.

We must be controlled by the Holy Spirit, not by people. The Word tells us that the fear of man—including the fear of man's rejection—will prove to be a snare. And it's not pleasing to the Lord.

Hurt people hurt other people, and misery loves company. If people are miserable, they often like to make those around them miserable, too. Maybe the person rejecting you has been through a lot of rejection himself and has never learned healthy ways of relating to people. As you take a stand and remain rejection-proof, the Lord can use you as an example in his life.

Refuse to Adopt Others' Issues

Another important practice along these lines is to refuse to adopt someone else's issues as your own. If someone has an issue with you, it's a reflection on a problem with him, not you! It never fails; if someone has an "issue with women," it just seems to rise to the surface if he gets around me too closely. I'll admit that I'm not exactly a pushover. I used to be, but those days are history. I know who I am in Christ, and I'm fine-tuned in my focus to fulfill the call of God on my life. Yes, I know how to be submissive to all of those in authority over me, men and women alike. Yet respecting authority is not mutually exclusive with being bold and confident in the Lord. My bold character and confident outlook make some people nervous. And you'd better get ready—when you, too, are bold and confident, not prideful or arrogant, you will cause those who are still in their box of insecurity to be a little shaken as well!

Just remember not to let anyone else's issue become your issue. The truth is, you have enough issues of your own to deal with, and so do I! Just keep focusing forward as you work toward becoming "rejection-proof."

WALKING FREE FROM REJECTION

Stand on the Truth

Again, Isaiah 41:9-10 says, *"I took you from the ends of the earth, from its farthest corners I called you. I said, 'You are my servant'; I have chosen you and have not rejected you. So do not fear, for I am with you; do not be dismayed, for I am your God. I will strengthen you and help you; I will uphold you with my righteous right hand."*

That's powerful and encouraging. Father has chosen us—He will never reject us. If someone else rejects us, it doesn't even matter because Father has not rejected us. He has chosen us. When I first came to understand this truth, I began saying out loud, "I'm not rejected—I'm accepted. I'm accepted by Christ." As we speak the Word—the truth—we are renewing our minds. Out with the old lies and in with the truth! I would write out Scriptures on large index cards and put them around my apartment. Whatever room I was in, I would have a Scripture to quote and pray over myself. Once we speak the truth long enough, it becomes a part of us. The Word of truth gets in our hearts, our minds, and our spirits.

The following are a few of my favorite Scriptures I like to quote. You should try quoting these yourself.

"[God] *hath made us accepted in the beloved"* (Ephesians 1:6b KJV).

"God has said, 'Never will I leave you; never will I forsake you'" (Hebrews 13:5b).

"The Lord your God is with you, he is mighty to save. He will take great delight in you, he will quiet you with his love, he will rejoice over you with singing" (Zephaniah 3:17).

"How great is the love the Father has lavished on us, that we should be called children of God! And that is what we are!" (1 John 3:1).

"[Jesus said,] 'All that the Father gives me will come to me, and whoever comes to me I will never drive away'" (John 6:37).

"Though my father and mother forsake me, the Lord will receive me" (Psalm 27:10).

Knock Down the Walls

When we experience rejection, the flesh tries to come up with carnal defense mechanisms in order to handle the pain. One of my most popular defense strategies was to put up a wall around myself—a barrier to protect me from people—so that I would never get hurt again. The biggest problem with putting up walls is that no one can get in, including those who really love and care about us. When we're trying to block out those who would hurt us, the people we ought to be in relationship with end up getting blocked out as well. Although the walls we construct around ourselves may prevent us from getting hurt, they also isolate us. It's lonely behind the wall! Love cannot get in or out, and that isn't how God designed us to live.

Walls cannot make you rejection-proof. They only isolate you in a lonely existence, setting you up to fall for an unhealthy relationship when someone finally breaks through a chink and causes your wall to come crashing down. At that point, you're vulnerable, and you may begin a relationship with the first person who comes along—not smart!

The truth is, the Lord is the only one who can make you rejection-proof. Confidence in His unfailing love will buoy your self-esteem, no matter the season. And when you're trusting in God, staying attuned to His Holy Spirit, you can maintain healthy boundaries in your relationships with no need for walls. Healthy boundaries are important, and it's wise to protect your heart, keeping your guard up around those who might take advantage of you. But erecting walls is never an effective method.

The apostle Paul exhorts, *"Be on your guard; stand firm in the faith"* (1 Corinthians 16:13a) because *"your enemy the devil prowls around like a roaring lion looking for someone to devour"* (1 Peter 5:8b). The devil sometimes uses people to bring about your destruction, whether their methods are physical, mental, emotional, or spiritual. This is why you and I must be on guard and remain aware of the enemy's schemes. But if you build a wall, you'll blind yourself to the enemy's schemes, and he will catch you off guard when you least expect it.

Emotional walls are a carnal attempt to keep you from getting hurt again. I can't promise that you will never get hurt again. After all, Jesus was despised and rejected by people (Isaiah 53:3), so we should expect the same treatment. But, I can promise you that building "walls" is not the way to go. God used several special friends at different times in my life to "love" my walls down. These special women of God are still in my life today.

The Lord is saying to you today, "No more walls!" Stop trying to control all of your relationships due to your fear of rejection. Let the love of God tear those walls down—there are too many people who love you and care about you, and you don't want to block them out. Let the Lord love you through the people of His choosing, some of whom you already know, and others whom He will bring into your life in a later season.

Choose today to forgive all of those who have hurt and rejected you. The very thing you hate, you become, if you don't forgive. Extend forgiveness to those as Father has forgiven you. Call on the name of the Lord and allow Him to shower you with His love. He wants to make you rejection-proof, but you first have to lay your pain at His feet. Forgive

The only way to experience true freedom from rejection and other experiences that wound our souls and crush our spirits, when those experiences are inflicted by other people, is to walk in forgiveness. Otherwise, we will remain bound by bitterness toward those who have hurt us.

Isaiah 48:18 says, *"If only you had paid attention to my commands, your peace would have been like a river, your righteousness like the waves of the sea."* One of our Father's commands is to forgive others, as He has forgiven us (Matthew 6:14-15).

#6

Forgive your offenders and fix
your eyes on the truth.

POINTS TO PONDER

1. There are two types of rejection: actual rejection and perceived rejection. What is the difference between these two
   types of rejection? Can you think of a time in your life when
   you have experienced either of these types of rejection?

2. Knowing who you are in Christ will build your self-esteem
   and confidence. Why is this true, and how can you arrive at
   this place?

3. Using the right weapons and knowing who your real enemy
   is will enable you to win the battle. List the weapons mentioned in Ephesians 6:17 and Galatians 5:22-23 and then de-
   scribe how one (or more) of these weapons will help you fight
   the stronghold of rejection.

4. Putting up emotional walls is an attempt to keep from getting
   hurt again. How can walking in forgiveness cause you to experience true freedom from rejection?

***Meditate on these Scriptures, speak them aloud, and commit them
to memory:***

> *"You are my servant"; I have chosen you and have not rejected
> you. So do not fear, for I am with you; do not be dismayed,
> for I am your God. I will strengthen you and help you; I will
> uphold you with my righteous right hand.* (Isaiah 41:9-10)

For our struggle is not against flesh and blood, but against the rulers, against the authorities, against the powers of this dark world and against the spiritual forces of evil in the heavenly realms. (Ephesians 6:12)

I praise you because I am fearfully and wonderfully made; your works are wonderful, I know that full well. (Psalm 139:14)

Be kind and compassionate to one another, forgiving each other, just as in Christ God forgave you. (Ephesians 4:32)

Chapter 7

TOTAL TURNAROUND IN YOUR MARRIAGE AND RELATIONSHIPS

People everywhere are suffering from broken relationships. Husbands and wives are at odds with each other. Friends are giving each other the "silent treatment." Conflict seems to be a normal part of every relationship. And I believe that, more often than not, that conflict stems from misinterpretations and misperceptions, similar to "perception deception," which we discussed in the previous chapter. When we jump to conclusions rather than leave space for the other person to defend him or herself, we risk erecting barriers that shouldn't be there—and that are very difficult to tear down.

DON'T RUSH TO JUDGE

This is how the birth of Jesus Christ came about: His mother Mary was pledged to be married to Joseph, but before they came together, she was found to be with child through the Holy Spirit. Because Joseph her husband was a righteous man and did not want to expose her to public disgrace, he had in mind to divorce her quietly. (Matthew 1:18-19)

If anybody had reason to be suspicious, it was Joseph. Imagine being engaged, only to find out that your wife-to-be was pregnant—and not by you! I'm sure that Joseph dealt with all manner of suspicion and hurt when he first found out. He was ready to break it off, just as I'm sure any other man would have done. But then, his perspective shifted when he received a special visit.

> But after he had considered this, an angel of the Lord appeared to him in a dream and said, "Joseph son of David, do not be afraid to take Mary home as your wife, because what is conceived in her is from the Holy Spirit. She will give birth to a son, and you are to give him the name Jesus, because he will save his people from their sins." (Matthew 1:20-21)

When Joseph discovered what was really going on, it shifted his entire perspective! Any anger and frustration he may have harbored surely disappeared when it became clear that his fiancée was carrying the Son of God. Because he had the whole picture, not just a misconception based on the way things looked in the natural, Joseph was able to remain faithful to Mary. Because he had the whole picture, Joseph woke up and *did what the angel of the Lord had commanded him and took Mary home as his wife* (Matthew 1:24).

Now, for most of us, the "big picture" isn't going to involve something quite as spectacular as Mary's. But it's true that there's usually more to the story than meets the eye. If we are quick to judge, and if we jump to draw conclusions about the behavior of our friends and family members without getting to the bottom of the story, we're prone to take offense easily and to place blame where it doesn't belong.

Granted, other people will hurt you. Your friends won't always have your best interests at heart. Your family members may act out of envy or resentment in their treatment of you. I'm only suggesting that you consider where you yourself may be responsible, at least in part, for the tension that arises in your relationships. It's usually a two-way street! And the way that you react to the people who hurt you, either intentionally or by accident, factors significantly into the outcome.

CONSIDER THE MOTIVATION, NOT THE MANIFESTATION

Along the same lines, it's sometimes best to concentrate on the intentions of someone rather than on how those intentions play out. Let me explain. Actually, I'll let my friend do the talking:

> My husband is very devoted to me. He is also extremely dedicated to his job, which is more demanding in certain months of the year. It was during one of these particularly busy seasons that we were planning to meet in the city after work on a Friday for a dinner date. I was really looking forward to the evening, and, as I often do, I envisioned exactly how our date would play out. (Meanwhile, I have learned time and again that it's better not to develop a preconceived idea of most things because I tend to be more flexible and easygoing when I don't have a picture in my mind of how things ought to go.) Anyway, we met up, and, wouldn't you know, things didn't go as I had planned. We ended up at a different restaurant from the one I'd had in mind, with an atmosphere that was romantic enough, but we were seated near the door—I never like sitting near the door. Then, I couldn't decide what I wanted—sounds petty, I know, but I'm plagued by indecisiveness in many areas, especially when it's time to pick from a menu. Our food came too fast, I ate too fast, and we were out of there too fast; I'd envisioned lingering over our dinner as we enjoyed an engaging discussion, when silence prevailed for most of the meal.
>
> When we got home, we went straight to bed—at 9:00 on a Friday night. Lying in bed, I felt frustrated, disappointed, and tempted to cry. But then, I felt the Lord nudging me to look at the bigger picture. I realized the sacrifice my husband had made by taking me out on a Friday night, after what had been a very long, very

trying, very tiring work week. I realized that treating me to a nice dinner was his way of making me feel special, his way of conveying his love in a time when he was short on other resources, such as energy and topics of conversation. Seeing the evening in this way—as a gift and a sacrifice, regardless of how far short it fell of my expectations—totally transformed my attitude, replacing my bitter frustration with sheer gratitude for my loving, selfless husband. Instead of bursting into tears of self-pity, I kissed my husband and snuggled in for a restful night's sleep. Changing my perspective truly made all the difference.

Have you ever felt like my friend did in this situation? Have you ever been tempted to wallow in self-pity when someone failed to live up to your expectations?

God looks at the motives of our hearts (1 Samuel 16:7), and that's what we should strive to do with our loved ones. Sometimes, no matter what they do in their attempts to meet our needs or show us love, they fail—at least, in our opinion. Sometimes, no matter what *we* do in our attempts to meet the needs of our loved ones or to show them our love, *we* fail—we never measure up! In those instances, we're the ones who are asking them to cut us some slack. We're the ones saying, "At least I tried! Don't I get any credit?" So let's step back and consider the intentions of our loved ones rather than the manifestation of those intentions, especially if our assessment of the outcome invites tears or a tantrum.

LOOK TO THE LORD

A friend of mine has one of the most powerful testimonies I know of concerning marriage. So, I'm going to step aside and let her share from her heart, in hopes that you will learn from her incredible example.

Marriage is something that many of us look forward to with high hopes and view through rose-colored glasses. No matter how realistic we try to be, once we are married, we are rudely awakened, at some point, out of our dream of the perfect marriage. For some, this "waking up" happens during the honeymoon; for others, it may occur after the first year or two.

I was rudely awakened out of my seemingly peaceful marriage when my husband and I had been married ten years. Not every marriage has the same kinds of issues as ours did, but the keys to turnaround that God showed me are effective, no matter your marital situation and the peaks and valleys you and your spouse encounter. We had been married about eight years when we began dealing with the issue of infertility. After attempting in vitro fertilization, we conceived. We were so excited, and we really believed God was answering our prayers for a baby. About eight to ten weeks into my pregnancy, God gave my husband a dream in which He clearly told him that our baby was a boy, and his name was Samuel, with strong ties to Samuel in the Old Testament. Two days later, I found out that our baby's heartbeat had stopped.

Looking back now, I can see how God was preparing us through the dream to release Samuel to the Lord, just as Samuel's mother, Hannah, had to release him to the Lord. At the time, however, it just seemed like a cruel trick. I wish I could say that we had understood clearly right away and turned him over to the Lord. Instead, things became more difficult for us. Life kept on going. My husband and I were both very involved in ministry at our church, and things were starting to fall apart in the church leadership. We also had very weighty jobs outside of church.

Bottom line: we were involved in many stressful situations in our jobs and at our church. I tried to work through my grief, despite the busyness. My husband saw me grieving and said he thought he needed to be strong for me, so he decided to shut down his grief, not realizing what a toll that would take on him. He has since then realized that he didn't understand grief or what it could do to him.

About a month and a half after we lost our baby, my husband made the first of a few sexual indiscretions over a ten-month period. It led to sexual addiction patterns that were not consistent but were nonetheless devastating to him—and, eventually, to me, when he told me about them. All of this culminated in him having a brief but life-changing affair. During this time, we were preparing to adopt a child. I knew "generally" what he was struggling with, but not to the extent that it had grown. I was so focused on our adoption process. We were both simply longing for hope and happiness in our life again, so it was easy to ignore some of the obvious signs that we were in trouble.

By the grace of God, we were amazingly blessed with our daughter not long after we completed our adoption paperwork. About a month and a half after our daughter was with us, my husband tearfully told me he'd had an affair. Initially, I was so in shock, I tried to comfort him, but the shock soon wore off and gave way to anger, and rage, and despair. My husband assured me that he did not love her and that he wanted to try and save our marriage. I wanted to believe him, but his actions seemed to speak louder than his words. I had a million questions, and the more honest answers I got from my husband to these hard questions, the more I realized how deceived I had been. I knew the issues he was struggling with weren't going to go away overnight. I was crying out to God and trying to imagine how I was going to proceed. It was at that point that God spoke to me so clearly. He said, "I want you to stay. Will you stay?" My first thought was, *You've got to be kidding!* I knew I had scriptural rights to leave, yet I could not escape the weightiness of the Lord's question to me. I knew that if God was asking me to stay, He was offering me a higher path. I understood I could choose the lower path, and no one would blame me, but I sensed God was calling me to trust Him in a way I never had before. I argued with God, "But I can't trust him, Lord, and I may never be able to trust him!" I heard the Lord say, "But you can trust Me. Trust Me!" Those words somehow gave me such peace because I realized that God must know something about my husband's heart that I didn't know at that point. I knew that if God was saying "Trust Me," I could trust Him.

As I look back now, I see the Lord's gentle, restorative hand in giving me that choice. He didn't say, "You will stay"; He said, "Will you stay?" In my position, having the choice to stay was healing and empowering all by itself. I was partnering with God in something that was beyond my ability to do. I could not fix my marriage; I could not heal it; but God could. He had the keys to turning around my marriage, and He wanted to restore what had been broken.

It was at that point that I turned around in my heart, looked at God clearly, and decided I would trust and obey Him, even though I didn't understand how it was all going to work. I said yes to my Lord Jesus, and a peace settled in my heart about one thing: no matter what was going to happen, I could trust God. Not "I can trust God if He restores my marriage," or "I can trust God if He does what I want Him to do," but "I can trust God no matter what the outcome of my circumstances." I discovered the first key to turnaround in my marriage that day: trusting obedience to God. I stopped trying to figure out what to do and started crying out to God and listening to hear His voice. When He spoke, I heard what He said, and I decided to do what He was asking me to do, out of trust in Him. A shift occurred in my heart the day I trusted Jesus with my marriage.

As time went on, and all the emotions of anger, hurt, and pain came up toward my husband, I felt stuck and unable to forgive him. One day during this time, I heard the Lord say, "Will you love My son?" I knew God was referring to my husband as His son. Being a new mom, I was beginning to understand what parental love felt like, and it touched my heart to think of my husband as God's son. Then, I thought, *Well, I guess that makes my husband my brother in the Lord.* When I looked at it like that, I could love him as a brother who had some serious issues that could destroy him. I also began to see the enemy (the devil), rather than my husband, as THE enemy. It says in First Peter 5:8, *"Be self-controlled and alert. Your enemy the devil prowls around like a roaring lion looking for someone to devour."* So, my husband was my brother, and my enemy was the devil. The Lord was reordering my thinking to what was true according to Him and how He saw it. Prior to that, I'd seen my husband as the enemy.

It's easy for us to view things through our emotions or our circumstances or our own "common sense" reasoning, but God wants us to see things through His perspective. In John 14:6, Jesus says, "I am the way, the truth and the life." We can trust what God says to be true because He is Truth. I think it is important to mention here that when I said yes to God, I did not know if my husband was really remorseful and wanting to save our marriage or if he was living a double life of pervasive sexual addiction and was unrepentant. There are often marriages in which the offending spouse really has no intention of repenting and wants to continue living a double life of sexual promiscuity. In my case, it became evident as time went on that my husband wanted to repent and work toward restoring our marriage. Even if he had not really wanted to do that, I would have been in the right position by hearing, trusting, and obeying God as I faced that reality as well. God wanted me to trust Him, regardless of the outcome of our marriage.

One day, the Lord gave me a picture of my marriage, and it looked like this: Jesus, my husband, and I were in a circle, holding hands. The Lord said, "This was your marriage covenant with Me on the day you got married." Then I saw my husband let go of my hand, and we were standing in a line now, holding hands; I was on one side of Jesus, holding His hand, and my husband was on the other side of Jesus, still holding His hand. The Lord said, "I am holding both of your hands. Even though your covenant has been broken with each other, I have not broken My covenant with both of you. I've got you, and I'm not letting go. The only way that there is no hope for our covenant is if either of you lets go of My hand. As both of you trust Me, you will be able to hold hands again." From this picture, I understood that faith was another key to turnaround in my marriage. It says in Second Timothy 2:13 that when we are faithless, He will remain faithful. Through God's faithfulness to me, I was able to respond in faith to Him. Again, I had to choose, and with every step of faith in God, I realized that I could not control my spouse's choices. I couldn't make him hold my hand or God's hand, and, at that point, I couldn't even take his hand again, in my own strength. But I found the strength to take my husband's hand again through the strength Christ gave me. Philippians 4:13 says, *I can do all things through Christ who strengthens me*" (NKJV). So, the restoration of our marriage covenant did not occur just with the passing of time. I've heard people say, "Time heals," but it's really Jesus who heals our hearts, not time. Time affords us some emotional distance from the event that caused us hurt, but, ultimately, it cannot heal us. Many days, I did not feel like acting loving toward my husband. But, out of faith in God, I chose to love him over and over again. Eventually, there came a day when I began to feel genuine love for him, and it would last for a short while. Then, I would have to love him in faith again, until the distrustful episodes became less and less frequent. I also began to recognize the enemy at work in my thoughts. I began to focus on my faith in God by speaking out the opposite of what I was feeling and hearing from the enemy or my fleshly fears. God sees us much differently than we are, even at our worst moments. He sees us through His Son Jesus. It says in Second Corinthians 5:21, *"God made him who had no sin to be sin for us, so that in him we might become the righteousness of God."* I began to speak out who my husband really is in Christ. I would put my husband's name in Scripture and speak it out loud. I also did this for myself, and I continue to pray and declare the truth in this way. By doing this, I align myself with Jesus, who is the Truth. We are to abide in the Vine daily, and when I speak the truth, I am doing just that. Jesus said in John 15:5, *"I am the vine; you are the branches. If a man remains in me and I in him, he will bear much fruit; apart from me you can do nothing."* I must speak the truth in faith. Often, what I am saying, I don't see or experience in my life yet, but I believe it will come to pass eventually. It's not wishful thinking or magic, but we are exercising our faith in what God says is true. We agree with Him instead of what is happening in our natural circumstances.

After the initial season of freely expressing my anger, hurt, sadness, and fear to the Lord, there came a day when I started to realize that I had not caused my husband to struggle with sexual addiction or to have an affair. Even though my husband (and other people) always said his sins were 100 percent his fault, it often "felt" like somehow it was more of a reflection on me, my failures, and that I was actually the problem (all lies of the enemy that, in my deep brokenness, I believed). This new revelation was important because it freed me from taking responsibility for his issues and from a lot of unrealistic guilt. It also positioned me to take responsibility for my issues, which would have to be faced regardless of whether we were married or not. If I faced my issues and made myself accountable to God's loving, corrective voice, as well as a godly, trustworthy, objective mentor who would hold me accountable to look at my issues, I would need to humble myself. I began to understand that humility would become a powerful key to turnaround in my marriage. When I began to humble myself, I aligned myself with God in a way that made me see things more clearly. God is love, and humility connects us with Love Himself. I began to think more about what I needed to get right in my own life, and I left my husband's issues to the Lord. Now, this did not mean I ignored his issues. Each time I made a choice to humble myself, I actually had more of an ability to speak to him respectfully, without fear or panic or anger, when it was time for me to confront him about something or share my heart.

Confession and repentance of my own sin was and is another powerful key to turnaround in my marriage. I remember when I first started confessing and repenting of my sins, it didn't seem fair. I would think, *Well, he was the one who messed up; why am I the focus here?* But I quickly learned that I needed to be accountable to someone. I chose a godly counselor who would be objective and not side with me against my husband and who had faith to believe God could restore my marriage. My husband and I also saw a marriage counselor who did not side with either of us but confronted us both equally on our issues. The Bible says, *"Confess your sins to each other...so that you may be healed"* (James 5:16a). A big part of our turnaround toward each other was confession and repentance to God, to other godly mentors, and, eventually, to each other. As our trust grew, we became more able to be vulnerable and confess our sins to each other. It was a long process, one that still continues today and will continue until we go to be with the Lord.

Worship times have always been a key area of importance in my life and our marriage. What I have found to be a very powerful key to turnaround in my marriage is my own private worship time with the Lord. During my darkest days, God met me in worship of Him and filled me with His love and joy and peace that sustained me through many hard, confusing days as He was turning around our marriage. I also had similar experiences while praising and worshipping God in a group of people. The Bible says in Psalm 22:3 (KJV) that God inhabits the praises of His people. I would feel His love when I praised Him and worshipped Him, and He would often touch me in a way that I was able to release much pent-up emotion about my losses and hurts. It was a safe place I could go to and be vulnerable with Him, and it still is for me today. Instead of my husband being my focus, Jesus became my focus as I worshipped Him.

God has begun to weave the keys to turnaround into my life and my marriage. These keys are trust and obedience to God, faith in God, humility, confession, repentance, and worship. It is a process that will go on until I go to be with the Lord. I am so grateful for His patience and love for me and my husband in this process, and He does the same for everyone who chooses to believe He will. Choosing turnaround in our marriage is not a one-time choice, though. It is a moment-by-moment choice that is made over and over again, like breathing. The fruit of our choices—what they produce—will stand in eternity, so we want to make the right ones. Regardless of your situation or what your spouse chooses, if you choose to use these keys, you will reap His eternal blessings and experience a turnaround in your life.

———

What an incredible testimony! My friend learned that a relationship with God is all that you need, and when you place your trust fully in

Him, whatever happens in your earthly relationships won't faze you. She was talking about her marriage, but the same principles apply in your relationships with your kids, your siblings, your parents, your friends, your coworkers, and so on. When you are fully satisfied in your relationship with God, you are less swayed by the waves of "drama" in your other relationships and you are better able to sit back and surrender to Him instead of insisting on having your own way. Remember, His ways are best!

#7 — Make God your priority relationship, and the rest will fall into place.

POINTS TO PONDER

1. Why do you think looking at the motivation and intent of the heart, with regard to relationships, is so important? How are our relationships positively affected when we put our expectation in the Lord?

2. God wants us to view every aspect of life, including our relationships, from His perspective. We can trust what He says to be true because He is Truth. How does this build up your faith?

3. Are you in a broken relationship and feel that you just don't have the strength to forgive and trust the one who has caused you hurt? Read Philippians 4:13 to find where you can get that strength.

4. During painful times of broken relationships, our times of worship are crucial. Why do you think this is true?

Meditate on these Scriptures, speak them aloud, and commit them to memory:

> *The Lord does not look at the things man looks at. Man looks at the outward appearance, but the Lord looks at the heart.* (1 Samuel 16:7b)

> *My soul, wait thou only upon God; for my expectation is from him.* (Psalm 62:5 KJV)

> *Trust in him at all times, O people; pour out your hearts to him, for God is our refuge.* (Psalm 62:8)

> *I can do all things through Christ who strengthens me.* (Philippians 4:13 NKJV)

Chapter 8

TOTAL TURNAROUND IN YOUR TEENAGER

I have always said that being a single mom is the hardest thing I have ever done. But the difficulty level went up a notch when my daughter became a teenager! Being a single mom of a teenage daughter definitely takes the cake. It reminds me of the first year of marriage—it's the best of times and the worst of times!

Still, in spite of the difficulties and frustrations, "Mom" is my favorite of all of the hats I wear. I believe it's important for parents to keep our focus on all that we love about our role, especially when our children are in their teens. Just as in the first year of marriage, when it's best to focus on all the reasons we married our spouse—all the things we love about him or her—during the teenage years, when our children and our homes go through so many changes, we need to stay focused on the fact that we love our children. Just remember, this season of "teenage-isms" will pass, just like every other season.

AVOID THE "EASY ROUTE"

If you focus on the fact that the season of your son or daughter's adolescence is only temporary, it will keep you from feeling completely overwhelmed and discouraged, and you will be less likely to give in to the temptation to take the "easy route" in raising your precious teenager.

I know how easy it is to default to the "easy route" in parenthood. The easy route is the path of least resistance; it means allowing your kids to do what they want, when they want. It's letting them call the shots for the sake of your own sanity, as well as for your ego—along the easy route, you're less likely to hear such exclamations as "You're so mean!" and "That's so unfair!" The easy route requires a lot less energy on the part of the parent, and it's appealing in the moment. But it's ultimately destructive, and it takes far more time and energy to "fix" all of the problems that result from taking the easy route. There is a high price to pay for taking the easy route—a price that may include drug rehab programs, school expulsions, juvenile detention homes, and even imprisonment.

The alternative to taking the easy route is to "stay on it," as I like to say. Parents who "stay on it" set a standard for their children—an uncompromising expectation of behavior for everyone living under their roof—and they are involved in their children's lives. Staying on it isn't easy, but it is well worth the investment of time, energy, and prayers.

No matter what you are facing today with your children, stay encouraged in the Lord, and "stay on it" in their lives. God is going to bring total turnaround in the life of your teenager, if you'll only stay the course and commit to being involved. Above all, you must entrust your children to God, trusting that He has them in the palm of His hand.

> *Can a mother forget the baby at her breast and have no compassion on the child she has borne? Though she may forget, I will not forget you! See, I have engraved you on the palms of my hands....* (Isaiah 49:15-16)

God has your children's names engraved on the palms of His hands. He is thinking about them constantly! He never forgets or neglects them. Even if things are going downhill and you fear the worst, God is still in control. Even if it seems that their raging hormones, roller-coaster emotions, and stubborn wills are calling the shots, remember, God is still on His throne. He'll never abdicate to anyone, including your teenager. So, don't sweat it!

WEATHERING THE CHANGE

During the teenage years, the name of the game is change. None of us really likes change. The sweet little angel born to you to twelve years ago has suddenly undergone a transformation—or, rather, has found him or herself in the midst of a major transformation. Over the course of adolescence, everything changes—bodies, thoughts, friends, schools, emotions—everything!

As parents, we find ourselves shaking our heads and asking ourselves, "What's happening?" The answer is, "A lot!" Adolescence is the bridge from childhood to adulthood, and there is no shortage of steps to take across that bridge. During the teenage years, our children grow up! And we, as parents, need to let them. Yes, we need to supervise the growing-up process, but our surveillance needs to happen "undercover." I hardly ever let my daughter out of my sight (even though she usually doesn't know it). As a teenager, she enjoys a greater degree of freedom than she did in childhood, but she still has well-defined boundaries. I keep a close eye on the music she listens to, the kids she hangs out with, and all that's going on at her school and in her youth group at church.

Today, the passage through these years of significant change is harder than ever. Our kids find themselves under pressure like never before—pressure to achieve, in academics and athletics; pressure from the culture, which tells them how to dress and what to do to be "cool"; and pressure from the enemy, who tries to lure them into a lifestyle of sin and compromise.

Is it easy for them? No! Is it easy for us parents? No! But, remember—you don't need "easy." All you need is "possible"—and with God, all things are possible. This, too, shall pass. This season is only temporary!

Remember, This Is Temporary

Everything in life is subject to change, the only exception being God Himself. Our circumstances can change overnight, so that life as we once knew it becomes just a distant memory. Within a few months' time, I went from living in a household with two incomes to being without any income at all. At the same time, I went from being without any children to having a child—and being left to raise her on my own. When change happens, it happens fast!

When we are faced with challenging circumstances in life, we need to remind ourselves that they are only temporary. One night, when my daughter was very young, I sat on the floor, sobbing, because I was overwhelmed by the responsibility to provide financially for my daughter, coupled with the stresses of caring for her 24/7. That night, in the midst of my distress, God spoke to me and very clearly said that my situation was temporary. His message came at just the right time—just when I felt that my current season would never change. His message meant that I wasn't going to die in the middle of my storm, but that there were bright and beautiful days awaiting me on the other side of this temporary season filled with storms.

When something is temporary, it is not permanent. Temporary means "for a time only." The experiences and circumstances of this life can be painful and perplexing; more often than not, we don't understand them. But the one thing we can be sure of is that they are temporary. The Lord was basically saying to me, "This is only a season." It was temporary, as surely as springtime lasts only until summer begins, and as autumn follows summer. The seasons of life are in constant flux. Winter always gives way to spring, and that fact alone should encourage us during the cold, blinding blizzards of life.

The key is to fix our eyes on the knowledge that a new season is coming, even if we don't see any "leaves starting to turn" or other indicators of its arrival. *We fix our eyes not on what is seen, but on what is unseen. For what is seen is temporary, but what is unseen is eternal"* (2 Corinthians 4:18).

It's so true. We must fix our eyes on the unseen because the "seen"—our current circumstances—are only temporary.

Sure enough, my season of distress and despair gave way to a new season that brought with it an improved financial situation. The circumstances that had so overwhelmed me back then are long gone. That's not to say that I'm immune to overwhelming circumstances in other aspects of life. Believe me, I experience a fair share of frustrations! But, whenever a challenge comes my way, I've learned to raise my hands in surrender and say, "Temporary!"

I found myself doing this a lot when my daughter became a teenager. What a relief that the teenage years are only temporary! However, I have found that the more challenges we face in a given season, the faster that season seems to pass. So, I try not to wish away my daughter's teenage years but instead relish every day, challenges and frustrations and all.

Yes, life is sometimes hard, but God is always good. In the words of Paul, *"We are hard pressed on every side, but not crushed; perplexed, but not in despair; persecuted, but not abandoned; struck down, but not destroyed"* (2 Corinthians 4:8-9). My translation of this Scripture is: "Things are hard, but they could be a whole lot worse. Yes, we are hard-pressed, but we aren't crushed. We are persecuted, but we aren't abandoned. We are struck down, but—be encouraged—we aren't destroyed! Yes, life is hard, but God is good. Not only could things be worse, but what we are facing is temporary."

Trust God in Every Season

Not only do we need to realize that trying circumstances are temporary, but we also need to remember that when we surrender to the Lord in the midst of trying circumstances, He gets the glory. When we persevere through trials and tough times in a way that honors God, He gets the glory. When our trust is in Him, even the most difficult seasons of life can work for us rather than against us, for He works *"all things"*—good and bad—for the benefit of those who love Him (Romans 8:28).

So, in the stormy seasons of life, draw close to the Lord and let Him lift your faith to a new level. What you're facing is temporary! And if you submit to Him in the midst of this season, you will grow in spiritual maturity so that you will be ready for each subsequent season.

The children of Israel failed to realize that the desert was temporary. One little trial caused them to lose their vision for the Promised Land. One little discomfort to their flesh, and they lost sight of the fact that their temporary circumstances were leading them to the next season of life—the land of "more than enough." Raising teenagers will definitely kill your flesh, and my daughter really is a great kid! Many of you parents are facing great challenges with your teenagers. Just remember that God's grace is sufficient for you, for His power is manifested in your times of weakness. The apostle Paul conveyed this very idea in Second Corinthians 12:9-10:

> [The Lord] *said to me, "My grace is sufficient for you, for my power is made perfect in weakness." Therefore I will boast all the more gladly about my weaknesses, so that Christ's power may rest on me. That is why, for Christ's sake, I delight in weaknesses, in insults, in hardships, in persecutions, in difficulties. For when I am weak, then I am strong.*

Stay encouraged, for God is going to turn it all around for you and for your teenager.

When you're raising teenagers, you must maintain a positive attitude, as the Holy Spirit empowers you. One way to do this is to keep your focus on the vision that God has given you for each precious child. He has great plans for your teenage son or daughter—don't lose sight of them! Keeping that vision before you will bring strength and sustenance for the "wilderness" experience that many teenagers take their parents through on the route to adulthood.

The caterpillar isn't a particularly attractive creature. It has to go through many changes before it turns into a beautiful butterfly. But, after it's on the other side of the transition period, everyone sees the beauty in the butterfly and perceives the value in all of the changes it underwent. No matter what stage of the teenage "metamorphosis" you find yourself in with your teenager, be encouraged—you will see the fulfillment of all that God has shown you for your child.

Set an Example

Many parents, myself included, find themselves worrying constantly about their teenagers. Worry doesn't change anything. Worry cannot bring about a positive turnaround. The only thing worry will do is put a strain on your relationship with your teenager, who is apt to view you as a nag or a paranoid parent. Remember what the Bible says about a nag?

> It is better to dwell in a corner of the housetop [on the flat oriental roof, exposed to all kinds of weather] than in a house shared with a nagging, quarrelsome, and faultfinding woman. (Proverbs 21:9 AMP)

A nagging woman (or man) is annoying! Parents who are prone to nagging, quarreling, and faultfinding should not expect positive responses from their teenage children. Someone might say, "I have a quarrelsome teenager." Is that any surprise? Being quarrelsome is a trait of most teenagers; it's part of the season they are in. They are like a baby chicken trying to peck its way out of an egg so that it can transition from being a chick to a full-fledged hen or rooster. As our teenagers peck their way out of the "egg" of adolescence, they are plucking your nerves! Peck, peck, peck; pluck, pluck, pluck! Yes, they may take "quarrelsome" to a new level, but you can't afford to respond with the same spirit. You need to set a positive example of how to handle change and persevere through challenges. You might say, "That's the problem—I don't have a clue." Well, join the club with every other parent who has ever raised a teenager! But, through the grace of God, through the principles from His Word, and through much prayer and fasting, you and I will get through this season successfully.

Quarreling back doesn't work. I've tried it, and—believe me—it only makes things worse. Actually, I think my daughter enjoys trying to get under my skin, and she knows she's succeeded when I react in a quarrelsome way. When I was clued in to that fact, I totally changed my approach.

In the midst of the changes our teenagers go through, they face a daily struggle within themselves. It didn't take me long to figure out that my daughter was engaged in a battle of emotions, choices, and change, and that she was trying to draw me into the fight. On the surface, it seemed that she was trying to draw me in as her adversary, when, in reality, she was really reaching out because she needed a stabilizing force to support and guide her through the struggle. In many cases, when our teenagers are "acting out," they're really crying out for our help, whether it's in the form of a hug, a listening ear, or an active advocate. If we jump into battle on the offensive, echoing our teenagers' screams and shouts with our own, everyone loses. But when we heed the Spirit and react in a patient, godly manner, we model an effective way of communicating, and we take great strides toward reconciliation. We even may open up opportunities for intimacy that otherwise would not have occurred.

Our kids learn more from our life example than from our lectures. That's why it's so important to model biblical ways of managing stress, weathering change, and dealing with difficult circumstances. How do our children see us interacting with others when disagreements arise? How do they see us handling challenges? What do they see us doing when we're stressed? Whatever we do, they will likely follow suit!

Don't Worry; Just Stay on the Wall

Middle school is a challenging experience for teenagers these days, especially difficult for teenage girls, who are dealing with physical changes, including the start of their cycles, and mood swings. Eighth grade was a particularly difficult year for my daughter, and I was presented with many opportunities to worry about her. There were many times when I would wake up in the middle of the night, concerned about her. Every time I would find myself beginning to worry, the Lord would jump into my business, and thankfully so! Time and time again, He would tell me, "Everything is going to be all right!" "Don't worry, I've got this." "Don't worry; just stay on the wall in prayer."

Prayer is the best gift you can give your children. I have learned to keep my mouth closed and pray. If you want to stay up all night, fine—just make sure you're praying rather than panicking. Don't pray in worry or fear. Pray in faith. Pray the Word over your teenagers. Pray and then obey. Listen for what the Lord tells you to do, and then carry it out. Pray, obey, and keep quarreling away!

WATCH YOUR WORDS IN THE "WILDERNESS" OF ADOLESCENCE

Don't lose your good attitude by getting bent out of shape because of your teenager's bad attitude. Don't allow words to fly out of your mouth in response to the words flying out of your teenager's mouth. The teenage years are a time when you will need self-control more than ever. This is a season in which you must be especially choosy as you pick your battles. Learn not to sweat the small stuff. Learn to bite your tongue to avoid responding out of anger and frustration, no matter what comes out of your teenager's mouth.

Stay calm, cool, and collected. Take some time to breathe—and pray—before you respond. And choose your words wisely, for *reckless words pierce like a sword, but the tongue of the wise brings healing*" (Proverbs 12:18). Never react out of your flesh to your teenager's actions and exclamations. Rather, act out of your spirit—a spirit submitted to the Lord. Ask yourself the question that our teenagers are asked at youth group: "What would Jesus do?" You know that Jesus would never answer shouts with shouts. He was always calm and composed; He responded out of love to everyone He met. Okay, parents, let's admit it: we all have a lot of homework to do! But it will be well worth the effort when we get a passing grade in this area.

"May the words of my mouth and the meditation of my heart be pleasing in your sight, O Lord, my Rock and my Redeemer" (Psalm 19:14). This

prayer of the psalmist should be our own as well, especially concerning our teenage children. We must guard our hearts and our mouths when we relate to our teens, so that we do not harbor attitudes or voice words that might wound their spirits. One way to maintain a right attitude toward our teen, and to speak the right words to him or her, is by cultivating our relationship with God through daily Bible reading, prayer, and worship.

Hebrews 4:12 says, *"For the word of God is living and active. Sharper than any double-edged sword, it penetrates even to dividing soul and spirit, joints and marrow; it judges the thoughts and attitudes of the heart."* As we study God's Word and maintain a life of prayer and worship, He will reveal to us the attitudes of our heart. Then, our response should be that of humble repentance for any heart attitudes that don't reflect love and gratitude.

Admit When You're Wrong

Parents don't like to admit it, but there are times when it's the parent who's wrong, not the child. Whether it's a wrong decision or a wrong way of responding—in anger rather than in love—be sure to humble yourself and ask forgiveness of your teenager. Even when you've blown it big time, you can actually increase your teenager's respect for you if you acknowledge your mistake and ask for forgiveness. Your teen also will grow in maturity as a result of seeing you model righteous behavior. It may not happen overnight, but he or she will follow in your footsteps.

Sometimes, our kids will sit back and wait to see if we are going to stay the course. They like to test us. If we practice humility and acknowledge our wrongdoing only once or twice, they'll conclude that we were merely putting on a show. They won't be convinced. But when we adopt this attitude as our lifestyle, and when our kids see us living it day in and day out, they will follow suit.

When my daughter has spoken disrespectfully or acted in an unrighteous way, more often than not, she comes to me of her own free will and asks for my forgiveness. I like to think that this is partly due to my own example. I have always tried to humble myself, by the grace of God, when

I have acted wrongly or done something to damage our relationship. And my efforts have paid off: my daughter respected my ability to admit my wrongdoing, and she has learned to follow my example.

Our kids model what they see us doing. If we yell and scream back, they will follow our example—they will yell and scream. In my house, I refuse to yell and scream. I refuse to waste energy in that way, and I refuse to let the enemy steal my joy. Do I get upset from time to time? Of course! Do I get frustrated and angry? Yes, indeed. But I learned, way back before having children, not to yell or scream. It doesn't do any good, and it actually grieves the Holy Spirit—never a good thing!

> *And do not grieve the Holy Spirit of God [do not offend or vex or sadden Him], by Whom you were sealed (marked, branded as God's own, secured) for the day of redemption (of final deliverance through Christ from evil and the consequences of sin).* (Ephesians 4:30 AMP)

Guard Your Joy

I choose to guard the anointing and the presence of the Lord in my life. Be wise to the enemy's schemes. Don't allow him to steal your joy! When you get angry and start yelling, the enemy has a good laugh because he knows he's gained the upper hand.

Nehemiah 8:10 says, *"Do not grieve, for the joy of the Lord is your strength."* When you are grieving over the challenges of any season of life, and when you grieve the Holy Spirit by your sinful actions or reactions, it gives the enemy a prime opportunity to steal your joy. And the joy of the Lord is your greatest source of strength. Why in the world would you allow the enemy to steal even an ounce of your strength? I don't know about you, but I need every ounce of my strength to accomplish all that the Lord has called me to do for His kingdom. I can't afford to have my strength depleted by the enemy and his diabolical schemes.

Great joy is found in the presence of the Lord. As you worship the Lord, as you pray to Him, and as you meditate on His Word day and night, you can maintain the presence of the Lord in your heart and in your home. Your teenager will be the beneficiary of the overflow of the presence of the Lord in your life. On the other hand, your teenager also will reap the consequences of the lack of God's presence and joy in your life. The choice is yours. Choose joy!

Cry Out for Wisdom

Soon after my daughter turned thirteen, just when she was beginning the adventure of adolescence, I found myself praying for her and crying out to God on her behalf, asking Him to give me wisdom to raise her and turning over to Him the concerns that had been weighing on my heart. I was worried because of the things I was seeing happen around her and the influences she was being exposed to.

Thank God for the Holy Spirit. He really does lead us into all truth (John 16:13). He really does teach us all things (John 14:26). And He really does give us any and all wisdom we need. It's ours for the asking!

James 1:5 says, *"If any of you lacks wisdom, he should ask God, who gives generously to all without finding fault, and it will be given to him."* Did you hear that, parents? Every mother and father with a teenager at home should be shouting for joy right now! We never fully understand how much wisdom we really lack until we have a teenager on our hands. When our children become teenagers, they begin to think their parents don't know anything. In a sense, they're right, because we lack wisdom based on life experience for raising teenagers! And we are in desperate need of God's infinite wisdom. Thank the Lord that He makes it available to us, through the power of the Holy Spirit. And all of the parents said, "Amen!"

We have this assurance, that, when we ask God for wisdom, He will grant it to us in abundance. But we must believe and not doubt that He will do so.

But when [a person] *asks* [for wisdom from God], *he must believe and not doubt, because he who doubts is like a wave of the sea, blown and tossed by the wind. That man should not think he will receive anything form the Lord; he is a double-minded man, unstable in all he does.* (James 1:6-8)

Many of you have asked God for wisdom, but you've blocked it from reaching you because you've wondered whether it would. Don't doubt God! Don't allow the enemy to plant his poisonous seeds of doubt in the garden of your mind. Just do what God has put in your heart to do, trusting Him to bring turnaround in every area where change is needed in your relationship with your teenager. Be fully persuaded that God has the power to turn anything around—and then watch Him work!

I want to share some nuggets of wisdom the Lord has given me in raising my teenage daughter. The first thing I know is, I don't know it all. The second thing is, I know I need God's wisdom, and more of it every day. If we keep both of these things in mind, we can raise God-fearing children who will become world changers for the Lord.

NUGGET #1: BUILD THE ARK FOR YOUR CHILDREN

Years ago, I did a series entitled "Building the Ark of His Presence." In this series, I talked about how the presence of the Lord in our lives builds the present-day ark for us. Just as in the days of Noah, when he and his family sought refuge in the ark from the flood that destroyed the rest of the world, the ark is a place of security—a safe haven from all of the destruction happening in the world around us. Today, as we build the ark of the Lord's presence in our lives, we can successfully weather the storms of life and find protection from the devastation and destruction going on in the world around us. We build the ark of the Lord's presence by worshipping Him, praying to Him, and meditating on His Word of truth. Maintaining our personal devotions with God keeps us living in the ark of the Lord's presence and enjoying the protection it offers.

Just as Noah built the ark to shelter himself and his family, we must build the ark of the Lord's presence for our own children. And we can begin the building process long before our children are born. By working on our relationship with the Lord and by praying for our children before they are even formed in the womb, we begin building the ark of the Lord's presence in their lives.

Don't get under condemnation if you weren't walking with the Lord when your children were born or if you came to the Lord just a few years ago. It's never too late to build the ark of the Lord's presence for yourself and your children. Yes, it's true that the earlier you build, the better; but, remember: God is the God of turnaround, and you have always been in the palm of His hand, even before you accepted Him as Lord and Savior of your life. He accepted you into the palm of His hand the day He died on the cross for you, so He's got you covered!

> God saw how corrupt the earth had become, for all the people on earth had corrupted their ways. So God said to Noah, "I am going to put an end to all people, for the earth is filled with violence because of them. I am surely going to destroy both them and the earth. So make yourself an ark….Noah did everything just as God commanded him….And Noah and his sons and his wife and his sons' wives entered the ark to escape the waters of the flood….And after the seven days the floodwaters came on the earth. (Genesis 6:12-14, 22; 7:7, 10)

Noah didn't wait for the rain to start falling before he built the ark. Instead, he began to build at the Lord's command. The ideal time to start building the ark of the Lord's presence for our children is before they arrive (their birth) and before the storms arrive in their lives (their teenage years). As parents, it's our job to build the ark for our children ahead of time, as Noah did.

I am going to bring floodwaters on the earth to destroy all life under the heavens, every creature that has the breath of life in it. Everything on earth will perish. But I will establish my covenant with you, and you will enter the ark—you and your sons and your wife and your sons' wives with you. (Genesis 6:17-18)

When you are in covenant with the Lord, your whole household is blessed! When you are in covenant with God, you can build and enter the ark of His presence. Your family is blessed by the ark you build.

God told Noah that He was going to establish His covenant with him, and that the blessing of that covenant would extend to his entire family—even his daughters-in-law. God went on to say that after Noah built the ark, he should enter it in order to find protection from the destruction that was coming on the world. Noah's obedience to build the ark ultimately protected his family members from destruction.

Noah did everything that God had commanded him (Genesis 6:22; 7:5). God offered the covenant and blessings of obedience to Noah, but it depended on Noah's choice. Noah made the right decision when he chose to obey God's commands. I'm sure it wasn't easy. Remember, before the flood, it had never rained before! Here was Noah, building this big boat, because God told him it was going to rain so hard that the earth would be flooded.

Parents, you know how everything we do is embarrassing to our teenagers? You know how we are called "weird," "strange," and "out of touch" with the real world? Well, we are in good company with Noah! I can't imagine what his children must have thought, not to mention his daughters-in-law, when he started constructing the ark. I bet old Noah really weathered some serious in-law jokes back in his day.

But, in spite of it all, Noah obeyed the Lord, following His instructions to a "T."

...Noah was a righteous man, blameless among the people of his time, and he walked with God. (Genesis 6:9)

Our obedience to the Lord brings us into the place of favor with God. Obedience to the Lord always leads to righteousness. The righteous heart of Noah ended up saving his entire family!

As you build the ark of the Lord's presence in your heart and in your home, you are assembling God's plan of deliverance and salvation for your entire family, teenagers included.

> *The Lord then said to Noah, "Go into the ark, you and your whole family, because I have found you righteous in this generation."* (Genesis 7:1)

Your teenagers might not want to have anything to do with you and your boat, but you just keep on building! They might think you are crazy; they might be embarrassed that you are the Christian parent you are. But, honey, you just keep on building!

That very boat Noah's children made fun of—the very ark they wanted nothing to do with—was the very boat that saved their skins. When the rain started falling, Noah's kids stopped laughing and ran right toward it. It may not be raining yet, but with the first cloudburst, your kids will come running—trust me!

When Noah and his family had taken shelter inside the ark, it says, *"Then the Lord shut him in"* (Genesis 7:16b). Noah and all of his precious family were shut inside the ark under the protection of God's hand at the appointed time, just as God had told Noah. No one was laughing then! No one was calling Noah the "mean dad." No longer did Noah's kids call him "strange" or "weird." And all of his children and their spouses were saved.

Keep building the ark of the presence of the Lord in your heart and in your home! Your teenagers might not want anything to do with it now, but you just keep building, looking forward to the day when the rain starts to fall and your kids come running to what you have built.

> *This is how you are to build it: The ark is to be 450 feet long, 75 feet wide and 45 feet high. Make a roof for it and finish*

the ark to within 18 inches of the top. Put a door in the side of the ark and make lower, middle and upper decks. (Genesis 6:15-16)

Noah received some very detailed instructions from God, and he obeyed all of them. God is a God of detail, and if He gives us instructions, it's important that we leave nothing undone. If Noah had not carried out the Lord's instructions to the last detail, his boat would have sunk! But, because he had adhered to every specification God gave him, the ark stayed intact through the entire storm. It didn't capsize or sink. I didn't say that it didn't "stink"—with all those animals on board, I'm sure it was more than a little smelly. But Noah and his family were probably so relieved to make it through the storm that they didn't mind.

Again, Genesis 6:22 says, *"Noah did everything just as God commanded him."* The detailed instructions for building the ark were very important, and so are the detailed instructions that the Lord gives us for raising our children. (If it helps, try keeping a journal in which you record and reflect on your communication with the Lord, including the instructions He gives to you. That way, you'll be more likely to follow through with those instructions!) It's important that we obey His voice all the time, not only when it's convenient or when we're feeling particularly ambitious about ark-building. No, we must continue building the ark for ourselves and our children, according to the Lord's instructions and according to His timetable.

I always say that hearing the voice of God is easy; it's obeying His instructions that's the challenging part. It's challenging because it often kills our flesh. Obedience to God is rarely convenient, and it's often the opposite of what we feel like doing or even what we believe we ought to be doing. But Noah set aside his personal preferences, obeyed God with blind faith, and was blessed as a result. We should do the same.

NUGGET #2: KEEP YOUR KIDS UNDER THE GLORY CLOUD

The concept of blind faith ties in well with the second nugget I want to share with you in regard to raising teenagers. One day soon after my daughter entered adolescence, I was praying for teenagers—those I knew, specifically, and those across the nation, in general—and asking God for wisdom on how to raise a teenage daughter. It was then that the Lord spoke to me about teenagers, saying, "You must keep them under the glory cloud!" This was God's specific instruction—that we, as parents seeking to build the ark of the Lord's presence in our children's lives, must keep them under the glory cloud.

There are many conflicting voices that try to "cloud" our teenagers' thoughts, minds, hearts, attitudes, and daily choices. But, we must keep them under the cloud of God's glory. As parents, if we don't have the cloud of God's glory in our lives, if we aren't under His glory cloud on a regular basis, there won't be a glory cloud for our kids to get under. If we don't experience the presence of the Lord on a regular basis, how can we expect our children to? They must see us experiencing regular "cloud bursts" of His glory.

If we don't get our children under the cloud of God's glory on a regular basis, then the cloud of depression, the cloud of misjudgment, the cloud of compromise, and others will threaten to "cloud out" God's presence and voice in the lives of our children.

Do our children ever hear us pray? Do our children see us dance before the Lord? What is our attitude toward worship? We must stay under the glory cloud ourselves, with a childlike faith that expresses itself through earnest worship. That way, our children will get splashed by our "cloud bursts" on a regular basis, whether or not they want to! But, once they have tasted and seen, they will know that the Lord is good (Psalm 34:8).

The book of Second Samuel records an instance when David danced before the Lord, in the presence of His glory cloud, in a time of thanksgiving. *"David, wearing a linen ephod, danced before the Lord with all his might, while he and the entire house of Israel brought up the ark of the Lord with shouts and the sound of trumpets"* (2 Samuel 6:14-15). David was child-like in his worship. He danced before the Lord with all his might. He wasn't just doing a little swaying; he was "getting down" in worship before the Lord. Trust me, you want your kids to worship the Lord with all their might, free of the inhibitions of self-consciousness. When they see you worshipping freely, without reservations, they will feel their spirit-man rise up within them, prompting them to dance worshipfully before the Lord.

If you don't model unrestrained worship, and if you restrict your children's expressions of worship, they'll find another place to express themselves through dance—and it won't be a God-honoring place. You need to keep them under the cloud of glory, at home and in your worship services. Don't take your children to a church that's spiritually asleep or, worse, dead! If you are attending a spiritually dead church, do your best to pray resurrection power over it; and then, if it stays dead, move on. You can't have your children at a spiritually dead church, or you will raise spiritually dead children who will grow up to be spiritually dead teenagers and adults.

During your children's teenage years, especially, it is important to keep the glory cloud over your house through regular times of family devotions, worship, and prayer. It's also vital for your children to be connected to a church where the worship services are alive. Church attendance should be a priority at all times, but especially during adolescence.

Please understand that I'm not legalistic about church attendance and related issues. I believe that there's a balance. There are times when God takes us somewhere that prevents us from attending our church's services. Sometimes schedule conflicts can't be avoided. I'm not talking about those times. I'm talking about those times when you're tempted to stay home because you or your children "just don't feel like going." If you follow the leading of your flesh in those instances, you set an example for your children—and, pretty soon, none of you will be at church at all. If your children wake up on Sunday morning and ask, "Are we going to church today?" it's a good indicator that you need to make church attendance a higher priority for your family.

Even when I'm exhausted from a week of ministry, I always drag myself out of bed to get to my home church service on time. If you find that you and your children attend church begrudgingly, it could be a clue that you are in a spiritually dead church. When the glory cloud of God is in a church, when the presence of the Lord is there, you can't wait to jump up and go dance in the river!

We need to have regular times of prayer and Bible study. Then, we need to encourage our teenagers and children to do the same. We shouldn't expect their devotions or prayer times to be just like ours. Praise God if they are, but we shouldn't be discouraged if they aren't.

There have been many times when God has prompted me to include my daughter in my prayer times. In my natural mind, I tend to think, *But my prayer times are personal—they're for me and God alone.* But the Lord says, "Take her with you to your place of prayer." He knew that it was better for me to take my daughter to my place of prayer from time to time, instead of going alone to experience God's glory while my daughter sat in the living room watching television. We need to get our children under our own glory cloud of God from time to time.

There were times when Destiny would sit in the corner, mad because she didn't want to be there under the glory cloud with me. But I have learned that if you keep your children under the glory cloud long enough, they will get wet, and, once they get wet, they won't be able to resist diving in themselves.

Your kids may have an attitude when you drag them to church, but keep on dragging them! As long as the glory of God is there, they will get wet. Put them in the front row, near the "spout" of water from the glory cloud. That's what I have always done with Destiny. During the Sunday morning service, she always sits with me, up front—not in the back with her friends. Even when I'm preaching, she's in the front row. From time to time, her attitude sits there with her, but don't worry—the glory cloud always washes it away. Let the glory of the Lord arise, and the attitude will fall. Just keep those teenagers under the cloud of God's glory!

NUGGET #3: SET A STANDARD AND KEEP IT

As parents, we must set the standard for our households and our children. It goes without saying that we ourselves must first live by the standards we set. We need to practice as we preach! We shouldn't ever say, "Do as I say, not as I do." That never works. Our words and our actions must correspond. We are setting the standard for our teenagers, first and foremost, by what we do, what we say, and how we act. They may outwardly resist our words, but they're going to end up following our act.

We must pray to God and hear from Him about the standards He would have us live by, above and beyond those set for us in His Word, the Bible. Once we have prayed and heard from the Lord on the standards He wants us to set for our house, we must communicate them clearly, enforce them consistently, and endeavor to follow them ourselves.

Teenagers need to know their boundaries just as much as young children. I don't believe in having legalistic rules, but I strongly believe in setting high standards of excellence for righteous, holy living. Living a holy life never goes out of style, no matter what your teenager may say to try to convince you otherwise.

Choose You This Day

> But if serving the Lord seems undesirable to you, then choose for yourselves this day whom you will serve, whether the gods your forefathers served beyond the River, or the gods of the Amorites, in whose land you are living. But as for me and my household, we will serve the Lord. (Joshua 24:15)

We have to be bold about whom we will serve, and we have to raise our teenagers to be bold standard setters. If our teenagers never see us being bold about our faith, they will never be bold about theirs.

People in the world are bold about serving their gods. People who practice other religions are very bold about serving their gods. We as Christians need to be bold about serving our God—the King of all kings and the Lord of all lords. I don't know about you, but as for me and my house, we will serve the Lord!

Get the Mixture Out

I believe we are entering a time when our choices will make it or break it for us. We must set a standard for our teenagers by our own example of living a life without mixture—that is, by refusing to tolerate sin or to compromise our standards.

Mixture and compromise can cause us to misinterpret the voice of God or to miss it entirely. There was mixture in Lot's heart, and, as a result, he didn't even bother consulting God on an important decision.

> *Lot looked up and saw that the whole plain of the Jordan was well watered, like the garden of the Lord, like the land of Egypt, toward Zoar. (This was before the Lord destroyed Sodom and Gomorrah.) So Lot chose for himself the whole plain of the Jordan and set out toward the east. The two men parted company. Abram lived in the land of Canaan, while Lot lived among the cities of the plain and pitched his tents near Sodom.* (Genesis 13:10-12)

We know Lot had mixture in his heart because the Word says that he *"chose for himself."* Choosing for ourselves is never smart! This is a lesson we must model for our teenagers. Lot saw what looked good in the natural. He saw what looked like God, and he chose for himself. His choice was made without consulting God on the matter. Had he surrendered the decision to God and waited for His voice, he would have realized the error in making the selection he did. Mixture in Lot's heart nearly cost him his life.

If we have mixture in our hearts, we will often abide such sinful attitudes as ungodly anger, unforgiveness, and bitterness. We can't afford to allow deadly emotions to fill in our hearts—it's mixture! We can't allow a little bit of sin and compromise to sneak into our lives—it's mixture. The Word says the little foxes come to ruin the vine or the fruit of our lives (Song of Songs 2:15). When we have mixture in our hearts and in our lives, we tend to make bad choices. As parents, we have to keep the little destructive foxes out of our homes, our hearts, and the lives of our teenagers.

Abram, on the other hand, sought God on his every move. Abram had a pure heart before the Lord—without any mixture. Abram made an altar to the Lord wherever he went. He heard God's voice and followed in obedience.

> *So Abram left, as the Lord had told him; and Lot went with him. Abram was seventy-five years old when he set out from Haran. He took his wife Sarai, his nephew Lot, all the possessions they had accumulated and the people they had acquired in Haran, and they set out for the land of Canaan, and they arrived there.* (Genesis 12:4-5)

Abram arrived at his destination because he had sought God on his every move. He let God choose for him. He didn't choose for himself. Distractions and discouragement try to prevent us from reaching our destiny in God. But, as we keep mixture out of our hearts and our lives, we will reach our God-ordained destination. God has a plan for our precious children, and it depends largely on the choices they make. That's why we need to emphasize the importance of making right decisions, especially during their teenage years.

I believe you and I need to be transparent and real with our kids. Don't try to hide your mistakes from them. Be honest about the times you've messed up and the consequences that you faced as a result. As always, pray before sharing anything with your children, to make sure that God agrees in the wisdom of doing so. When you've heard from Him and you're ready to share, be sure to be real, to practice humility, and to speak in a spirit of love.

Keep the Standard, No Matter What

God has given me some very clear standards for me and my daughter to live by. Teenagers love to say, "But everyone else is doing it!" My answer to this objection has always been the same: "But I'm not everyone else's momma! I'm your momma, and you're not doing it."

We should never judge someone else's standards or lack thereof. But neither should we compromise our standards because of someone else's. That's what our teenagers face every day: the temptation to compromise their standards—the very standards we have spent years instilling in them. As parents, we must stick to our standards, if we hope to model for our children how to stand up for them.

When God puts His standard on your heart, it's not easy to maintain them with your teenagers. Other parents and even family members have told me that I'm being too strict. But I know better. I have to build the ark for my daughter according to the specific instructions I have received from the Lord. Other parents can build their arks the way they think they should build them, and I earnestly pray they will stay afloat, but I am answerable to God, and I must make sure to build according to the blueprint He has given me in prayer.

One example of an area in which I've been accused of being "too strict" is the music we listen to. Whether it's a CD or the radio, Destiny and I listen exclusively to Christian music. We don't compromise that standard. Has it been easy? No! Has my daughter fought it? You bet! But I'm still standing on the standard God instructed me to employ with my teenager.

God has shown me time and time again that music is a major way in which the enemy ensnares young people. Music that is not honoring to God opens the door to the enemy's attempts to snare our kids in all kinds of sin. If you'll recall, Satan was the "worship leader" in heaven before he fell. And he fell due to his rebellion against God. That's what sin is—rebellion against God. Much of popular music today, outside of the Christian realm, promotes rebellion against godly principles. Some country music talks about sleeping with JoJo's wife after getting drunk at the local bar—real edifying, right?

Why would we let our kids listen to music that instills principles that contradict everything we have taught them over the years? Even the "golden oldies" awaken love—make that lust—entirely too early, in my book. Why do you suppose it is that almost every young vocalist sings love songs? Because the producers know what sells—and it's all about the bottom line for them. For me, however, it's about my daughter living a holy life, separated unto the Lord, without compromise. As for me and my house, we will serve the Lord!

I limit my daughter's television watching and Internet usage. She may be fourteen, but she isn't old enough for Facebook, in my book. Call me old-fashioned, but my teenage daughter has no business posting cute pictures of herself on the Internet for the whole world—predators included—to see. If she wants to see the faces of her friends, they are welcome at our house anytime. When you establish and reinforce the standards that you receive from the Lord, you usher in the glory cloud over your children and your home.

Nugget #4: Let Them Talk

When they reach adolescence, our children need to talk more than ever before. Our children need us when they are infants and toddlers, but I'm convinced that they need us even more when they are teenagers, albeit for different reasons.

I pick up my daughter after school as often as I can. I'll rearrange my work schedule so that I may pick her up, even if it means doing additional work at home in the evening, because it's worth it to me to create some quality time for the two of us to talk. One thing I never do is ask questions. I used to ask questions, but the answer was always "Nothing" (with an occasional "Okay"). "What did you do today?" "Nothing." "What did you learn today?" "Nothing." "How was your day?" "Okay." Finally, I got smart and stopped asking questions.

Instead, I simply tell her I love her and that I missed her during the day. That's it. Then, I just wait and listen. Sometimes, It takes her until dinner or bedtime to start telling me about her day. When I don't ask questions, she tells me everything, eventually. But that depends on my being available. So, I make myself available, ready and willing to listen whenever she wants to talk. Parents, this is a golden nugget! Make yourselves available. Don't ask questions; just let your teenager talk.

Sometimes, your teenage son or daughter will want to talk, only to tell you why you should change your standards. Be sure to listen and then respond in love—and stick to your guns! Of course, it's important to be flexible when flexibility is called for. And that brings me to my next "nugget"—the importance of picking your battles.

NUGGET #5: CHOOSE YOUR BATTLES WISELY

Our kids are wise, and we should respect their intelligence and value their opinions, just as we expect them to do for us. I have actually made a lot of changes as a result of having listened to my daughter. For example, I have altered my requirements regarding the way she maintains her bedroom. The spiritual atmosphere of her room is vital to her growth as a young Christian woman and is therefore important to me. But I have learned to choose my battles wisely, and one thing I no longer fight her on is the physical cleanliness of the room. That's an area where I can afford to compromise. If she wants to live in a pigpen, that's fine by me—it's her room. As long as there aren't a bunch of bugs crawling around, I can handle it. I don't do bugs, but clothes, shoes, and other items I can easily step over and around. I make sure to enter at my own risk, about three times a week, tops.

It's important to give our children the room to make decisions for themselves. That's why we need to pick our battles. We should compromise where we feel comfortable doing so. Just be sure never to compromise where their spiritual development is concerned.

NUGGET #6: SHOW YOUR LOVE

Most teenagers resist physical affection from their parents. They act as if they don't want you hugging and kissing them. But adolescence is when they need your love more than ever. Just make sure you aren't demonstrative with your love at the wrong time! If their friends are around, it's the wrong time for hugs and kisses. It's also the wrong time to refer to yourself in the third person as "Mommy" or "Daddy." (I learned this the hard way.)

But when there isn't an audience, be sure to pour on the hugs. They may push you away at first, but give it time. They want your love and affection on their terms, but they need to know that it's available when they need it.

They are faced with bullying situations, cruel friends, academic challenges, peer pressure, comparison, and many other areas of stress and anxiety. Your unconditional love gives them a greatly needed sense of security, even if they don't realize how much they need it. Even if your teenager is pretty happy-go-lucky, like mine, he or she probably has plenty of fears and insecurities beneath the surface. The enemy tries to bombard their impressionable minds with lies and untruths. Let your love set the stage for them to talk to you and to receive your affirmation. Let your love set the stage for their security and self-confidence in a world of uncertainty outside the walls of your house.

Never assume that your children know you love them; tell them every day, as many chances as you get. And don't just tell them with your words—tell them with your actions, as well!

NUGGET #7: SPEND QUALITY TIME WITH THEM

You've probably heard it said that "love" is spelled T-I-M-E. One major way in which we demonstrate our love for our children is by spending quality time with them. They appreciate it more than you know, even if it takes their becoming parents themselves to realize how much.

Quality time can also include those instances when you show up for your kids as a show of support, even if you aren't doing something together. They may pretend not to notice you in the stands at their basketball game or in the audience at the school play. They may not address you in front of their teammates and friends. But, trust me—they are glad to see you there.

The quality of time spent with your kids is far more important than the quantity of time. It's great to have plenty of both, but if you can't spend a lot of time together, be sure that you are fully present and focused during the times you are together. Give your kids your undivided attention—and demand the same from them. Turn off your cell phone and your iPad, and ask them to do the same.

I try to schedule a short weekend trip or an overnight for Destiny and me every couple of months. I have a demanding schedule, with staff members, ministry partners, volunteers, and other people always trying to get ahold of me. That's why, when I go out of town with my daughter, I turn off my cell phone—to eliminate any distractions that might diminish the quality of our time spent together.

There are some weekends when we take a trip and, at the outset, think that we don't have the time or the money to go. Other times, we just don't want to go because we've been getting on each other's nerves. But, every time we go away together, we grow closer to each other, we enjoy our time, and we both are glad we went.

Quality time with no outside distractions is a key piece of advice for married couples, and it's just as important for your relationships with your kids. They really do need you during their teenage years more than ever, and spending time without any distractions or deterrents is a vital part of staying connected.

NUGGET #8: HAVE FUN WITH THEM

This should be an easy "rule": just have fun! I am a very focused person. I am a very hard worker, and I take my work for the Lord very seriously. I like things to be done right. I am an achiever and goal setter by nature. But one thing my daughter has taught me is how to have fun.

I believe in working hard, but I believe that playing hard is just as important. When it's the middle of the work week, it's a struggle for me to take off and go play. But I have had to learn to draw the line when I've worked enough. I have learned how to set boundaries on my work. And when my work is done, we go crazy! We play, we giggle, we go for ice cream—we just enjoy being together.

There will always be something else that needs to be done. There will always be someone else who needs to be ministered to. There will always be another person who needs my attention. So, I have learned to draw healthy boundaries, for the sake of my daughter, for the sake of my health, and for the sake of God's glory. It is my hope that doing so will give me the stamina to keep preaching until I'm ninety, if the Lord tarries.

If there are tensions between your teenager and you, try taking a break and having some fun together. Don't discuss the "hot topic" at hand. Just go do something you both enjoy, and allow the experience to reconnect you. That way, the "hot topic" will have a chance to cool down, so that you can discuss it calmly and considerately.

NUGGET #9: REMEMBER, PRAYER CHANGES EVERYTHING

Prayer is the most important nugget of all. Pray for your teenager—pray without ceasing!

> *Rejoice always, pray without ceasing, in everything give thanks; for this is the will of God in Christ Jesus for you.* (1 Thessalonians 5:16-18 NKJV)

> *Pray in the Spirit on all occasions with all kinds of prayers and requests.* (Ephesians 6:18a)

Your teenager needs your prayer covering more than just about anything else. Remember, you are engaged in spiritual warfare, and the battle for the hearts of your teenagers is fiercer than ever. This is why you should pray without ceasing. Prayer changes things! Remember to pray against ungodly influences. Pray and curse the spirit of rebellion in the life of your teenager. Pray for God to handpick your children's friends. Pray for their future spouse. Pray for them to hear God and to follow His leading in every decision.

Pray without ceasing for your teenagers. Ask others to pray for you, that you would hear the voice of God in raising your teenager. And don't forget to ask God daily for wisdom in raising your child. The Word promises that He will grant you wisdom, as long as you remain confident of that fact.

> *If any of you lacks wisdom, he should ask God, who gives generously to all without finding fault, and it will be given to him. But when he asks, he must believe and not doubt, because he who doubts is like a wave of the sea, blown and tossed by the wind. That man should not think he will receive anything from the Lord; he is a double-minded man, unstable in all he does.* (James 1:5-8)

Don't doubt yourself. Don't doubt your discernment when it comes to hearing from the Lord. Don't doubt your choices concerning your teenager when they are made based on God-given wisdom, even if someone else says that you are being overly strict.

When my daughter was young, there was a church where I was happy to speak and minister, but I wasn't comfortable allowing Destiny to attend their children's church. Everyone else seemed to think I was being overprotective—and that's the opinion my natural mind had formed. However, I couldn't shake the sense that God did not want her there. Years later, it was discovered that someone had been molesting children in that setting. I thanked the Lord that I had followed His leading rather than dismissing it!

Follow the Lord's leading, which is always confirmed by a sense of peace. If you don't have peace, you don't need to know why—just trust your discernment. Pray and ask God for wisdom, but don't be double-minded. Stand in faith, and keep on standing!

BUILDING THE ARK IS UP TO YOU; GETTING INSIDE IS UP TO YOUR KIDS

As parents, we have the weighty responsibility of building the ark of the Lord's presence in our hearts and homes, in order for our families to be blessed. Our children's destiny depends on it! But we should never feel pressured to secure their salvation, since that isn't our job. Our job is to build the ark, not to force our children inside. Once we have constructed the ark of the Lord's presence and ushered in His glory cloud, we invite our children in, and then we step aside and let the Holy Spirit do His work. Our children will never get in unless it's of their own volition. As long as we keep them under the glory cloud, they will want to be in the ark of the Lord's presence that we have prepared for them. But the choice is theirs.

Again, a key to total turnaround for your teenager is wisdom. As you seek the Lord for His wisdom and also implement the "nuggets" of wisdom I have shared in this chapter, you will see the Lord bring total turnaround in the life of your teenage children, as well as in your relationship with them. Stay encouraged, for God is turning the ship around!

Build the ark of the Lord's presence for your teenager.

POINTS TO PONDER

1. When we are faced with challenging circumstances in life, we need to remind ourselves that they are temporary. What effect can just knowing that a new season is coming have on you?

2. Prayer is the best gift that we can give our children. Can you think back to a time when you prayed in faith for your child and saw God perform a turnaround in his or her situation?

3. How do you build the "ark of the Lord's presence" for your children, and what will it do for them?

4. Seeking God about the standards He would have you live by, and then keeping those standards, will allow you to live a life without mixture before your children. This will usher in the glory cloud over your children and your home. What standards has God directed you not to compromise on?

Meditate on these Scriptures, speak them aloud, and commit them to memory:

We fix our eyes not on what is seen, but on what is unseen. For what is seen is temporary, but what is unseen is eternal. (2 Corinthians 4:18)

May the words of my mouth and the meditation of my heart be pleasing in your sight, O Lord, my Rock and my Redeemer. (Psalm 19:14)

If any of you lacks wisdom, he should ask God, who gives generously to all without finding fault, and it will be given to him. (James 1:5)

Rejoice always, pray without ceasing, in everything give thanks; for this is the will of God in Christ Jesus for you. (1 Thessalonians 5:16-18 NKJV)

Chapter 9

TOTAL TURNAROUND IN YOUR FINANCES

God wants to bring total turnaround in every area of your life, including your wallet and your bank accounts. Many people find it easy to walk by faith in every area except for their finances. Money can be the most diffi-cult thing to surrender to God. Yet He longs to perform a total turnaround in this realm as much as in every other realm of your life.

If you are one of those people who have always struggled financially, or who have always struggled to walk by faith in the area of finances, then I want you to ask the Holy Spirit to reveal to you the root cause of your struggle. Maybe you have been operating with a poverty mind-set. Maybe you have a control issue or a trust issue in the area of finances because of the financial circumstances of your growing-up years. For many of you, a turnaround in the area of your finances may begin in your mind.

Sometimes, it's our mind-set that sets the stage for lack. Sometimes, it's fear or a lack of faith that is really the area in which we need a turnaround. No matter what the underlying issues may be, God wants to heal us and set us free.

When my daughter was born, I became a single mom overnight—and went from two incomes to none at all. My husband and I had both been earning a salary, but I could no longer work full-time with a baby in tow. As for my husband, he took all of his income with him when he left us.

So, here I was, walking by faith without any income. Needless to say, God put His finger on a lot of fears that I had in my life. I never realized I had fear in this area before, but God revealed it. God showed me that I had a fear of not being provided for. When I was young, my parents divorced, and my mother struggled to provide for my brothers and me. As a result, I never had the assurance that "Daddy" was going to pay the bills. So, when I became a Christian, I didn't have the assurance that my heavenly "Daddy" would pay the bills, either.

I had to learn to doubt my doubts and face my fears. It was at this time that I learned to trust God at a level that I had never known before. It was a process, but I learned to overcome the fear of not being provided for. I learned that the Lord would always provide for my needs, as long as I walked in obedience to do what He told me to do, when He told me to do it. For the first time, I was able to testify to the truth of Philippians 4:19: *"My God will meet all your needs according to his glorious riches in Christ Jesus."*

God's Place of Provision

Whether we realize it or not, we have preconceived ideas of how God's provision will be brought about for our lives. These preconceived ideas usually come from the system of the world in which we have been raised. People who have grown up in government housing unconsciously believe that their provision comes from the government. Working-class people generally believe that their provision comes from their paycheck. Business owners and investors often have the mind-set that their provision comes from their investments, their customers, or their savings.

In reality, all of us receive our provision from the Lord. Maybe your income does currently come from one of those three sources. But that's just a means or a source in which your provision is currently being funneled through. And if you view your source as your provider or your means of provision, as soon as your financial season changes, you will be in sad shape!

Again, God is your provider, and His provision for you always comes at His place of positioning. If God wants you in Arizona, you'd better not be searching for a job in Florida. If God wants you working in retail, you'd better not be taking a different job. God's provision for you will be manifested when you are in the right place, at the right time, with the right heart motive!

THE LORD WILL PROVIDE

The Lord tests us from time to time to see if we will obey His voice and His leading. He tests us in order to reveal the nature of our hearts to ourselves, so that we may see whether repentance is needed.

One of the earliest examples of God testing the obedience of one of His children is recorded in Genesis 22:1-5:

> Some time later God tested Abraham. He said to him, "Abraham!" "Here I am," he replied. Then God said, "Take your son, your only son, Isaac, whom you love, and go to the region of Moriah. Sacrifice him there as a burnt offering on one of the mountains I will tell you about." Early the next morning Abraham got up and saddled his donkey. He took with him two of his servants and his son Isaac. When he had cut enough wood for the burnt offering, he set out for the place God had told him about. On the third day Abraham looked up and saw the place in the distance. He said to his servants, "Stay here with the donkey while I and the boy go over there. We will worship and then we will come back to you."

God was testing Abraham to see if his son Isaac meant more to him than God Himself. If we aren't careful, the fulfillment of our vision may end up meaning more to us than the One who gave us that vision and brought its fulfillment—God Himself! But Abraham remained obedient and passed the test. By following God's instructions, and by his willingness to sacrifice his son in obedience to God, he proved that his faith was genuine and his priorities were right. He also proved that he trusted in God, to the point of believing that God would raise his son to life again, if Abraham followed through with the sacrifice, in order to fulfill His promise to him. Abraham didn't doubt, and he didn't disobey. He was prepared to do what God said, when and how God said to do it!

Fortunately for Abraham, his obedience was rewarded before he had a chance to slay his son.

> *When they reached the place God had told him about, Abraham built an altar there and arranged the wood on it. He bound his son Isaac and laid him on the altar, on top of the wood. Then he reached out his hand and took the knife to slay his son. But the angel of the Lord called out to him from heaven, "Abraham! Abraham!" "Here I am," he replied. "Do not lay a hand on the boy," he said. "Do not do anything to him. Now I know that you fear God, because you have not withheld from me your son, your only son." Abraham looked up and there in a thicket he saw a ram caught by its horns. He went over and took the ram and sacrificed it as a burnt offering instead of his son. So Abraham called that place The Lord Will Provide. And to this day it is said, "On the mountain of the Lord it will be provided."* (Genesis 22:9-14)

Abraham feared God with reverence and respect to the point that he obeyed His voice, even if it would mean the death of his promised son. By way of an extreme lesson, Abraham learned to trust God as his provider.

God provided for Abraham, and He will provide for you today, because God never changes. (See Hebrews 13:8.) The Lord was the provider of His people in Bible times, and He is the provider of His people's needs today! He provides...

- the desires of our hearts (Psalm 37:4),

- our every need (Philippians 4:19),

- the strength that we require (1 Peter 4:11),

- redemption (Psalm 119:11),

- food, water, and sustenance for animals, as well as people (Psalm 147:9; Isaiah 43:20),

- prosperity and peace (Jeremiah 33:9),

- escape from danger and temptation (Jonah 1:17; 1 Corinthians 10:13), and

- everything for our enjoyment (1 Timothy 6:17)—all at His place of positioning!

If Abraham had decided to go to another mountain, he would have missed the ram in the thicket. If Abraham had decided the mountain was too far of a walk, the ram would not have been in place. If Abraham had decided that obedience to God's command was just too much for him, he would have missed out completely! But Abraham obeyed, and God totally turned his situation around.

> *The angel of the Lord called to Abraham from heaven a second time and said, "I swear by myself, declares the Lord, that because you have done this and have not withheld your son, your only son, I will surely bless you and make your descendants as numerous as the stars in the sky and as the sand on the seashore. Your descendants will take possession of the cities of their enemies, and through your offspring all nations on earth will be blessed, because you have obeyed me." (Genesis 22:15-18)*

Obeying the Lord is a secret key to turnaround in any situation. Whatever your need—be it a sacrificial ram or a salary increase—the Lord will provide it, if you'll just be obedient to His leading.

CLOSE THE DOOR TO LACK

When you find yourself in need of a total turnaround, it often feels as if everything is upside down in that area of your life. The good news is, God majors in turnarounds, especially when everything seems to be upside down—that's often an indication that He's working to make everything right side up! The kingdom of God is the "upside down, right side up" kingdom, and the wisdom of the world is turned on its head.

> *For the foolishness of God is wiser than man's wisdom, and the weakness of God is stronger than man's strength.* (1 Corinthians 1:25)

> *For the wisdom of this world is foolishness in God's sight.* (1 Corinthians 3:19a)

In the kingdom of God, you give up to go up; you lose in order to receive (Mark 9:35). You die in order to live (Colossians 3:5). So, don't be alarmed when things appear to be upside down—God is just positioning you for a new season, for the next level.

Eliminate Mixture

During the transition, it's crucial that we keep the mixture out of our lives. In the day of Ahab, everything became affected due to the mixture of sin and compromise that entered into the land and the hearts of the people. Ahab did not intend to replace the worship of the Lord with the worship of Baal, but he intended to mix them together—just as many people today allow secular practices and beliefs to seep into their spiritual lives. Righteousness and unrighteousness together, worship of the one true God of Israel and the worship of pagan gods together, equals mixture. Ahab imported the Baal worship of his wife Jezebel into the kingdom he was ruling over. When we allow ourselves to worship any god other than the one true God—the King of kings and Lord of lords—we open ourselves up to mixture, which is dangerous and often deadly.

As a result of the mixture in the land, God spoke to the prophet Elijah:

> *Now Elijah the Tishbite, from Tishbe in Gilead, said to Ahab, "As the Lord, the God of Israel, lives, whom I serve, there will be neither dew nor rain in the next few years except at my word." Then the word of the Lord came to Elijah: "Leave here, turn eastward and hide in the Kerith Ravine, east of the Jordan. You will drink from the brook, and I have ordered the ravens to feed you there." So he did what the Lord had told him. He went to the Kerith Ravine, east of the Jordan, and stayed there. The ravens brought him bread and meat in the morning and bread and meat in the evening, and he drank from the brook.*
> (1 Kings 17:1-6)

First off, the land and all the people in it were experiencing lack as a result of their sin and compromise, which led to mixture. God raised up a righteous man, Elijah, to speak forth the Word of the Lord. He prophesied the drought. The land was about to experience great lack, but God was going to supernaturally sustain the prophet. God always takes care of His people, no matter what is happening around them. Don't forget it! If the world is in famine, if the world is having a financial crisis, your right relationship with the Lord and your stand for righteousness will cause the hand of God and His provision to be with you, no matter what.

God spoke to me during a time of prayer at the end of 2010, and He told me that He wanted the church—the body of Christ—to get the mixture out and to get the power back in. Mixture is simply compromise that tolerates or even sanctions sin. We must get the mixture out of our lives! It's the material equivalent of being spiritually lukewarm, something the Lord detests, as He said to the church at Laodicea: *I know your deeds, that you are neither cold nor hot. I wish you were either one or the other! So, because you are lukewarm—neither hot nor cold—I am about to spit you out of my mouth"* (Revelation 3:15-16). We must get mixture out of our hearts, out of our homes, and out of the church—the body of Christ.

Joshua 24:15 says, *"...choose for yourselves this day whom you will serve, whether the gods your forefathers served beyond the River, or the gods of the Amorites, in whose land you are living. But as for me and my household, we will serve the Lord."* We must choose whom we will serve, and then serve with all of our heart. I believe that God wants to use righteous people to lead as an example. We must be individuals who refuse to open a door to mixture. Like Elijah, we must allow the righteousness in our lives to expose mixture in the world around us.

Walk in Obedience

After the Lord gave Elijah the prophetic word for the land, He gave him a word of instruction for himself. He told Elijah to leave and to hide east of the Jordan. God also promised that supernatural provision would be there to sustain him. Obedience to the voice of the Lord always leads to abundant blessings. Immediately, Elijah obeyed and went, and, sure enough, supernatural provision was there waiting for him. Elijah had his own personal delivery service there in the Kerith Ravine. The ravens brought him bread and meat twice a day—every morning and every evening. The ravens were never early, nor were they ever late, just like the Lord who was ordering their every delivery. And the brook provided all the water Elijah needed for that season!

You don't have to have big resources to do something big for God. When God is in the mix, your small resources are more than enough, because He is the God of more than enough. One definition of *resource* is "a means of accomplishing something." God will always give you what you need to accomplish what He wants you to accomplish—always! Throughout the Bible, God just about always did big things with small resources. He rarely did big things with big resources.

Elijah was about to do big things for God, but first, he had to prove that he trusted in God's provision. When God puts our trust to the test, He usually starts in the area of provision; if we can't trust God for our provision or with our resources, then we can't trust Him in any other area.

Elijah passed the test and received his provision because his trust was true. He trusted in God's limitless abilities instead of his own perceived lack. So often, people don't do great things for God because they keep looking at what they don't have. "We don't have the money," they say. Well, God owns it all! "We don't have the workers we need"—well, you and God are the majority, so claiming a lack of adequate workers is a cop-out. "We don't have the time"—well, are your priorities in order? Are you being a good steward of your time? We must do what God tells us to do, one step of obedience at a time. When we have a lot of resources at our disposal, it's tempting to rely on ourselves rather than depend on God. Let's stop looking at what we don't have, and start using what we do have for the glory of God.

Cultivate a Heart of Gratitude

Jesus' feeding the five thousand is one of the best biblical examples of God using small resources to accomplish great ends. "...*Taking the five loaves and the two fish and looking up to heaven, [Jesus] gave thanks and broke the loaves. Then he gave them to the disciples, and the disciples gave them to the people*" (Matthew 14:19). Jesus took what He had—that's where most people quit. They look at their resources and become depressed and discouraged; they feel sorry for themselves, and they may try to manipulate others to give them resources. The key is to start with what you have and then look to the Lord—not to man!

Jesus looked up to heaven—He didn't look down—and you, too, must look up. This is where your faith and your trust come in. Then, Jesus gave thanks. Thank God for what you have! Stop complaining about what you don't have and start praising God for what you do have. A grateful heart—a thankful attitude—is always a forerunner of an increase in blessings. If you aren't thankful for what you have, why would God give you more?

Last, Jesus took a step of faith. Although He had only five loaves and two fish, He started giving out what He had—now, that was a true step of faith! When we take a step of faith and just start doing what we know we should do, the Lord's provision will always be there.

In the case of Jesus' feeding the five thousand, *"They all ate and were satisfied, and the disciples picked up twelve basketfuls of broken pieces that were left over. The number of those who ate was about five thousand men, besides women and children"* (Matthew 14:20-21). God is always the God of more than enough and when we have the mind-set of trust, we understand this principle completely! God can feed the multitudes with our miniscule resources, if only we will trust Him to do so.

Take the Righteous Path

Righteousness is simply doing the right thing. Obedience to the Lord and to His voice will always lead us in paths of righteousness (Psalm 23:3).

> *Do not offer the parts of your body to sin, as instruments of wickedness, but rather offer yourselves to God, as those who have been brought from death to life; and offer the parts of your body to him as instruments of righteousness.* (Romans 6:13)

Sin is no longer our master when we accept Christ into our lives. We are no longer slaves to sin, but we become instruments of the righteousness of God.

> *Don't you know that when you offer yourselves to someone to obey him as slaves, you are slaves to the one whom you obey— whether you are slaves to sin, which leads to death, or to obedi- ence, which leads to righteousness?* (Romans 6:16)

Obedience to the leading of the Holy Spirit will bring about righteousness in your daily life. The Holy Spirit will nudge you and show you how to act, what to say, and how not to respond so you can live a life of righteousness.

Romans 6:19 says, *"...Just as you used to offer the parts of your body in slavery to impurity and to ever-increasing wickedness, so now offer them in slavery to righteousness leading to holiness."* Righteousness reflects your relationships and dealings with people. Holiness reflects your relationship with the Lord. It all starts with obedience. Obedience to the Lord will always lead you in the paths of righteousness—your daily life and actions toward others on this earth. Your righteousness, in turn, leads to holiness. When you live righteously in your relationships with people, you are headed in the right direction for living a holy life before the Lord. You can't qualify as living holy if you don't treat people in a "righteous" way.

If you cheat people out of money, if you don't treat people fairly, you will have a hard time living in the Holy of Holies before the Lord. But, when you live a righteous life, you can experience the presence of the Lord and you can live with holiness in your heart.

YOUR PROVISION WILL NEVER RUN DRY

Change is often a required obedience to our turnarounds. Sometimes the Lord speaks to our hearts concerning a change in us that He is requiring. At other times, God speaks to us to make a change from the place in which we have grown comfortable. It's usually right after we get "comfortable" that God says, "Okay, it's time to change!" The change will always usher us into the new season. The change will always bring us into the next level. Changes require great obedience. We obey by saying good-bye to our comfort zones and hello to our potential zones. We obey by releasing the old and embracing the new.

Think about Elijah. He needed a change of scenery in order to receive provision from the Lord.

Some time later the brook dried up because there had been no rain in the land. Then the word of the Lord came to [Elijah]:

"Go at once to Zarephath of Sidon and stay there. I have commanded a widow in that place to supply you with food." (1 Kings 17:7-9)

I can imagine that the prophet Elijah was just beginning to adjust to his new accommodations and his new favorite restaurant and delivery service, the "Ravine Ravens," when God announced the new plan of action. The place Elijah called home was about to change, the means to his provision was about to change, and his daily menu was about to change, as well.

Why is it that we don't like change? I believe it's because we get comfortable in our surroundings and secure with the status quo. We tend to derive our identity and our security from stability. No wonder God likes to shake things up in our lives—we need to learn that our identity and our security come from Him alone. Every aspect of our lives is subject to change, the sole exception being our heavenly Father. And, while we may receive our sustenance in a variety of ways, the ultimate Source is always the same: Father God. Remember, the Lord of lords and the King of kings is your provider, no matter the means by which He gets His provision to you.

The seasons of life will change; our surroundings will change; but our Source and Sustainer remains constant at all times.

Movin' On and Goin' Up

When your "brook" dries up—when your source of provision runs dry—it doesn't mean that you have done something "wrong." If you have been walking in obedience to the Lord's instructions, and your funds are cut off, it means that God is ushering you into a new, more fruitful season, just as He did with the prophet Elijah. God wanted to use Elijah somewhere else, and so, when the prophet's assignment changed, his source of income shifted. Most of the time, when your assignment changes, it's because you have been faithful in fulfilling your previous assignment. On the other hand, if you aren't faithful, you'll get stuck where you are or you'll keep on wandering, like the children of Israel. Most of them never made it to the next season of fruitfulness because they refused to obey.

Elijah the prophet was "movin' on up"! He knew in his heart that what God had done for him before, He would do again—and again and again, if need be! As we remember God's faithfulness in our previous seasons, we can maintain our confidence that He will continue providing for us as long as we walk in obedience to His leading. We don't have to understand His leading; we don't have to agree with His leading; we don't even have to like His leading. We only have to obey His leading, just as Elijah did.

> So [Elijah] *went to Zarephath. When he came to the town gate, a widow was there gathering sticks. He called to her and asked, "Would you bring me a little water in a jar so I may have a drink?" As she was going to get it, he called, "And bring me, please, a piece of bread." "As surely as the Lord your God lives," she replied, "I don't have any bread—only a handful of flour in a jar and a little oil in a jug. I am gathering a few sticks to take home and make a meal for myself and my son, that we may eat it—and die."* (1 Kings 17:10-12)

When Elijah first arrived at his new assignment, it didn't look too great in the natural. It looked as though Elijah's source of provision—the poor widow—didn't have enough to sustain her son and herself, let alone Elijah, too. If Elijah had assessed the situation through his natural eyes, he could have easily become depressed. After all, his source of provision was about to throw in the towel and die. That's not too encouraging!

Rather than allowing the spirit of fear to take root in his life, Elijah was quick to encourage the widow.

> *Elijah said to her, "Don't be afraid. Go home and do as you have said. But first make a small cake of bread for me from what you have and bring it to me, and then make something for yourself and your son. For this is what the Lord, the God*

of Israel, says: 'The jar of flour will not be used up and the jug of oil will not run dry until the day the Lord gives rain on the land.'" (1 Kings 17:13-14)

One simple instruction, and the widow's heart of obedience totally turned everything around. Elijah commanded her not to give in to the spirit of fear. In the same way, you must command yourself not to give in to the spirit of fear when it comes to your provision. And then, Elijah instructed her to give first and then take the rest for herself and her beloved son.

Fear tries to keep us from giving when it seems like our barrel is just about empty, but that's the time we must give the most! It was the widow's giving that caused her to always have enough. It's our seed and our giving that will sustain us. The widow obeyed Elijah's instructions to give, and she never again suffered lack.

She went away and did as Elijah had told her. So there was food every day for Elijah and for the woman and her family. For the jar of flour was not used up and the jug of oil did not run dry, in keeping with the word of the Lord spoken by Elijah. (1 Kings 17:15-16)

GIVING AND LIVING GOD'S WAY

The Word of God contains a great deal of wisdom on how to handle our finances. When we are obedient to follow the biblical principles of money management, we can enjoy debt-free living. God wants us to experience a total turnaround in our finances and to enjoy financial freedom, which comes after all debt has been shed.

Most people tend to think that financial freedom is being debt-free and having lots of money. You can be debt-free and have a lot of money and still not experience what I call financial freedom. Many people who grew up during the Great Depression feared lack no matter how much money they accumulated. This is because they had adopted a depression mind-set. They had allowed the spirit of fear to infiltrate their minds. The spirit of fear comes to steal, kill, and destroy in every area of your life (John 10:10). It will steal your peace, your sleep, and your joy.

The spirit of fear aims to cripple you, financially and otherwise, in order to destroy your life. But Jesus came to free you from that toxic spirit, so that you might enjoy life in all its abundance (John 10:10). God wants you to be free to trust Him, no matter your circumstances. Remember, God is the God of turnaround!

Being debt-free comes from walking in obedience every day—from managing your money God's way. Let's explore some principles from His economy, as outlined in the Bible.

Don't Rob God

> "Will a man rob God? Yet you rob me. But you ask, 'How do we rob you?' In tithes and offerings. You are under a curse— the whole nation of you—because you are robbing me. Bring the whole tithe into the storehouse, that there may be food in my house. Test me in this," says the Lord Almighty, "and see if I will not throw open the floodgates of heaven and pour out so much blessing that you will not have room enough for it." (Malachi 3:8-10)

Many people will claim the promises of God, but they aren't standing on His Word and living it out. Sooner or later, they'll find that it doesn't work that way! Lots of people like to quote Philippians 4:19, saying, *"My God shall supply all* [my] *need according to His riches in glory by Christ Jesus"* (NKJV). I think that's great. I believe we need to think the Word, speak the Word, and do the Word. But if you aren't doing the Word by living out its principles, it's fruitless to speak the Word. For instance, if you keep claiming, "My God shall supply all my need according to His riches in glory," but you don't give back to Him through your tithes and offerings, then your disobedience overshadows your proclamation of His promises. Faith without works is dead (James 2:20, 26). You have faith in God's promises—great!—but you need some obedient action on your part to prove it.

According to the passage from Malachi, those who withhold their tithes and offerings from God don't just deprive Him of their financial stewardship; they rob Him outright! Robbing and stealing is always wrong, especially from God. This is why Malachi 3:9 says that "you are under a curse" if you don't give your tithes and offerings. If you are under a curse, you can make $100,000 a year and still not have enough to meet your needs unless you honor the biblical principle of giving back to God.

How much is a tithe, you ask? It's one-tenth of your income, or ten percent. I have had people tell me they were going to give three percent of their income to the Lord's work. I had to be honest with them and inform them that they were operating in partial obedience, but God wants total obedience. We can't redefine the word tithe to fit our own perceived financial needs. And we can't afford to "tithe" less than ten percent in those times when we find ourselves in need of a financial turnaround! For it is during those times of financial strain that we can least afford to disobey. Many people say, "I can't afford to tithe." I always say, "None of us can afford not to tithe!"

Malachi 3:10 commands us, *"Bring the whole tithe into the storehouse."* I believe this is because the Lord knew that there would be times when His people would be tempted to bring just part of the tithe into the storehouse. Partial obedience doesn't get us anywhere; it only frustrates and discourages. But immediate, total obedience brings great blessings into our lives and into our hands.

The Lord said that you should "test" Him in this. You can "test" God in the area of giving, for you will always see the fruits of your obedience (or disobedience). You may not experience a financial turnaround the moment you start tithing and giving offerings, but you can trust God to bring a turnaround in His perfect timing. As you continue in your acts of obedience and "test" God, He will always pass the test with flying colors!

We Reap What We Sow

Remember this: Whoever sows sparingly will also reap sparingly, and whoever sows generously will also reap generously. Each man should give what he has decided in his heart to give, not reluctantly or under compulsion, for God loves a cheerful giver. (2 Corinthians 9:6-7)

As far as our offerings go, God put no limits as to how much we can give—He just gave us the above passage. Our tithe is ten percent, but our offerings can be as much as the entire ninety percent that's left! The choice is up to us, but we should remember that when we sow generously, we reap generously. In the same vein, when we sow sparingly, we reap sparingly. In other words, our harvest will be the size of our seed. If we sow a small seed, we can expect a small harvest. If we want a big harvest, we should sow a big seed!

God loves a cheerful giver. Don't give and then act like a poor victim about your giving. Don't give because someone has manipulated you or taken advantage of you. But give as the Holy Spirit leads you to give, and then get excited about your obedience to follow through.

BIG Seed Reaps BIG Harvest

I can remember the first time I gave a seed of $1,000 as my offering. I was totally freaked out after I realized what I had done. Crossing over to sowing a seed of $1,000 was a difficult step for me to take. But, once I took that step, I came to realize that you can't "out give" God. The more I gave, the more God put in my hand. God loves a cheerful giver, and if we obey His voice and get excited about our obedience, He will use us miraculously to fund His kingdom's work.

I also remember the first time I gave $10,000. I haven't given that amount many times since, but I do hope to be able to sow generous seeds more often. The first time I gave $10,000, I was in Mexico with Dr. Marilyn Hickey. I'm a giver, I enjoy giving, and I believe I even have the gift of giving. Yet, on this trip, I knew I had exhausted my giving many times over. I went to the service that night without my checkbook. I don't even think I had it with me on the trip. I thought, *Well, if I don't have my checkbook, I won't be tempted to give.* Folks, there is no such thing as being "tempted to give." But there is such a thing as being "tempted *not* to give." And the devil will never tell you to give to the Lord's work—just remember that.

Again, on this particular night, I did not have my checkbook with me because I didn't want to be tempted to give. I don't know what I was thinking, but it definitely was not a "God thought." Needless to say, it was that night that the Lord told me to give an amount greater than any I had ever given before—$10,000!

The moral of the story is, if we think we are going to slip by without giving as much, chances are, we will be required to give more than ever. I'm convinced it's all part of a test of obedience. God loves us so much, and He wants to bless us radically through our obedience.

That night, the Lord told me to give $10,000 using my credit card. I had forgotten that I had my credit card with me, but the Lord hadn't forgotten! I had never given using my credit card before, especially when I did not have the funds to pay for the charge when the bill came in.

For the rest of that night following the offering, I felt faint, to say the least! Then I started to feel a little nauseous. I knew the right response would be prayer, so I started pacing back and forth in my room, thanking God for putting the funds into my hand before the bill arrived to pay for the charge I had just made. Then, I started feeling dizzy all over again. I forced myself to pray the Word and quote His promises over me and the act of obedience I had taken.

God is an on-time God. He is rarely early, but He is never late. And yet, I must say, this was the one and only time I can remember God being a tad bit early! Before my credit card payment was due, someone miraculously gave me $10,000. I shouted, I praised, and I never went back to leaving my checkbook at home—not because I didn't want God to tell me to give more, but because I didn't want to miss out on my blessing!

Give Obediently

True financial freedom is having the ability to obey the Holy Spirit with your giving. God wants you to be free to give, whether that giving is in the form of money, time, resources, talents, or something else.

True financial freedom comes from self-control to live within your means. True financial freedom is having peace that the Lord, and the Lord alone, is your Provider. True financial freedom is living life free from the spirit of poverty.

Poverty is defined as "the condition or quality of being poor; indigence; need; deficiency in necessary properties or desirable qualities, or in a specific quality, etc.; inadequacy...smallness in amount; scarcity." A spirit of poverty not only keeps your mind in a place of lack, but it also causes you to feel deficient, inadequate, and small. The spirit of poverty keeps you bound in your areas of perceived lack, often to the point where you become stuck in unproductivity.

The truth is, you can do all things through Christ who strengthens you (Philippians 4:13 NKJV). The truth is, your *God shall supply all your needs according to His riches in glory by Christ Jesus*" (Philippians 4:19 NKJV). And the truth is, the only thing that can limit you is the limits you allow the enemy to put in your mind. There are no limits as to what God can do in you, through you, and for you. So, get your mind set on the Word and His promises, for He is about to turn things all around for you!

Give Like God Gave

God did not give sparingly—God gave it all! "All" included His one and only Son. *"He who did not spare his own Son, but gave him up for us all—how will he not also, along with him, graciously give us all things?"*

(Romans 8:32). I believe we need to give like God gave. We should be willing to give it all!

If God gave it all for us by giving His Son Jesus, how would He not also give us all things graciously? We settle for so much less than what God wants to give us. And often we settle for small when we choose to sow small. Start sowing big, and then reap big harvests for the glory of God!

God gives us what I call "steps" of giving in the Word. Not only are we to give our tithes and offerings; we are also to give what the Bible calls our "firstfruits."

> *Honor the Lord with your wealth, with the firstfruits of all your crops; then your barns will be filled to overflowing, and your vats will brim over with new wine.* (Proverbs 3:9-10)

I believe in devoting the firstfruits of our day to the Lord by spending time with Him in prayer, in reading the Word, and in worship each morning. I believe the Lord wants the firstfruits of our week and the firstfruits of our year, as well. And I believe in sowing an offering of the firstfruits of our income.

Whenever we put God first, the rest is always blessed! I believe we can give our way to blessings. We don't give to get, but we obey the Lord's voice and give because we love God. I sowed myself right out of a big financial pit and I sowed my way to total turnaround. And what God did for me, He will do for you, too—He is just waiting on your obedience.

FINE-TUNED FOCUS IN FINANCES

Almost nobody likes the word *diet*. But, when you really think about it, a diet is just a fine-tuned focus on your weight and health. In the same way, *budget* is an unpopular term, but it's just a fine-tuned focus on your finances. It causes many people to cringe, but a God-inspired "budget" can lead to financial freedom like you've never experienced before. Fine-tuning your focus on your financial stewardship can lead to a miraculous turnaround in your bank account. That's because focus causes us to bear fruit.

Maybe you have tried to get out of debt—multiple times. Maybe financial freedom seems like an unreachable dream. I want to encourage you today—focus can take you all the way to the place of great fruitfulness and unlimited success when you set out to do what the Lord has put in your heart to do.

Focus is a forerunner of favor, and favor is a forerunner of fruit. Many people are trying to be fruitful, but they aren't focused. You have to be focused in order to have favor because favor opens the door to fruitfulness. So, it's focus, favor, and then fruit. When you try to be fruitful in your business, your ministry, or your family without being focused, you will get discouraged and want to throw in the towel. If you are trying to be fruitful without the favor of God and the favor of man, you are trying to do things in your own strength. That's how people get burned out, discouraged, and feeling like failures.

Favor Ensures Provision for Nehemiah

Nehemiah is a great example from the Bible of someone who was focused and had great favor, and so was extremely fruitful in the task he set out to do.

> They said to me, "Those who survived the exile and are back in the province are in great trouble and disgrace. The wall of Jerusalem is broken down, and its gates have been burned with fire." When I heard these things, I sat down and wept. For some days I mourned and fasted and prayed before the God of heaven. Then I said: "O Lord, God of heaven, the great and awesome God, who keeps his covenant of love with those who love him and obey his commands, let your ear be attentive and your eyes open to hear the prayer your servant is praying before you day and night for your servants, the people of Israel. I confess the sins we Israelites, including myself and my father's house, have committed against you....O Lord, let your ear be

attentive to the prayer of this your servant and to the prayer of your servants who delight in revering your name. Give your servant success today by granting him favor in the presence of this man." (Nehemiah 1:3-6, 11)

Prayer is the most important part of focus. If you don't have a strong, consistent prayer life, you will be trying to maintain a life of focus in your own strength. But, when you have a powerful prayer life, you will have strong focus through the power of the Holy Spirit.

Nehemiah had a powerful, faithful prayer life, first and foremost. Ministry is about meeting the needs of the people. When Nehemiah heard about the great need, he had a heart to meet that need. He had a desire to minister to them through meeting their need. Because he was a man of God, the first thing he did was get on his face and call out to God in prayer—proof of true focus. In his time of prayer, he first repented of any sin in his heart and in the hearts of the Israelites. He understood that unconfessed sin would not only hinder his ability to communicate with God but also diminish his favor with Him.

So, first, Nehemiah was focused in prayer, and then he asked for the Lord's favor. He knew that if he had the favor of God, he would have the favor of man. You can't help but have the favor of man when you have the favor of God. People just bless you, and they don't even know why. People who don't even like you bless you anyway when you have the favor of God!

When Nehemiah went before the king, the king noticed that something was bothering him. Nehemiah's heart was burdened for the people and he responded to the king by saying, *"Why should my face not look sad when the city where my fathers are buried lies in ruins, and its gates have been destroyed by fire?"* (Nehemiah 2:3b).

Nehemiah spoke what was on his heart to the king, and God's favor was with him.

The king said to me, "What is it you want?" Then I prayed to the God of heaven, and I answered the king, "If it pleases the

*king and if your servant has found favor in his sight, let him
send me to the city in Judah where my fathers are buried so that
I can rebuild it."* (Nehemiah 2:4-5)

Not only did Nehemiah find favor in the eyes of God, but, because he
had the favor of God, he had the favor of man. Man gave him everything
he needed and more to fulfill the vision that God had placed in his heart.
Nehemiah was extremely fruitful.

> *...It pleased the king to send me; so I set a time. I also said to
> him, "If it pleases the king, may I have letters to the governors
> of Trans-Euphrates, so that they will provide my safe-conduct
> until I arrive in Judah? And may I have a letter to Asaph,
> keeper of the king's forest, so he will give me timber to make
> beams for the gates of the citadel by the temple and for the
> city wall and for the residence I will occupy?" And because the
> gracious hand of my God was upon me, the king granted my
> requests. So I went to the governors of Trans-Euphrates and
> gave them the king's letters. The King had also sent army offi-
> cers and cavalry with me.* (Nehemiah 2:6-9)

Not only did Nehemiah get everything he needed, but he also received
an abundance of supplies and manpower. He was given a backup of army
officers and cavalry. Nehemiah was focused on the vision that God had put
in his heart, and he had found favor with God—and, again, that always
results in the favor of man. It was this twofold favor that led Nehemiah to
a fruitful ending.

"So the wall was completed on the twenty-fifth of Elul, in fifty-two days"
(Nehemiah 6:15). The wall that had lain in ruins for nearly a century and
a half was rebuilt in only fifty-two days! Now, that's fruitfulness! When
you are focused on the will of the Father, favor and fruit will follow. Once
you are focused, God will see to it that you have favor. And that favor will

bring about any financial provision you need. Once you have favor, then fruit—great fruit—will follow.

What Nehemiah accomplished seemed impossible, but it wasn't. The people were discouraged and just thought they would have to live the way they had been living for nearly a century and a half. But, God! God raised up a man who had found favor with Him through his obedience, God provided for his needs, and God made sure he went forth and accomplished all that the Lord had for him.

Your financial situation may seem impossible. Your needed turnaround may seem unlikely. But, God! Nothing is impossible for the Lord. Your financial turnaround is just up ahead. Don't give up—total turnaround is for you today.

Faithfulness Prompts Ruth's Financial Turnaround

Another Bible character who received abundant provision in the midst of great lack was Ruth. Widowed at a young age and left to fend for herself and her mother-in-law, Naomi, Ruth had limited options when it came to earning a living. Yet, because of her obedience to the Lord and her faithful commitment to her mother-in-law, Ruth found her "Boaz blessing."

> *Boaz said to Ruth, "My daughter, listen to me. Don't go and glean in another field and don't go away from here. Stay here with my servant girls. Watch the field where the men are harvesting, and follow along after the girls. I have told the men not to touch you. And whenever you are thirsty, go and get a drink from the water jars the men have filled." At this, she bowed down with her face to the ground. She exclaimed, "Why have I found such favor in your eyes that you notice me—a foreigner?" Boaz replied, "I've been told all about what you have done for your mother-in-law since the death of your husband—how you left your father and mother and your homeland and came to live with a people you did not know before. May the Lord repay*

you for what you have done. May you be richly rewarded by the Lord, the God of Israel, under whose wings you have come to take refuge." (Ruth 2:8-12)

Boaz ended up marrying Ruth, thereby inviting her to partake of his wealth and resources (Ruth 4).

Because of this inspiring story, a concept known as the "Boaz blessing" has come about, loosely defined as a place of abundant financial provision resulting from the obedience, commitment, and faithfulness of an individual. So many women are waiting for a man to arrive on the scene and be their "Boaz blessing," but they don't realize that the Boaz blessing arrives only when the character and integrity of Ruth have been worked in them.

I can honestly say that I have crossed over into the Boaz blessing in my life, even though I'm as single as single can be. I'm a single mom with no prospects in sight! Yet, I have received my Boaz blessing. Why? Because the abundant provision in a Boaz blessing doesn't come from man—a specific man, such as a boyfriend or husband, or people in general—it comes from God. The Boaz blessing is really part of a biblical principle known as the law of sowing and reaping. In a nutshell, it says, "You reap what you sow." Ruth sowed provision and faithfulness into the life of her mother-in-law, Naomi, and she reaped provision and faithfulness from Boaz in return. In her case, her Boaz blessing came through a man, yes; the key word here is *through*. Boaz himself was not the blessing; he was just the channel through whom God sent His blessings to His faithful daughter Ruth.

Regardless of the channel, your Boaz blessing always comes from the Lord. Just because Ruth was married to the "channel" of her Boaz blessing doesn't necessarily mean that you will be, too. God uses many different channels to get His blessings to us. And it's often the case that He uses the last channel we would have expected. So, just rest assured that He will get you hooked up with the right channels once you have stepped into the right season of your life.

Ruth received her blessing in the right season. Ruth 1:22 says, *"So Naomi returned from Moab accompanied by Ruth the Moabitess, her daughter-in-law, arriving in Bethlehem as the barley harvest was beginning."* It just so happened that Ruth, while being faithful and loyal to her mother-in-law, arrived in Bethlehem as the barley harvest was beginning. Did you get that? She was neither a day early nor a day late! Don't tell me that God is not an on-time God. He most certainly is! He's never early, and He's never late. His timing is perfect, even if it doesn't correspond to our own personal timetable. And yet we say, "Where are You, God?" and grow impatient, all because He seems to be "delaying" in sending our blessing. God doesn't delay! He knows exactly when to deliver our blessing, and we should trust Him to get it to us right on time.

I have been a single mom since my daughter was two weeks old. The first few years were very challenging in many ways, especially in the area of our finances. Every month, I would stress myself out worrying that I would be late with my mortgage payment. Believe it or not, my payments were never late! Of course, they were never early, either; often, the money came in on the very day the payment was due. It took me awhile to learn that I could trust God to provide, and so, month after month, when the due date arrived, I would freak out! I would threaten God to get a job at Walmart—where, I assumed, the stress level would be low—if I couldn't make my mortgage payment. And yet, every month, God came through for us—to my utter shock and disbelief. This went on for a couple of years. What can I say? I was a slow learner. Eventually, though, I learned the lesson: God is always right on time.

His provision for Ruth was right on time! There's no record of her worrying about her provision or provision for her mother-in-law. She just kept going forward in her faithfulness. As we take one step of obedience at a time, faithfully following where the Lord leads us, His provision will always be there—right on time.

There are no coincidences in God, only divine appointments. And we'll never miss those appointments if we just keep doing the right thing.

When we are following the Lord's leading, we can't help but trip over His blessings for our lives, just as Ruth nearly ran right into her Boaz blessing. Again, she wasn't thinking about herself; she wasn't looking for her blessing. She was just working hard at doing the right thing—the "righteous" thing. When our focus is on God and our hearts are obedient to Him, there won't be any risk of sidestepping His blessings and abundant provision for our lives.

Ruth ended up owning the very field where she had gleaned after the harvesters. That's what I call total turnaround! When you are walking in obedience to the Lord and trusting Him to provide, it's only a matter of time until you will "trip over" a total turnaround in your finances. Obedience is the key!

Don't rob God but seed your need.

POINTS TO PONDER

1. God promises to provide all our needs, but we often doubt that He will. Have you found yourself doubting His provision? Why do you think you were doubtful?

2. What prompted Ruth's financial turnaround, and how did she obtain her "Boaz blessing"?

3. Every farmer knows that sowing seed is the only way to reap a harvest. If we sow big seed, we can expect a big harvest. When was the last time God radically blessed you because of your obedience to sow a big seed?

4. Fine-tuned focus on your finances, otherwise known as following a budget, can lead to financial freedom. What is focus a forerunner of?

Meditate on these Scriptures, speak them aloud, and commit them to memory:

My God will meet all your needs according to his glorious riches in Christ Jesus. (Philippians 4:19)

"Bring the whole tithe into the storehouse, that there may be food in my house. Test me in this," says the Lord Almighty, "and see if I will not throw open the floodgates of heaven and pour out so much blessing that you will not have room enough for it." (Malachi 3:10)

Remember this: Whoever sows sparingly will also reap sparingly, and whoever sows generously will also reap generously. Each man should give what he has decided in his heart to give, not reluctantly or under compulsion, for God loves a cheerful giver. (2 Corinthians 9:6-7)

Honor the Lord with your wealth, with the firstfruits of all your crops; then your barns will be filled to overflowing, and your vats will brim over with new wine. (Proverbs 3:9-10)

Chapter 10

TOTAL TURNAROUND
IN YOUR HEALTH

If you are in need of a total turnaround in your health, you're in good company! Millions of people today are in need of physical healing or improved health. I want to challenge you today—don't accept the status quo! Stop agreeing with the report of man and receive instead the report of the Lord, *"by whose stripes you were healed"* (1 Peter 2:24 NKJV).

I have experienced firsthand the overwhelming sense of fear and frustration that accompanies a negative report from doctors and other medical professionals. And I also know the overwhelming joy and humility that come from witnessing a miracle from the hand of the Lord in my body. Take heart—what the Lord has done for me, He will do for you, too. He is no respecter of persons (Acts 10:34 KJV). His favor is for all of us!

I first want to say that Jesus is the cure to all sickness. My brother received a bad medical report after being cancer-free for one year. As I was praying for him to receive his miracle, I also began to pray that the Lord would reveal the cure for cancer. As soon as I prayed that request out loud, the Lord immediately answered me and said, "I already have revealed the cure to cancer—I AM!"

Wow! For years, I had known that the Lord is the Healer—the Great Physician—and the answer for everything. And yet the fresh revelation I received while in prayer that day really shook me. The Lord has already revealed the cure to cancer and all sickness and disease!

Then the Lord began to show me some root causes of cancer, such as anger, bitterness, stress, and sin. He said, "I'm the answer." He was referring to the love and forgiveness He freely offers all people. When we accept His love and forgiveness, we don't need to carry around our deadly emotions and sinful behaviors any longer. We don't need to be stressed out all the time—we can cast all our cares on the Lord!

> *Cast your cares on the Lord and he will sustain you; he will never let the righteous fall.* (Psalm 55:22)

> *Cast all your anxiety on* [God] *because he cares for you.* (1 Peter 5:7)

We can live a life free of the crippling sicknesses brought on by ungodly emotions. Yes, Jesus is the cure to cancer!

The Lord then told me, "Satan has tried to bring a curse on man with cancer, but I am the cure." Never before had I realized how similar the words *cure* and *curse* were. The only difference is one little letter *s*. Satan tries to bring a curse by adding his signature—*s*—and Jesus remains the cure, removing that *s* and the sin and sickness it stands for.

Then the Lord led me to read a passage from the book of Deuteronomy that says:

> *For they did not come to meet you with bread and water on your way when you came out of Egypt, and they hired Balaam son of Beor from Pethor in Aram Naharaim to pronounce a curse on you. However, the Lord your God would not listen to Balaam but turned the curse into a blessing for you, because the Lord your God loves you.* (Deuteronomy 23:4-5)

The enemy will try to get people, situations, and circumstances to pronounce a curse on you. But, God! God is the God of your turnaround. God turned around the curse that Balaam tried to bring. And He will turn around the curse of sickness that the enemy is trying to bring upon you. God turned Balaam's attempted curse into a blessing because of His love for His people.

God is going to turn Satan's attempted curse on you into a huge blessing for your life—all because of His great love for you! Yes, what Satan meant for evil, God will use for good (Genesis 50:20).

GOD'S PEOPLE UNTOUCHED

I am continually amazed by the love of God and His hand of protection on His children. Every time God brought about a plague in Egypt, His children were untouched!

> *Then the Lord said to Moses, "Get up early in the morning and confront Pharaoh as he goes to the water and say to him, 'This is what the Lord says: Let my people go, so that they may worship me. If you do not let my people go, I will send swarms of flies on you and your officials, on your people and into your houses. The houses of the Egyptians will be full of flies, and even the ground where they are. But on that day I will deal differently with the land of Goshen, where my people live; no swarms of flies will be there, so that you will know that I, the Lord, am in this land. I will make a distinction between my people and your people. This miraculous sign will occur tomorrow.'"* (Exodus 8:20-23)

God always makes a distinction between His people and the people of the world. Maybe you need a turnaround today from the plague of financial crisis. If so, God will cause you to be untouched, and you will thrive while the rest of the world is thrown into crisis. You will be untouched in your physical body, and you will thrive in health and long life, while the rest of the world is experiencing sickness and disease. You will remain untouched by the plagues of floods, tornadoes, and hurricanes when the world around you is affected. Yes, the people of God sometimes suffer, but never without purpose. He will never let any harm befall you and me from which He cannot save us!

BELIEVE THE REPORT OF THE LORD

The prophetic voice of God speaks forth His report—what God is saying today. The prophetic voice of God today will always line up with His written Word. But, if someone reads or teaches and studies His Word without having a prophetic ear to hear what the Lord is saying today, it can be flat and without any anointing. You don't study the Bible like you do a textbook. You don't teach from the Bible like you would instruct students enrolled in a math class.

When you have a relationship with the Lord, when you have cultivated a powerful prayer life, you have union and communion with the Holy Spirit. It's this relationship of intimacy that allows you to hear the prophetic voice of the Lord on a regular basis. You and I must each hear and know what God is saying to us today. That way, if we receive a negative report from man—be it in regard to our health or another aspect of our lives—we may discern in our spirit what God's report says, that we may believe Him.

The Lord's report will always align with His written Word, the Bible, which tells us that the price for our healing was paid more than 2,000 years ago by the Son of God, Jesus Christ.

> [Jesus] *Himself bore our sins in His own body on the tree, that we, having died to sins, might live for righteousness—by whose stripes you were healed.* (1 Peter 2:24 NKJV)

Notice the use of the past tense in the above verse—you *"were healed."* Your healing has already been taken care of! All you must do today is simply receive your healing by faith. And faith comes by hearing the Word

(Romans 10:17 NKJV). When you hear the prophetic voice of the Lord, faith rises within you!

Don't dismiss the reports of doctors altogether—they're useful in that they give an indication of how you ought to pray. I don't believe that believers should live in denial. If you have received a diagnosis in the natural, don't view it as an unavoidable destination—use it as an aid to detailed prayer! It's easier to fight when you know your enemy. When you are able to name the thing that is attacking your body, you can take it to the Lord in prayer and turn the battle over to Him. Denial won't get you anywhere, but neither will fear. So, don't fear the doctor's diagnosis—simply stand in faith that God will turn it around.

Facts, such as a doctor's diagnosis, exist in the natural realm. But faith exists in the supernatural realm, and faith changes the facts! Let me repeat: Your faith in the Lord's report—in His holy Word—changes the facts. The supernatural realm is far more powerful than the natural realm. Don't deny the facts; change them with your faith!

The Word tells us that God's children hear Him because they know His voice (John 10:27). Without the prophetic voice of the Lord, things become lifeless and dead. Without His prophetic insight, you can become overwhelmed and tempted to accept a grim diagnosis with resignation. Don't let that happen! Never give in to the report of man. Stand up and fight in faith! The battle isn't over until God has won. Remember, you're on the winning team! When God is on your side, just the two of you are the majority, no matter how many foes (or negative diagnoses) are coming against you.

How do you maintain your faith in the face of an intimidating diagnosis? One way is to surround yourself with faith-speaking people. Don't allow others to speak death over you. Remember, the power of life and death is in the tongue (Proverbs 18:21). Speak life over yourself by quoting the Word of God. Stand on His promises and keep on standing. You are in a spiritual battle, but cheer up—you're on the winning side!

RECEIVING IS THE FIRST STEP

God wants you to receive your miracle today! And receiving is the first step. You can't go on to the second and third steps if you don't take the first step. When you are given a gift, you must reach out and receive it. If you are going to be the one who is the recipient, you have to receive it for yourself. You must reach out and take it. You reach out and grab it! Like salvation, healing is a gift you reach out and receive. You can't earn it; you freely receive it as a gift. Maybe you find yourself in need of healing today. It may be that, in order to be healed, you first need some work on your "receptor." Many people have a difficult time receiving even the best things God has for them.

Know that the Lord wants you to receive His gift of healing for you. Don't think for a minute that God loves anyone else more than you. Some people believe that God will heal everyone else but not themselves. They feel unworthy of His healing touch. Again, it has nothing to do with merit! The truth is, none of us deserves anything good from the Lord, and yet He showers us with the blessings of salvation, wholeness, health, and more—not because we deserve them but because He loves us so much. His Son Jesus was the only one worthy of receiving eternal life, and He passed along that blessing to all of mankind by paying the ultimate price—His very life. *"He who did not spare his own Son, but gave him up for us all—how will he not also, along with him, graciously give us all things?"* (Romans 8:32).

JESUS HEALS—YESTERDAY, TODAY, AND FOREVER

Jesus went throughout Galilee, teaching in their synagogues, preaching the good news of the kingdom, and healing every disease and sickness among the people. News about him spread all over Syria, and people brought to him all who were ill with various diseases, those suffering severe pain, the demon-possessed, those having seizures, and the paralyzed; and he healed them. (Matthew 4:23-24)

We have the teaching and the preaching down, but what about the miracles? We must never forget that Jesus healed every disease and sickness. God is pouring out His Spirit, and today is the day of miracles! Jesus is the same yesterday, today, and forever (Hebrews 13:8). Jesus healed people in the Bible, and He still heals people today! We simply need to receive His healing.

The good news of Jesus healing the sick spread all over, and it spread fast! Have you ever noticed how fast bad news spreads? Don't be overwhelmed or discouraged about the quick spread of bad news, but be a spreader of the good news!

On the way to your total, miraculous healing, you will hear many victorious medical reports. Shout at every good report! Spread every victory along the way. Don't hold back from celebrating the good report just because you aren't totally out of the woods yet. You get out of the "woods" one step at a time, and the first step is to receive through faith the miraculous healing the Lord has for you.

Build Your Faith for Healing

God wants to build your faith, but you need to take an active role in the building process. Faith comes by hearing the Word of God (Romans 10:17), while doubt comes by hearing the word of the enemy. You must choose to hear the Word of the Lord on a daily basis. The tougher your battle, the more of the Word you need. If you are standing in faith for your life on a minute-by-minute basis, you need to be meditating on the Word minute by minute. And always remember, the battle is not yours, the battle is the Lord's—even if you are battling for your life moment by moment!

"But the Pharisees went out and plotted how they might kill Jesus. Aware of this, Jesus withdrew from that place. Many followed him, and he healed all their sick" (Matthew 12:14-15). Jesus healed all the sick. He didn't pick favorites! We all have the favor of God, and Jesus wants to heal everyone. Though the Pharisees were trying to kill Jesus, He kept on reaching out and healing others. This Scripture shows us how to keep our eyes off of

ourselves and on the Lord. I have learned a key to healing: we should pray for others to receive their miracle, every chance we get!

My Personal Healing

In May of 2001, I received a negative report from the doctors. I had been suffering with pain and other related symptoms for many months, and I finally received a diagnosis: my T10 vertebra had been totally destroyed, causing vertebrae T9 and T11 to come crashing together. I had a 100 percent compressed fracture at T10.

I was sent to the University of Virginia Medical Center, and I walked into the office on my own, without a wheelchair, despite the excruciating pain it caused me—much to the shock of the surgeon. After he examined me, he said that he needed to get me stabilized immediately because the slightest jolt to my already fragile back could produce devastating results. He also said that he wanted to determine why this had happened to me so that we could prevent it from happening again.

He went on to tell me that I would need two major surgeries and that I would be essentially "out of commission" for over a year. I responded quickly, blurting out what was on my heart: "I'm a single mom of a very energetic toddler! I can't be out of commission for an hour, let alone a whole year." He then encouraged me to move in with a friend or family member who could help me during my extended recovery time.

The surgeon explained that one of the major surgeries would involve inserting a rod in my back. He also said that they would need to remove one of my ribs so that it could be ground down into a new T10 vertebra for me. That wasn't exactly a good report! Again, I responded quickly. "Do you believe in miracles?" I asked him.

After some hemming and hawing, he said, "I'm not sure."

I told him I believed in miracles—and that I was going to get one! Actually, I needed two miracles: one for each surgery. I went on to tell him that I was going to go home and pray about what God wanted me to do.

He scheduled a follow-up appointment, when I was to come back and give him my decision.

I left the office that day feeling overwhelmed, but I was nonetheless determined to hear from God! My great friend Laura said that Destiny and I could move in with her so that she could help me during my recovery. Her offer was a huge blessing. Yet I still wasn't convinced that having surgery was the route the Lord wanted me to take.

Every morning, I would rise early and go into my prayer closet—the bathroom, where I would sit on an old comforter on the floor—to seek a word from the Lord. I would pray and ask God to show me His will in this situation. I knew then, and still believe, that God often uses doctors to bring about miracles, but I also knew that I should never let a surgeon cut me if I hadn't received a word from the Lord to confirm that it was His will.

As I kept seeking the Lord, I continued to go back and forth. I was in pain, and I wanted relief. I knew that God could do a miracle and make it all go away. Yet I began to waver, thinking that maybe I should just go ahead and schedule the surgeries.

About six weeks later, during my morning time in my prayer closet, I felt completely overwhelmed, both by the pain I was suffering and by the quandary I was in regarding whether to have the surgeries. It was then that the Lord spoke to me, saying, "Have you given up on believing for your miracle?"

At that moment, I knew my answer! I knew that God was telling me not to give up but to keep on believing for my miracle. Ironically, my answer came in the form of a question from the Lord. Whenever God asks you a question, it isn't because He doesn't already know the answer; He simply wants you to look inside your heart and discover the answer for yourself. I finally knew that I was supposed to keep standing in faith for my miracle!

I called the surgeon's office and cancelled the follow-up appointment I had scheduled. My plan was to call and reschedule it after my miracle had manifested. And that's exactly what I did—several years later. That's right; my follow-up appointment did not occur one or two months later but in late 2004!

You see, it was in my prayer closet that I received my miracle by faith, yet that miracle did not manifest until November 4, 2004. From the summer of 2001 until November 2004, I stood on the word that the Lord had given me.

During those years of standing in faith, I kept praying for every sick person I could find! Despite my ongoing pain, I kept recording my television programs; I kept speaking on praying for the sick and seeing them healed. I kept organizing services where I would see the power of God perform miraculous healings in the lives of other people, all the while still waiting for my own miracle to manifest. But every time I spoke the Word of God or prayed for someone else who needed a miracle, my faith was built up more and more.

Finally, after years of standing, it was my time! My miracle manifested! I ran home after the service that night to take my clothes off so I could examine my back. Sure enough, the huge knot I had previously had at the spot where the T9 and T11 vertebrae had come crashing together was totally gone.

Again, I had already received my miracle by faith—I'm convinced that receiving is the first step. I believe that you won't have to wait for years like I did. I don't understand why God does things the way He does. Maybe He wanted to "supersize" my faith, and the process took years—I don't know. All I know is that His ways are not our ways, nor is His timing our timing (Isaiah 55:8-9).

I waited until the end of December of 2004 to go back to the doctor. Honestly, I wanted to make sure that every symptom was gone. Even though I had been convinced that God would heal me, I was in shock when He finally did. I kept testing it out, trying to do things I hadn't been able to do before my healing manifested.

I was floating on cloud nine as I walked into the doctor's office for my appointment. I told him that I had received a miracle and would not need the surgeries. After giving me a physical exam, he said, "Wow! You can do things you couldn't do before!" He also said that he wanted to get an X-ray of my back. I was so excited because I couldn't wait to see the old X-ray compared to the new one.

When the surgeon came back into the exam room with the X-rays, he had a huge smile on his face. "Did you get this miracle here in Charlottesville?" he asked me.

"No; actually, I received this miracle in Hampton, Virginia," I replied, "but Jesus is the miracle Man, and He can do miracles anywhere!"

"I believe in miracles now!" said the surgeon. He sat down, shook his head, and added, "I need more patients like you." He continued to compare the old X-rays with the new ones, showing me how my back was totally stabilized and how the curvature was miraculously straighter than it had been before.

It was a glorious day! We talked for a long time, and I prayed that his heart's desire would come true—that he would have more patients like me who received miraculous healings.

It gets better. In December of 2012, I was rear-ended in my car and needed to have a thorough exam, including an MRI, to check for any damage to my spinal cord. I met with a renowned neurosurgeon who interpreted the results of my MRI. His first question to me was, "Who did your surgery at T10?" I told him, "I have never had surgery on my back. The Lord did my surgery." He didn't believe me, and so he asked me again, "Who did your surgery? It is picture-perfect." I was so excited that this renowned surgeon had proof of God's miraculous hand.

This is my prayer for all doctors across the nation: "Lord, heal the sick and grant miracles to all in need!" As you pray for others, standing in faith for their healing as you meditate on the Word of truth, you should expect healings to occur, in their lives and in yours.

Trust in the Lord with All Your Heart

When I was nineteen years old, a cousin of mine, who was only two months older than me, was killed in a snowmobile accident. I was a new Christian at the time, having come to salvation only two years prior, and I began to question God on the matter. I was confused as to why the Lord would allow such a tragedy to happen.

Then, one day, I was in prayer, and the Lord directed me to a Scripture passage I had never read before. It was Proverbs 3:5-6, which says, *"Trust in the Lord with all your heart and lean not on your own understanding; in all your ways acknowledge him, and he will make your paths straight."* That was just what I needed to hear. I never questioned God again—that is, in regard to that situation. When we stop leaning on our own understanding and start trusting God instead, we can have peace in the midst of every storm.

Recently, out of the blue, a cyst appeared on my daughter's face. It was an attack from the enemy, and it grew into a huge deal.

I stood in faith, believing that she would not need surgery. I have been praying over her ever since her birth that she would never have to be cut open or go through surgery. I kept praying the Word over her, and I stood on God's promises for total healing.

The longer I stood in faith, the bigger the cyst grew. I didn't understand it. I didn't want my baby girl to have to go through surgery. Plus, I didn't have the time or the money for such a procedure. I just wanted God to work a miracle. I wanted to wake up one morning, look at my daughter, and see that the cyst had totally disappeared.

Well, it didn't happen that way. We went the route of surgery. I nearly passed out when I saw the incision on her face—and also when I saw the bill for thousands of dollars. Destiny had a difficult recovery, too. Today, however, she is fine—totally healed! The cyst ended up being benign, praise God. I tell you all this as proof that God sometimes uses surgery to perform a miracle. He sometimes sends you along the route of medical procedures for the manifestation of your miracle. Never feel ashamed or condemned for taking medication or undergoing a medical procedure! Just make sure you have a word from the Lord on the matter. Once you have reached a place of peace from the Lord in regard to your decision, step forth in faith, trusting Him to bring about a fruitful procedure. Don't lean on your own understanding—trust God, for His ways are higher than your ways.

HANG ON TO HOPE FOR GOOD HEALTH

"Now hope does not disappoint, because the love of God has been poured out in our hearts by the Holy Spirit who was given to us" (Romans 5:5 NKJV). There's great power in hope. There's power to stand and power to persevere as long as you have hope. Get a strong grip on God's rope of hope—His Word—and don't allow anything to cause you to lose your grip.

Hope in God Will Never Fail You

The devil comes to steal, kill, destroy, and otherwise wreak havoc in your life (John 10:10). If he manages to steal your hope, sending you negative diagnoses and dire medical reports, you will be tempted to give up believing for your miracle. You will be robbed of joy and peace. Don't let the devil steal your hope!

If the devil can't manage to steal your hope, he'll try to get you to stake your hope on something other than God—something that will let you down. Don't fall for this tactic, either. *"A horse is a vain hope for deliverance; despite all its great strength it cannot save"* (Psalm 33:17).

Instead, place your hopes on the only one who will never let you down—your heavenly Father. *"Put your hope in the Lord, for with the Lord is unfailing love and with him is full redemption"* (Psalm 130:7). Don't merely hope *in* God; let Him *be* your hope! *"For You are my hope, O Lord God; You are my trust from my youth"* (Psalm 71:5 NKJV). He will never fail you!

When your hope is in the Lord, you are filled with joy and peace—to the point of overflowing! *"May the God of hope fill you with all joy and peace as you trust in him, so that you may overflow with hope by the power of the*

Holy Spirit" (Romans 15:13). The God of all hope will fill you with peace in the midst of the largest storms of your life, if you'll simply trust Him and refuse to let go of His rope of hope—His Word!

We have this assurance in Isaiah 40:31: *"Those who hope in the Lord will renew their strength. They will soar on wings like eagles; they will run and not grow weary, they will walk and not be faint."* What a glorious promise! Hoping in God gives us an unfailing source of strength and vitality.

God not only promises to give you all the hope you need, but He also will cause you to overflow with hope. Those other people in the waiting room at the doctor's office, those other patients getting treatment, and even the doctors themselves—all of them need the same hope you have! Allow the power of the Holy Spirit to overflow your hope into the lives of those around you. Share your rope of hope with them. That rope has limitless length, so go ahead and throw them a lifeline of hope!

Hope Trumps the Facts

> *Against all hope, Abraham in hope believed and so became the father of many nations, just as it had been said to him, "So shall your offspring be." Without weakening in his faith, he faced the fact that his body was as good as dead—since he was about a hundred years old—and that Sarah's womb was also dead. Yet he did not waver through unbelief regarding the promise of God, but was strengthened in his faith and gave glory to God, being fully persuaded that God had power to do what he had promised.* (Romans 4:18-21)

Against all hope in the natural realm, Abraham held on to hope and believed that God would fulfill the promise He had made to him. As a result, Abraham became the father of many nations. God's promise was fulfilled in his life, all because he hung on to hope without giving up, no matter what the "facts" were! The "fact" that both Abraham and Sarah were beyond the childbearing years did not cause Abraham to lose hope.

The truth of God always trumps the facts—and so does our hope, when we're hoping in God and His Word. The facts didn't cause Abraham's faith to weaken or his hope to dwindle in unbelief. Don't let your faith or hope diminish in the face of the "facts," either! Like Abraham, be *"fully persuaded"* that God has the power to do what He has promised, no matter what the facts may seem to say.

AS YOU AWAIT YOUR RESTORATION

"'I will restore you to health and heal your wounds,' declares the Lord" (Jeremiah 30:17a). God declares health and healing over us! What are you and I declaring about our own health? Even when the doctors declare sickness and disease over us, we must get in agreement with God and declare what He declares! The Word doesn't deny that we will experience sickness and other physical challenges. But it does declare that God will restore us to health and heal our wounds! And if He is restoring us, it's because something has deviated from the way God originally intended it to be.

Restore is defined as "to give back (something taken away, lost, etc.); make restitution of; to bring back to a former or normal condition, as by repairing, rebuilding, altering, etc.:…to put (a person) back in a place, position, rank, etc.: to bring back to health, strength, etc."

Get Close Enough to Touch Him

> And when the men of that place recognized Jesus, they sent word to all the surrounding country. People brought all their sick to [Jesus] and begged him to let the sick just touch the edge of his cloak, and all who touched him were healed. (Matthew 14:35-36)

We must get close enough to touch the Lord. The Word tells us that all who touched Him were healed. We touch the Lord by our faith; we touch the Lord in our worship; we touch the Lord when we draw close to Him through a personal relationship. We can't get close to Him through other people. Yes, others can teach us about Jesus and help show us how to get close to the Lord, but we can't hang onto other people's coattails as they touch the Lord. We must develop that relationship for ourselves.

Again, in order to receive our miracle, we must touch the Lord. And in order to touch the Lord, we must recognize who He is: the miracle Man! The Healer! The Son of God, who took the stripes on His back for our healing!

When we recognize who Jesus really is, we then realize we don't have to beg Him to heal us; healing is part of His nature. He wants to heal us. He has already paid the price for our healing; we simply need to receive it and unwrap the bows and paper from this beautiful, free gift.

Many people are prevented from touching the Lord because of doubt and unbelief. Don't buy the lies of the enemy. Don't allow the devil's lies to steal your hope. Reach out by faith and touch the Lord—He is passing by your way today! Reach out in prayer. Reach out in worship. Reach out in faith and be determined to touch Him. That's just what the woman with the issue of blood did in Mark chapter 5.

> *And a woman was there who had been subject to bleeding for twelve years. She had suffered a great deal under the care of many doctors and had spent all she had, yet instead of getting better she grew worse. When she heard about Jesus, she came up behind him in the crowd and touched his cloak, because she thought, "If I just touch his clothes, I will be healed." Immediately her bleeding stopped and she felt in her body that she was freed from her suffering.* (Mark 5:25-29)

The woman with the issue of blood had suffered for twelve years. She had consulted every doctor around and spent every dollar she had—only to find herself getting progressively worse. She was desperate for her miracle! That's actually not always a bad place to be. Sometimes, we don't get serious about "touching" God until we are desperate. In her desperation, she was determined to touch the Lord; she had tried everything else. She had exhausted every other option.

She pressed her way through many obstacles and distractions. She pressed her way through many challenges, just to touch the hem of Jesus' garment. And in an instant, she was healed. You may need to press your way through the "crowd" of negative medical reports, grim prognoses, and dire outlooks; you may need to press your way through pain and fear. But, if you do, you will touch Him and receive your miracle!

Most of the time, healing is progressive, as it was for my vertebra. However, on rare occasions, healing is instantaneous, as it was for this woman. Immediately her bleeding stopped, and she was relieved of her suffering.

It was God, not the doctors, who received the glory from her healing. The medical professionals couldn't do a thing for her, but God received the glory for her miracle. And He is going to get the glory from yours, as well.

Shout at Every Victory

When you are in need of a total turnaround in your health, you need to shout and praise God at every victory. I learned this key firsthand—not when I was in a battle for my health but when I was in the midst of a financial storm.

As a single mom of a newborn baby, I often found myself without diapers for Destiny or toilet paper for me. Now, I can fast and go without food for days, but I need to use the bathroom multiple times a day! So, whenever there was a fresh supply of toilet paper in the house, I would have a shouting party! I don't expect you to understand this if you have never been without toilet paper, but for all of you out there who have been through a season of lack in which the simple necessities of life are hard to come by, you know what I mean. As a matter of fact, I can hear you shouting with me right now!

God taught me to shout my praises to Him with every roll of provision. He taught me to have a grateful heart and have a praise party each time I would get a bar of soap I so desperately needed. The principle He was teaching me was that I should go ahead and shout at every little victory, as a way of reminding myself what God had done for me before.

> *Some men came and told Jehoshaphat, "A vast army is coming against you from Edom, from the other side of the Sea. It is already in Hazazon Tamar"* (that is, En Gedi). *Alarmed, Jehoshaphat resolved to inquire of the Lord, and he proclaimed a fast for all Judah.* (2 Chronicles 20:2-3)

Jehoshaphat received an alarming report. Whenever we receive a bad medical report, it's very alarming. Yet, we can learn how to act in our spirit and how not to react out of our flesh. Jehoshaphat was shocked and alarmed, yet he reacted out of his spirit rather than his flesh when he resolved to inquire of the Lord. He immediately called a fast, knowing that he needed to get a word from the Lord. When we react out of our flesh, we give fear free rein and are easily overwhelmed. But, when we act out of our spirit and seek the Lord and His direction, we can have victory!

After he proclaimed a fast, Jehoshaphat began to pray, acknowledging God for who He was. Fear always proclaims and magnifies the report in the natural, but faith always acknowledges and proclaims who the Lord is.

> *Then Jehoshaphat stood up in the assembly of Judah and Jerusalem at the temple of the Lord in the front of the new courtyard and said: "O Lord, God of our fathers, are you not the God who is in heaven? You rule over all the kingdoms of the nations. Power and might are in your hand, and no one can withstand you. O our God, did you not drive out the inhabitants of this land before your people Israel and give it forever to the descendants of Abraham your friend?"* (2 Chronicles 20:5-7)

Jehoshaphat was acknowledging all that the Lord had done in the past. As you acknowledge every battle the Lord has already brought you through, it builds your faith for the current battle you are facing. Stop and think about it—God has never let you down before. He has always brought you through! Remember every turnaround He has brought about in your life. Recall every time He has healed your body. Remind yourself of all the healings and physical miracles He has done for others. Feed your faith with all the past victories—and shout now for the one you are about to receive!

After King Jehoshaphat and the people had prayed and fasted, they received a word from the Lord. God gave them direction, just as He did for me in my prayer closet that morning.

> *He said: "Listen, King Jehoshaphat and all who live in Judah and Jerusalem! This is what the Lord says to you: 'Do not be afraid or discouraged because of this vast army. For the battle is not yours, but God's. Tomorrow march down against them. They will be climbing up by the Pass of Ziz, and you will find them at the end of the gorge in the Desert of Jeruel. You will not have to fight this battle. Take up your positions; stand firm and see the deliverance the Lord will give you, O Judah and Jerusalem. Do not be afraid; do not be discouraged. Go out to face them tomorrow, and the Lord will be with you.'"* (2 Chronicles 20:15-17)

Wow! That's powerful! I sure hope you didn't skip over that verse because you already knew it. If you did, you'd better go back and read it because it's a "now" word for you!

Don't be afraid because of the medical report you received. Don't be discouraged—it's just a blueprint of the enemy's schemes for you. Now you have the upper hand! All you must do now is take your position, standing firm on what the Word of God says about your situation. Let nothing move you—just keep standing! And remember, you won't even have to fight this battle; the Lord is going to fight it for you!

Don't wear yourself out by trying to fight the battle alone. All you have to do is stand and watch as God fights for you, every step of the way—just as He did for the people of Jerusalem.

Early in the morning they left for the Desert of Tekoa. As they set out, Jehoshaphat stood and said, "Listen to me, Judah and people of Jerusalem! Have faith in the Lord your God and you will be upheld; have faith in his prophets and you will be successful." After consulting the people, Jehoshaphat appointed men to sing to the Lord and to praise him for the splendor of his holiness as they went out at the head of the army, saying: "Give thanks to the Lord, for his love endures forever." As they began to sing and praise, the Lord set ambushes against the men of Ammon and Moab and Mount Seir who were invading Judah, and they were defeated. (2 Chronicles 20:20-22)

They went out early in the morning to face the enemy just as the Lord had instructed them. Your battles are won early in the morning in prayer! As you rise early and face the enemy in prayer, your day will be filled with victory.

The people of Jerusalem had faith in the Lord's promises, and they went out shouting and praising God for the victory. They took their position and they stood firm. They didn't try to fight the battle themselves; they simply praised God that He was going to fight for them. As a result, the enemy defeated themselves, while the army of Jerusalem enjoyed their God-given rest!

The fear of God came upon all the kingdoms of the countries when they heard how the Lord had fought against the enemies of Israel. And the kingdom of Jehoshaphat was at peace, for his God had given him rest on every side. (2 Chronicles 20:29-30)

Enjoy the rest of the Lord today. Don't wear yourself out "fighting" cancer or "fighting" the medical report. You don't have to "fight for your life" on your own; you simply need to stand in faith on the promises of God and rest in Him while you shout and praise Him for every victory!

Persevere in Praise

When we are standing for a total turnaround in our health, we need to persevere and keep on standing. We don't always understand the things God does, or why or how. We don't have to understand His ways; we simply have to trust Him.

Remember Isaiah 55:8-9: *"For my thoughts are not your thoughts, neither are your ways my ways,' declares the Lord. 'As the heavens are higher than the earth, so are my ways higher than your ways and my thoughts than your thoughts.'"* When we try to figure God out, we can get angry, frustrated, and easily discouraged. We must not grumble against God or fault Him for what's happening in our lives. It's not wrong to question, but it is wrong to allow our questions to cause a gap or a wedge between us and the Lord.

Dwell on the Goodness of God

I like the way the Amplified Bible translates Philippians 2:14: *"Do all things without grumbling and faultfinding and complaining [against God] and questioning and doubting [among yourselves]."* If we aren't careful, we can begin to find fault with God. We can begin to focus on all of the things we want God to do for us, forgetting that those things may not be His will for us. Let's not allow that to happen! We should praise God for all that He has already done, instead. Thanking Him for all He has already done enables us to cultivate a grateful heart. But thinking on what we wish He would do only fosters a spirit of anger, bitterness, and self-pity. That isn't the way to go!

> *He who dwells in the shelter of the Most High will rest in the shadow of the Almighty. I will say of the Lord, "He is my refuge and my fortress, my God, in whom I trust." Surely he will save you from the fowler's snare and from the deadly pestilence.* (Psalm 91:1-3)

If we are dwelling in the presence of the Lord, we can dwell on the fact that He will take care of everything. When we are dwelling in the Lord, we can rest on the knowledge of what is true about Him. We can say, "He is my refuge and my fortress." Through our words and our meditations, we internalize our belief that the Lord is taking care of us and protecting us. But, if we stop dwelling in His presence, we will be quick to say the wrong things about the Lord. We may start grumbling and complaining about what we are going through. We may begin to question God in a way that brings about anger and resentment in our hearts to God—and that's the last thing we need!

What we really need, especially in times of trial, is to be closer to God than ever before.

> *Consider it pure joy, my brothers, whenever you face trials of many kinds, because you know that the testing of your faith develops perseverance. Perseverance must finish its work so that you may be mature and complete, not lacking anything.* (James 1:2-4)

When I was challenged to persevere for those years while I was standing for my miracle, I can honestly say that God matured my faith. He taught me how to stand and keep on standing. And learning to stand benefitted many other areas of my life, as well. When we learn to persevere as we wait for the fulfillment of God's promises in one area of life, that perseverance causes us to mature in other areas, as well.

God wants us to be *"mature and complete"* in every area. Sometimes, His schooling takes us on a path we would rather not follow. I don't know about you, but I like the quick, direct route. Yet, that is rarely the route God takes me on! His guidance always takes me by way of the most effective route rather than the most direct.

The desire of God is always to mature our faith, to fulfill the desires of our heart, and to grow our character. He refines us and takes off the rough edges and He prepares us for all that He has ahead for us in our glorious futures in Him.

TRUST GOD TO PROVIDE THE POWER FOR YOUR TURNAROUND!

The prophetic voice of God has the power to turn any situation around. Read what the prophet Ezekiel had to say about an experience with the power of the prophetic word.

> *He asked me, "Son of man, can these bones live?" I said, "O Sovereign Lord, you alone know." Then he said to me, "Prophesy to these bones and say to them, 'Dry bones, hear the word of the Lord! This is what the Sovereign Lord says to these bones: I will make breath enter you, and you will come to life. I will attach tendons to you and make flesh come upon you and cover you with skin; I will put breath in you, and you will come to life. Then you will know that I am the Lord.'" So I prophesied as I was commanded. And as I was prophesying, there was a noise, a rattling sound, and the bones came together, bone to bone. I looked, and tendons and flesh appeared on them and skin covered them, but there was no breath in them. The he said to me, "Prophesy to the breath; prophesy, son of man, and say to it, 'This is what the Sovereign Lord says: Come from the four winds, O breath, and breathe into these slain, that they may live.'" So I prophesied as he commanded me, and breath entered them, they came to life and stood up on their feet—a vast army.* (Ezekiel 37:3-10)

The prophetic voice of the Lord turned things around and breathed life into the valley of dry bones. They were already dead. They weren't just dying; they were as dead as they could get. Yet, God turned it all around as He spoke the prophetic Word over the valley of dry bones and breathed life into them.

No matter how "dead" our situation looks, God can breathe His prophetic voice into the situation so that new life comes forth. He is the God who *"gives life to the dead and calls things that are not as though they were"*

(Romans 4:17). God is the God who gives life. He is all-powerful, and He can give life to everything—even things already dead! That's awesome. All He has to do is call things that are not as though they were. In other words, He can call it healed, healthy, and whole, even when it's dead. We need to do the same thing. Jesus said to His disciples, *"I tell you the truth, anyone who has faith in me will do what I have been doing. He will do even greater things than these, because I am going to the Father"* (John 14:12). We are supposed to be doing even greater works than the Lord did!

Start prophesying and speaking life to dead reports. The prophet Ezekiel prophesied as the Lord commanded him to an entire valley filled with dry bones. As he obeyed the command of the Lord, life—powerful life—came forth.

PROPHESY TO YOUR OWN "DRY BONES" SITUATION

The devil wants to bring death on you and on the body of Christ through sickness and disease. His goal is to debilitate the body of Christ. Don't accept his schemes! You need to know that the dry bones can live. You need to know that God can do anything. As you prophesy the Word of the Lord over yourself and your medical situation, God will bring forth new life.

In the passage from Ezekiel, we see God performing a creative miracle. He caused new tendons to be formed. He caused new flesh and skin to cover it and to grow. Then, He breathed new life into the entire being. God can resurrect the dead!

In a miracle service I was attending, a lady who had been diagnosed with breast cancer received a creative miracle. She had had one breast surgically removed to prevent the spread of cancer, but, during that service, the Lord supernaturally grew her a new one! I was there, and I witnessed it. I have seen the Lord cause legs to grow out that were inches shorter than the other leg. I have seen people who could not walk just jump out of wheelchairs as the power of God hit them. God can and will turn any situation around!

We must prophesy the Word of the Lord over our medical conditions and situations. As the Lord commanded Ezekiel to prophesy to the valley of dry bones, I believe the Lord is commanding us to prophesy over our own "dry bones" situations and speak forth life.

God wants to breathe new life into you, and He wants you to stand up strong and healthy as a part of His vast army!

> *Then he said to me: "Son of man, these bones are the whole house of Israel. They say, 'Our bones are dried up and our hope is gone; we are cut off.' Therefore prophesy and say to them: 'This is what the Sovereign Lord says: O my people, I am going to open your graves and bring you up from them; I will bring you back to the land of Israel. Then you, my people, will know that I am the Lord, when I open your graves and bring you up from them. I will put my Spirit in you and you will live, and I will settle you in your own land. Then you will know that I the Lord have spoken, and I have done it, declares the Lord.'"*
> (Ezekiel 37:11-14)

It was said that their hope was gone, yet, when the prophetic voice of the Lord came forth, their hope was restored. You must hear the prophetic voice of the Lord daily, for it brings fresh revelation and strong life to you!

When God breathed His resurrection power and life into the dry bones, they all knew it was God. God got all the glory! God is about to get glory in the earth today like never before. People will be more desperate than ever for their miracle and, as they turn to the Lord, He will get the glory.

If you are facing a situation that seems dead and lifeless, God wants to open the grave and speak forth His prophetic word of healing and life over you and your situation. As you continue to prophetically speak to your situation daily, resurrection life will come forth for all to see and glory will be given to the Lord. The prophetic voice always turns things around.

NO WEAPON FORMED AGAINST YOU SHALL PROSPER

No matter what the enemy tries to bring against you, It cannot prosper. God always wins!

Romans 8:28 says, *"And we know that in all things God works for the good of those who love him, who have been called according to his purpose."* The battle you have been facing—the challenge set before you—will not take you out! God is able to turn it around so that it works for your good. No, God is not the author of sickness and disease, but what Satan means for evil, God will use for your good.

You will come out stronger in your character. You will come out stronger in your faith. And I believe you will even come out stronger in your health. Don't quit now, for victory is just around the corner! The enemy will not succeed in his schemes against you as long as you stand and keep on standing.

When You Have Done All, Stand

As we stand against the schemes of the enemy, we must keep our full armor on! Yes, sickness and disease are major weapons in the enemy's arsenal, and he uses them to stall the body of Christ as it advances. The enemy wants to stop us from bringing forth the work of the Lord. Like the enemy did to Nehemiah, Satan attempts to stop our work by throwing distractions our way. And one of his most effective distractions is that of sickness and disease. If Satan can succeed at putting restraints on our physical bodies, it often gives him an edge over the other aspects of our lives—our emotions, our minds, and our spirits.

We must put on our full armor and stand. And then, when we have done all, we must keep standing!

> *Finally, be strong in the Lord and in his mighty power. Put on the full armor of God so that you can take your stand against the devil's schemes. For our struggle is not against flesh and blood, but against the rulers, against the authorities, against*

the powers of this dark world and against the spiritual forces of evil in the heavenly realms. Therefore put on the full armor of God, so that when the day of evil comes, you may be able to stand your ground, and after you have done everything, to stand. Stand firm then, with the belt of truth buckled around your waist, with the breastplate of righteousness in place, and with your feet fitted with the readiness that comes from the gospel of peace. In addition to all this, take up the shield of faith, with which you can extinguish all the flaming arrows of the evil one. Take the helmet of salvation and the sword of the Spirit, which is the word of God. And pray in the Spirit on all occasions with all kinds of prayers and requests. With this in mind, be alert and always keep on praying for all the saints. (Ephesians 6:10-18)

That's powerful! A key to total turnaround in your health is meditating on the Word of truth. The truth is that you are engaged in spiritual warfare. You must stand up and fight. You can't give in to sickness and disease. Even though the battle is not yours but the Lord's, and even though He is fighting for you, there's still a part for you to play: you must renew your mind to the truth of God's Word—on a daily basis! You must stand on the Word of truth, which will nourish your faith and hope.

There have been many times when I felt sick and I just wanted to go to bed and pull the covers over my head. Each time I was about to give in, the Lord would say, "Stand up and fight. This is war."

From time to time, I lose sight of the fact that I am engaged in a spiritual battle. Although we shouldn't get so caught up in the warfare that we lose sight of the presence of God, we need to be attuned to the enemy's schemes so that we may fend him off.

Meditate on the Word of Truth

Don't ever go to battle without your sword—the Word of God. If you aren't armed and dangerous, you won't stand a chance on the battlefield. You must keep your sword sharpened, and you do this by reading the Word, thinking the Word, and praying the Word daily. You do this by living out the charge in Joshua 1:8-9:

> *Do not let this Book of the Law depart from your mouth; meditate on it day and night, so that you may be careful to do everything written in it. Then you will be prosperous and successful. Have I not commanded you? Be strong and courageous. Do not be terrified; do not be discouraged, for the Lord your God will be with you wherever you go.*

As we meditate the Word of truth every day, our thinking will line up with the mind of Christ. As we speak the Word, we will be strong and courageous, not fearful and discouraged. Keep your sword sharp; don't let it grow dull due to lack of use.

> *The weapons we fight with are not the weapons of the world. On the contrary, they have divine power to demolish strongholds. We demolish arguments and every pretension that sets itself up against the knowledge of God, and we take captive every thought to make it obedient to Christ.* (2 Corinthians 10:4-5)

When the enemy attempts to develop a stronghold of sickness and disease in your life, you must demolish it with the weapons of the Lord. Demolish those thoughts that set themselves up against what God's Word has to say about your situation. Bring captive every thought that doesn't line up with the promises of God. Don't allow yourself to meditate on anything contrary to the Word of God—on thoughts such as, *I'll never make it through this alive.* Don't allow yourself to speak words of doubt and unbelief. Know that God is more than able to turn your situation around. Stand on His promises.

Prophesy new life to your valley of dry bones! Prophesy health and healing! You don't have to strive to be healed. You just have to receive your healing by faith.

Arm Yourself with the Right Weapons

The Word says in Second Corinthians 10 that we don't fight with the weapons of the world. Carnal weapons of anger, bitterness, and unforgiveness can actually cause us to lose the battle. Instead, we must arm ourselves with the righteous weapons of warfare, including love, joy, peace, patience, kindness, and longsuffering. Our weapons are the fruit of the Spirit, as described in Galatians 5:22-23. Our battle is not a battle against flesh and blood; our battle is a spiritual battle, and it must be won in the spirit.

The fruit of the Spirit are our powerful weapons that defeat strongholds. Unforgiveness, bitterness, and anger have been proven medically to cause cancer and other sickness and diseases. Stress produces many forms of sickness and disease. But love, joy, and peace also have been recorded as medically successful in healing sickness and disease. Remember, *"A merry heart does good, like medicine"* (Proverbs 17:22a NKJV).

Watch your weapons, and make sure you are armed and dangerous against the kingdom of darkness. God wants you on the winning side!

DIETARY TURNAROUND

God can give us keys to our total turnaround in our health if we are open to obeying His command and leading. Sometimes our turnaround can be achieved by our own choices. This is certainly true in the realm of our diets. Our eating habits are only one example of changes we can make that will assist us in walking in the divine health the Lord has for us.

Your Choices Are a Key to Your Turnaround

A few years ago, I was in need of a turnaround in a situation for my daughter, Destiny, who was in middle school at the time. If you are a parent, or if you can simply recall your own youth, you know that the middle school years can be a very difficult time! Destiny attended a private Christian school from kindergarten through fourth grade, and I homeschooled her for grades five through seven. When she reached the eighth grade, I knew it was God's time for her to return to school. So, I took her back to the private Christian school.

We were both in shock from the first day of orientation. Some of the sweet little angels from her fourth grade class had sure changed in the interim. Ten weeks into the school year, tired of watching my daughter be bullied for taking a stand for righteousness (yes, even at a Christian school), I cried out to the Lord in fervent prayer for a turnaround. He answered me with this message: "Your choices can bring about your own turnaround."

Sometimes, we labor in prayer, pleading with God to turn the situation around, only to find out that the key to our turnaround has been in our own hands—our own choices—all along. God was telling me that I had the power of choice: I could enroll Destiny in a different school. He was telling me that I didn't have to stay in the "muck," not even for the remainder of the school year. I was driving down the road one day when I heard the Lord say, "Leave now and don't go back."

So, that's just what we did. We left in the middle of everything. We didn't leave at the end of the quarter. We didn't leave at the end of the week. We didn't leave at the end of anything. We left immediately, in obedience to the voice of the Lord. And we never looked back. When God told Moses that it was time to leave Egypt, it was time to leave Egypt. Yes, we have good friends at that school; yes, we love the people there; but when God says "Go," we know that we must leave immediately.

Looking back now, I can say that taking Destiny out of that school was one of the best decisions I have made! For the remainder of the school year, we dealt with "normal" middle school issues. We didn't have to deal with bullying, division, and unacceptable behaviors targeting individual children.

Our year ended strong, my daughter has been radically blessed, and we both learned a valuable lesson. My daughter didn't want to leave in the middle of the year, but she learned that when God says "Go," we should never delay—not even by a single day! We don't have to understand or even agree with the command; we must simply obey.

Children who grow up in abusive homes or amid other undesirable conditions really have no choice; they must remain in those environments until they reach an age when they can make decisions for themselves. But, once you reach adulthood, you can make your own choices—with God's guidance. However, too many adults retain the "victim mentality" they developed during childhood. A victim mentality causes you to believe that you have no say in a matter—that your voice doesn't count. It causes you to resign yourself to remaining in a harmful situation. The truth is, you don't have to be a victim! You can make your own choices and decisions, according to God's will for you. When you follow His lead, He can cause your situation to undergo a total turnaround!

This applies to your daily diet. You alone determine the food that you ingest. Remember that your body is a temple of God's Holy Spirit, and take care of it accordingly!

Listen with Open Ears and a Receptive Heart

The Holy Spirit will lead us into all truth in every area, as long as we are open to hearing His voice. I know time and time again, the Lord has instructed me to limit my caffeine and my sugar.

Maybe the Lord has been trying to tell you to change your eating habits, yet you haven't listened to His leading. I want to encourage you to pray, and then obey. Your obedience to change certain things could be your key to your physical miracle.

We can be thin and trim and need to eat healthy. Unhealthy eating is not always reflected in our weight. I believe we should all weigh ourselves regularly to maintain a healthy weight because we must take care of our temple if we are going to live long and do the Lord's work. However, the scale doesn't reflect such details as caffeine intake, sugar consumption, and so forth.

As we obey the voice of the Holy Spirit, He will even assist us in our eating habits. After all, He wants us alive and well to do kingdom work for His glory!

Reap the Benefits of Physical Exercise

Many of you cringe just at the mention of the word *exercise*. It's really not a bad word. It could be worse—I could have typed the dreaded word *diet*. Actually, I never use that word. Instead, I say "healthy eating habits." It just sounds a lot less painful!

But exercise doesn't have to be strenuous. I don't do major workouts, but I do walk on my treadmill and around my neighborhood on a regular basis.

I actually can't do a major workout since I'm still standing in faith for God to grow me a new T10 vertebra. I'm totally healed—I strut around in my five-inch high heels whenever I want, in order to add to my stature of five feet three inches—yet there are certain exercises that aggravate my back.

I'm not saying you have to go "all out" in your physical exercise, but I am suggesting that you stay active and just do *something*. And walking from the couch to the refrigerator and back again for a snack doesn't count!

Experience the Wonders of Rest

God has designed our bodies to heal themselves as we sleep. It is so true! I tend to live life in fifth gear. I start early in the morning and I go strong all day. And then, when it's over, it's over.

My staff knows that when I begin to downshift from fifth gear, it takes me only about an hour before I'm in "park." When I begin to downshift, I had better be close to my bed. Otherwise, it isn't pretty!

Ironically, rest is an area I have had to work hard at mastering. I have really had to submit to the Lord's dealing with me in this area. I love what I do, and I have always been a hard worker. My mom and dad both raised me that way.

For a period of about two years, God drilled into me the importance of rest. My doctor was always telling me that I needed more sleep. It took awhile, and I'm not totally where I need to be with it, yet I have come a long way, baby!

Yes, we need rest and proper sleep so that we can be healthy servants of the Lord!

FAITH IS YOUR TITLE DEED

A key to total turnaround in your health is faith. Faith is your title deed to your miracle.

> *Now faith is the assurance (the confirmation, the title deed) of the things [we] hope for, being the proof of things [we] do not see and the conviction of their reality [faith perceiving as real fact what is not revealed to the senses].* (Hebrews 11:1 AMP)

The assurance and proof that you own something is your title deed! Faith is your title deed. In order to receive your total turnaround in your health, you have to get rid of the "if You can" attitude toward the Lord.

We must have the attitude that says, "Of course, God is going to do it!" True faith perceives things as real fact before they are revealed to the senses. In other words, they haven't manifested in the natural realm yet. We can't see them, touch them, or feel them. Faith doesn't have to see, feel, or touch. Real faith owns the title deed, and real faith knows that healing belongs to us.

A key to total turnaround in your health is hanging on to your title deed—your faith! Don't let anyone or anything steal your title deed. It belongs to you! Stay encouraged because God is about to bring total turnaround in your health for His glory!

The Word of the Lord to you is Psalm 118:17: *"I will not die but live, and will proclaim what the Lord has done."*

Hang on to your title deed of
faith for good health.

POINTS TO PONDER

1. God wants to build our faith. What is our active role in this building process, according to Romans 10:17?

2. Why is hope so powerful? What is God's "rope of hope"?

3. The Bible says in Mathew 4:23-24 that Jesus healed all the sick who came to Him. It also says that Jesus is the same yesterday, today, and forever (Hebrews 13:8). What can we expect, based on these truths?

4. Faith is your title deed to your miracle. What does a title deed prove? What exactly does this mean to you in regard to your health?

Meditate on these Scriptures, speak them aloud, and commit them to memory:

> [Jesus] *Himself bore our sins in His own body on the tree, that we, having died to sins, might live for righteousness—by whose stripes you were healed.* (1 Peter 2:24 NKJV)

> *So then faith comes by hearing, and hearing by the word of God.* (Romans 10:17 NKJV)

Now hope does not disappoint, because the love of God has been poured out in our hearts by the Holy Spirit who was given to us. (Romans 5:5 NKJV)

Now faith is being sure of what we hope for and certain of what we do not see. (Hebrews 11:1)

Chapter 11

Total Turnaround in Your Perspective

After being declared cancer-free, my brother, David, was diagnosed with cancer once again. The doctors were shocked. Somehow, his kidney cancer became metastasized and spread rapidly throughout his body. Two days after his fifty-first birthday, the report came in. Within eight months, he was placed in hospice care and ultimately went home to be with the Lord.

I was blessed to be able to spend a lot of quality time with him during the final months, weeks, and days of his life on earth. When the report came from the doctors that they were stopping all treatment because they had done everything they could do, he called me and asked for me to come home immediately. Within hours, I left Virginia and headed back to my hometown.

I sat with David, talking to him one on one and listening as he spoke from his heart. He confided in me, "I guess I'm a little afraid and a little worried." He went on to say that he didn't know what to expect when he died. He knew that he was going to heaven because he had rededicated his life to the Lord four months earlier, but he still wondered what he was going to experience when he died.

Most of us are afraid of the unknown, and that's all right. But that's also where trust comes in. I did my best to explain to David that death wasn't going to be painful for him. He had already endured the worst pain and suffering he would ever face as he battled bone cancer. I told him that death would be like going to sleep peacefully and waking up in the presence of the Lord with angels singing.

As we discussed heaven, I could tell that he was comforted. He then went on to say, "I'm just afraid that I haven't done enough for the Lord in this life." That statement has stayed with me. Even now, it rings in my ears. As a minister, I deal with birth, death, and everything in between on a regular basis. And I have yet to hear someone on his deathbed say, "I wish I would have put in just a little bit more time at the office," or "I wish I would have made just a little bit more money."

From the day David and I had that conversation, my view on daily life has been vastly different from before. Sometimes, as ministers, we can be so busy working for the Lord that we forget about what we are working toward—heaven! And the truth is, like my brother stated, the only thing that counts is what you and I have done for the Lord in this life. So if you tend to focus more on the world at hand than on eternity, it's time for a turnaround in your perspective.

A "Heavenly" Perspective on Working and Wealth

Command those who are rich in this present world not to be arrogant nor to put their hope in wealth, which is so uncertain, but to put their hope in God, who richly provides us with everything for our enjoyment. Command them to do good, to be rich in good deeds, and to be generous and willing to share. In this way they will lay up treasure for themselves as a firm foundation for the coming age, so that they may take hold of the life that is truly life. (1 Timothy 6:17-19)

Our hope should never be in our wealth, possessions, or status; our hope should always be in God. When we put our hope in wealth or anything else uncertain, it can open the door to the spirit of fear, which is often birthed out of uncertainty and instability. But, when our hope is in God—the God who is the same yesterday, today, and forever (Hebrews 13:8)—our hope is sure because its foundation will never be shaken.

As it says in First Timothy 6:17, God blesses us with good things for our enjoyment. Let's not be afraid to enjoy the blessings of the Lord—we are supposed to! But we shouldn't be content to please only ourselves. If we do, then it has become all about us. But we are blessed in order to be a blessing to others, as well. As we are rich in good deeds and liberal in sharing our blessings with others, we are laying up treasures for ourselves in heaven.

My brother was a very generous person. He often gave to the Lord's work and to those who were less fortunate. As we talked in the hospital that day, I was able to share with him that, even though he hadn't traveled around preaching the gospel, as I had, he had stored up treasures in heaven every time he gave to those who were less fortunate or seeded money into a ministry with the purpose of advancing the kingdom. The same is true for you today. You don't need to travel the globe as an evangelist to make a difference in the kingdom or to store up treasure in heaven!

> *Do not store up for yourselves treasures on earth, where moth and rust destroy, and where thieves break in and steal. But store up for yourselves treasures in heaven, where moth and rust do not destroy, and where thieves do not break in and steal. For where your treasure is, there your heart will be also.* (Matthew 6:19-21)

God wants our hearts to be with Him today. He wants us to store up treasures in heaven. As we keep our hearts' priority on the Father and His kingdom, we have no need to worry about what awaits us after death.

A "HEAVENLY" PERSPECTIVE ON YOUR TIME AND OTHER RESOURCES

No matter how much money you have, it will never be your greatest asset. Remember, God owns it all, so He could just drop a couple million your way at any time (get in agreement and start declaring that, right?). Money is nothing to God, and it's never a problem for the Lord. Therefore, it should never be a problem for you. If you keep your part of the covenant—if you tithe and give when God says give, if you walk in obedience with every dollar He puts in your hand—abundant provision will always be there for you, so fear not!

What is your greatest asset, then, if not your money? It's your time. Time is limited, which makes it a precious resource indeed. No one has more than twenty-four hours in a day. No one has more than seven days in a week—no one, not even God Himself! So, you must invest your greatest resource—your time—very wisely!

> *His work will be shown for what it is, because the Day will bring it to light. It will be revealed with fire, and the fire will test the quality of each man's work. If what he has built survives, he will receive his reward. If it is burned up, he will suffer loss; he himself will be saved, but only as one escaping through the flames.* (1 Corinthians 3:13-15)

Giving of our time to others is a wonderful investment in the kingdom, as long as what we do for the Lord is done from a pure heart and with upright motives. If we perform an act of service in order to be seen, we have already received our reward; but if we serve others out of a heart of obedience to God, with a desire to build up His kingdom, our works will receive great reward in heaven. This is one way of reading Matthew 6:1-4:

> *Be careful not to do your "acts of righteousness" before men, to be seen by them. If you do, you will have no reward from your Father in heaven. So when you give to the needy, do not*

announce it with trumpets, as the hypocrites do in the syna-gogues and on the streets, to be honored by men. I tell you the truth, they have received their reward in full. But when you give to the needy, do not let your left hand know what your right hand is doing, so that your giving may be in secret. Then your Father, who sees what is done in secret, will reward you.

Those whose works are burned up on the Day of Judgment will themselves be saved, but only as one just escaping through the flames. In other words, they just slid into heaven (the paraphrased gospel according to Danette). I don't know about you, but I don't want to "just slide" into heaven—I want to store up treasures every day that will last for eternity!

Just a few days after my conversation with my brother in his room at the hospital, I was teaching at a Kids' Club in one of the neighborhoods that our ministry has adopted. Our lesson was about obeying God, based on the example of Jonah. As I looked at all of the smiling faces of the underprivileged and fatherless children gathered there that day, I felt the presence of God so strongly, and I heard Him whisper to my heart, saying, "You are storing up treasures in heaven today!"

I will never forget that moment. Fear comes to paralyze you from launching forward in all that God has for you in His kingdom. The enemy tries to keep your focus on this life; he works to distract you when you think from a kingdom perspective. But, if you remain in the Word, you, too, can store up treasures in heaven.

Proverbs 28:27 says, *"He who gives to the poor will lack nothing, but he who closes his eyes to them receives many curses."* Don't close your eyes to the poor and the fatherless today. Don't ignore the plight of those around you. Reach out and make a difference! As you do, God will pour out more blessings on you than you could ever imagine. My life is proof of that!

First Corinthians 15:58 says, *"Therefore, my dear brothers, stand firm. Let nothing move you. Always give yourselves fully to the work of the Lord, because you know that your labor in the Lord is not in vain."* Never let anything move you away from doing the Lord's work. Don't allow any situation or circumstance to bring fear, which would attempt to shake your firm stand for the Lord and His work. And never let the enemy's lying declarations tell you your work for Him is in vain—it's not! As a matter of fact, you are being used by God to bring total turnaround in the lives of those all around you. So, you boldly tell the devil and his spirit of fear to go back to the pit of hell, where it came from. And you, you keep on keeping on, for you are about to take down the giants!

A "Heavenly" Perspective on Major Undertakings

The Lord prepared little David to do a great big job—a job so big that even the "big boys" didn't want to do it. The "big boys" feared, but little David stood. David's preparation didn't come the way you would expect. He never graduated from Yale or Harvard. He wasn't even prepared the same way the "big boys" were. Yet, he received his preparation simply from doing what he was given to do at the place he was instructed to do it.

> *The Lord said to Samuel, "How long will you mourn for Saul, since I have rejected him as king over Israel? Fill your horn with oil and be on your way; I am sending you to Jesse of Bethlehem. I have chosen one of his sons to be king." (1 Samuel 16:1)*

If you remember, Saul had lost his position because of his disobedience. He did not do everything the Lord told him to do. He feared man, not God. As a result, the Lord was about to anoint the next king. But everyone was surprised at God's choice.

> *Jesse had seven of his sons pass before Samuel, but Samuel said to him, "The Lord has not chosen these." So he asked Jesse, "Are these all the sons you have?" "There is still the youngest," Jesse answered, "but he is tending the sheep." Samuel said, "Send for him; we will not sit down until he arrives." (1 Samuel 16:10-11)*

All of the most likely candidates passed before Samuel. I can imagine that Jesse proudly brought his sons before Samuel, thinking he was bringing the best of the best. Yet, each time one of the sons paraded by, Samuel knew in his heart that he wasn't God's choice.

After seven different sons paraded by, I can imagine that both Jesse and Samuel were wondering what was going on. You see, little David wasn't even considered to be in the running! Samuel asked for Jesse's sons but Jesse didn't even view David as a possible candidate. Finally, Samuel asked, *"Are these all the sons you have?"* Samuel may have even begun to doubt if he was hearing right from the Lord.

God uses people whom others don't even consider! Little David was on the backside of the desert, just tending a "few little sheep." He was the youngest, he was the smallest, he was the least likely; yet, the Lord called for him! Little David was fearless, not fearful. He feared God and God alone. Little David had been raised up for such a time as this, and he had favor!

> *So he sent for* [David] *and had him brought in. He was ruddy, with a fine appearance and handsome features. Then the Lord said, "Rise and anoint him; he is the one." So Samuel took the horn of oil and anointed him in the presence of his brothers, and from that day on the Spirit of the Lord came upon David in power....* (1 Samuel 16:12-13)

The Lord said, *"Rise and anoint him; he is the one."* I believe the Lord is saying to you today—"Rise up! You are the one! I have called you for such a time as this!" You may be the least likely, but so was David. Little David had been trained and equipped. Little David had been prepared right where he was—being faithful over a few little sheep. But, in God's perfect timing, He anointed him and used him for an important job that only little David could do—defeat the giant.

When Eliab, David's oldest brother, heard him speaking with the men, he burned with anger at him and asked, "Why have you come down here? And with whom did you leave those few sheep in the desert? I know how conceited you are and how wicked your heart is; you came down only to watch the battle." (1 Samuel 17:28)

David's oldest brother became very angry and jealous of David. Sometimes when the family dynamic that has been in place for years changes, everyone's issues come out. They weren't used to David being out front. After all, their family dynamic had defined David as the "little guy" who could only do the "little stuff." But when God had called David to the forefront, the family dynamic shifted, and Eliab didn't like it! But David wasn't fazed, either by his brother or by his gigantic opponent.

David said to the Philistine, "You come against me with sword and spear and javelin, but I come against you in the name of the Lord Almighty, the God of the armies of Israel, whom you have defied. This day the Lord will hand you over to me, and I'll strike you down and cut off your head. Today I will give the carcasses of the Philistine army to the birds of the air and the beasts of the earth, and the whole world will know that there is a God in Israel." (1 Samuel 17:45-46)

Again, David was fearless and not fearful! David was fighting for the glory of God. He was at the right place, doing the right thing, with the right heart; as a result, he had the favor of God on all that he did. We have to be fearless and courageous. We have to be ready and willing to lay down our lives for the purposes of the Lord. As we do, we will be used greatly by God, like David was. He grew up to be the greatest king Israel ever had. Just because someone starts out as the least likely candidate for a major undertaking doesn't mean God hasn't appointed him or her for the task.

Are you the least likely? If you have the favor of God, get ready—today is your day for total turnaround! God has great feats for you to accomplish for the sake of His kingdom.

A "HEAVENLY" PERSPECTIVE ON SPIRITUAL WARFARE

Fear basically says that you don't think God is going to show up and you don't believe that God is in control. God always shows up when He is invited. And when you invite Him into your situation, you know that He will not only show up, but also that stuff is about to happen! It reminds me of a song by Carmen whose lyrics basically tell the devil that he's about to be "busted up." When God shows up, things happen! He always "busts up" the devil! Say it out loud: "Devil, I'm going to bust you up!" God has given you all power and authority—so exercise that authority. When you allow fear to control you, you are allowing the devil to "bust" you up! But today is your day for total turnaround—you "bust him up"! That's what God always does and greater works than these shall you do—if you believe!

When God is with you, you always come out on top! When God is with you, you know that everything is going to be all right because you and God are always the majority. When God is on your side, you already know the outcome! Little David and God were the majority against Goliath. You don't need a big army when you are serving a BIG God, so fear not!

Isaiah 41:10a says, *"...Do not be dismayed, for I am your God."* When the enemy succeeds at causing us to perceive rejection, we feel dismayed (afraid and discouraged). Fear and discouragement are some of Satan's favorite schemes to use against us. But we know that *"God has not given us a spirit of fear, but of power and of love and of a sound mind"* (2 Timothy 1:7 NKJV). God hasn't given us that spirit of fear; the enemy is the one who has thrown it at us. He's trying to cripple us with fear—fear of rejection, fear of failure, fear of people, fear of the unknown, and so forth. God has given us all power and all authority in the name of Jesus (Matthew 28:18). Let's not throw away our power by receiving a spirit of fear from the pit of hell! Father has given us power to overcome and power to handle everything that comes against us in this life. Jesus says to us, *"I have given you authority to trample on snakes and scorpions and to overcome all the power of the enemy; nothing will harm you"* (Luke 10:19). We are the ones with the power! My friend, never throw away the power Father has given you to any spirit of fear.

Not only do you have power, but you also have love and a sound mind. The enemy likes to mess with your God-given need to give and receive love. If you feel rejected—either actual or perceived—you shy away from giving and receiving love. You and I were created in the very image of God, and God is love (1 John 4:8). You were created to love and be loved. When you are bound up in fear, the enemy isolates you behind the wall of rejection and your needs are left unmet. It's like a car without gas or any other energy source—it's not very productive.

Not only has God given you and me power and love, but He also has made the provision for us to have a sound mind. The devil likes for the sound of his words to echo in your mind on a daily basis: no one loves you, you are all alone, you are different, you don't have any friends, and so forth. But, your heavenly Father has given you a sound mind—a mind that is filled with the truth about you and your situations. Fill your mind daily with God's Word.

Declare What God Says, Not What the Enemy Says

So many times, the root of our fear comes from our own words. What are we declaring over ourselves with our mouths? The enemy works hard to get us to "buy the lies" he throws our way. If we "buy the lie," we begin to declare the words of the enemy over ourselves and our situations. Instead, we should be declaring what God says in His Word.

The enemy whispers such lies as the following: "You are not going to make it." "You are going to die of this sickness." "You won't be able to make it financially." "You should just quit right now." If we aren't careful, we will internalize those lies in our thoughts, voice them with our mouths, and live them out with our actions.

But, God! God always declares victory, health, and blessings over His children, and you need to stay in agreement with Him. When you are in agreement with the Lord, you declare His words. When you are in agreement with the devil, you declare his lying words. With whom are you in agreement today? You may think you are in agreement with God, yet your words, your thoughts, and your actions are in agreement with the enemy. If that's the case, you need a total turnaround!

God not only restores your health, but He also restores everything in your life. God restores all! Fear does not declare God's power to restore. Fear declares the enemy's power to steal. Yes, the enemy comes to steal, kill, and destroy, but Jesus came to give you and me life—life more abundantly (John 10:10). Make sure your declaration is on the right side of the fight. Yes, it is a fight. It's a spiritual battle. But if you stand up and fight, everything is going to be all right. You stand up and fight with your declaration of victory promised in God's Word over every one of your situations.

We should always be declaring God's Word, God's works, and His illustrious acts! The way we live each day should be a declaration of God's goodness and great power. We declare God's works and power with our words, but also with our very lives, and this is the way we cast out the spirit of fear and defeat the devil.

Claim Your Inheritance of Eternal Life

"There is now no condemnation for those who are in Christ Jesus" (Romans 8:1). If you are in Christ, you can be confident that there is no condemnation—Jesus paid the price for your every sin! If you have not yet made that commitment, rest assured that God has secured a place for you in heaven with Him—it's yours for the taking! Add your name to the Lamb's Book of Life today by accepting Jesus Christ as your Lord and Savior. If you didn't do this already, you may use the prayer in Chapter 2. Today is the day of salvation!

#11   Set your sights on heaven.

POINTS TO PONDER

1. We sometimes think that money is our greatest resource. In reality, however, our greatest resource is our time. Explain why this is true and how this truth will affect your perspective on life.

2. When we invest in God's kingdom, we store up treasures that will last for eternity. Why is it so important that our acts of service be done from a pure heart with pure motives and from a heart of obedience to God? (Refer to Matthew 6:1-3.)

3. God likes to use people others don't even consider—people who are at the right place, doing the right thing, with the right heart. Looking at the life of David in First Samuel 17, what do you find particularly encouraging, and how does it help you to prepare for your turnaround?

4. We need to be fearless, not fearful. We are to fear God alone. Explain how declaring what God says and not what the enemy says will deliver you from a spirit of fear.

Meditate on these Scriptures, speak them aloud, and commit them to memory:

> *Do not store up for yourselves treasures on earth, where moth and rust destroy, and where thieves break in and steal. But store up for yourselves treasures in heaven, where moth and rust*

do not destroy, and where thieves do not break in and steal. For where your treasure is, there your heart will be also. (Matthew 6:19-21)

Therefore, my dear brothers, stand firm. Let nothing move you. Always give yourselves fully to the work of the Lord, because you know that your labor in the Lord is not in vain. (1 Corinthians 15:58)

God has not given us a spirit of fear, but of power and of love and of a sound mind. (2 Timothy 1:7 NKJV)

I have given you authority to trample on snakes and scorpions and to overcome all the power of the enemy; nothing will harm you. (Luke 10:19)

Chapter 12

TOTAL TURNAROUND IN EVERY AREA

God wants to give you a total turnaround in every area of your life, especially in the areas where you are struggling the most. Some people have an easier time trusting God to bring a turnaround in certain areas than in others. As I mentioned before, it's usually more difficult for men than women to believe in God for a miraculous turnaround in their finances. I believe that the reason is rooted in the God-given nature of men to be the provider for their families; many men mistake themselves for their source of provision. Women, on the other hand, tend to find it a challenge to trust God for turnaround in the area of emotions. And I believe that just about everybody struggles to find faith for a turnaround in the area of their health, especially if their bodies are wracked with throbbing pain.

Whatever your area of greatest challenge or deepest need, identify it, hand it over to God in prayer, and allow Him to build expectation in your heart because He truly wants to bring a turnaround in that area. He is the God who says, *"See, I am doing a new thing! Now it springs up; do you not perceive it? I am making a way in the desert and streams in the wasteland"* (Isaiah 43:19), and *"I am making everything new!"* (Revelation 21:5). Get ready—a new day is dawning!

And the key to seizing the new day, whatever the area in which you need turnaround, is a righteous life submitted to God, being ready to answer when He calls, and staying committed to setting a standard in the world.

THE SEASON OF "GET READY"

I love the book of Joshua. I have read it many times. However, I recently read it and, as God is so faithful to do, He showed me fresh new revelation. He spoke to my heart as I read it and He said, "'Get ready' is a season."

> After the death of Moses the servant of the Lord, the Lord said to Joshua son of Nun, Moses' aide: "Moses my servant is dead. Now then, you and all these people, get ready to cross the Jordan River into the land I am about to give to them—to the Israel-ites." (Joshua 1:1-2)

The Lord was not only telling Joshua to do the single action of "getting ready"; God also was outlining for him and the people, step by step, the process or season that they were in. So many times, when we come up against the season of "get ready," we think it's going to last a day or two. Often the season of "get ready" is a lot longer than we ever anticipated. Joseph was in the season of "get ready" a lot longer than he ever anticipated. He had the dream and got excited and started telling everyone. That didn't actually go over so well. As a matter of fact, that landed him in the bottom of the well—an empty well, at that! Yet, God used that empty well as a part of Joseph's season of "get ready."

Our little dog, Miracle (Mimi for short), is always ready to go. She also knows English. Well, she knows at least the word *go*. As soon as my daughter or I say *go*, Mimi runs downstairs and sits by the door leading to the garage. She understands better than my teenage daughter, who takes forever to get ready when I say "Let's go." But not Mimi!

Most of us are like Mimi. When God says "Get ready," we go stand by the door, waiting for Him to open it. We think the open door He spoke to us about will be swung wide open at any minute. So, we just want to sit and wait. Most of the time, when God says "Get ready," it's the beginning of a new season—the season of "get ready."

In the season of "get ready," it's often tempting to think that God has forgotten about us. We may begin to feel abandoned or overlooked. Yet, the opposite is true. We have been chosen by God, not neglected. That's why He's getting us ready! In the season of "get ready," we are about to experience total turnaround as we climb to the next level.

We may begin to feel forgotten, overlooked, and just plain discouraged when God doesn't open the door immediately. After all, He told us to get ready, so we tend to think that we should go sit by the door to indicate our readiness. In reality, the Lord knows that we are ready only after we have successfully passed through the season of "get ready." In other words, it's a process.

Don't lose sight of the fact that you are in a season of "get ready." Otherwise, you won't hang in there through the entire process. If you don't go through the process, you won't be ready when your "suddenly"—your sudden promotion, your sudden arrival, your sudden turnaround—arrives. Suddenly, you will be called out of the season of "get ready" and called into the new land, the new level, new season of promotion. God is always more interested in who you are as a person when you get to your new level than He is about the new level itself. You and I, on the other hand, tend to be far more interested in forging ahead and getting to where we are going. You and I forget that we must be dressed and ready, first and foremost. If we aren't first clothed in the character of Christ, we won't be able to handle the pressures and responsibilities of the new season once we get there.

Don't buy the lie that God has forgotten you or overlooked you. Just submit to the season of "get ready," for you are about to step into your total turnaround!

[The Lord said to Joshua,] *"I will give you every place where you set your foot, as I promised Moses. Your territory will extend from the desert to Lebanon, and from the great river, the Euphrates—all the Hittite country—to the Great Sea on the west. No one will be able to stand up against you all the days of your life. As I was with Moses, so I will be with you; I will never leave you nor forsake you. Be strong and courageous, because you will lead these people to inherit the land I swore to their forefathers to give them."* (Joshua 1:3-6)

God did not suggest but rather commanded Joshua to get the people ready, and then He showed him exactly what they were getting ready for. God said that their land would be extensive! In other words, God was preparing them for big stuff. All too often, our vision is too limited, our goals too small. If our goals don't sound impossible for us to accomplish, chances are we haven't made them big enough.

In the season of "get ready," God was expanding their vision and showing them details of His goals for them. God's vision for you will always bring you out of your comfort zone and into your potential zone. His vision and purpose for you will always be so big—so "impossible"—that you could never achieve them in your own strength. That's actually all a part of the preparation process—getting you to become totally dependent on the Lord. Because, without Him, you will never be able to reach your God-given goals. Don't just sit around thinking about your goals today; get in the presence of God and allow Him to birth His goals in your heart.

I was just finishing graduate school at the ripe old age of twenty-four when God told me that my ministry would involve television broadcasts and as well as books that I would author. In my natural mind, I never would have imagined myself doing either of those things. If I hadn't received my goals from God by faith that day, I might not be writing now. When the land God has given you to possess looks impossible, that's your first clue that it must be a God thing!

Just in the past couple of years, God has given me additional goals upon my completion of His earlier ones. The things God has told me I would do are so big that I'm just harboring them in my heart as Mary did in the Bible. But, I know from experience, God is able to cause us to accomplish anything that He has called us to! He has always done it in the past, and He will continue to do it if we don't quit in the season of "get ready"!

YOU ARE GOING FORWARD, NOT BACKWARD

Have you ever felt that you have been taking two steps forward and one step back? Well, even if you are, let me give you a reminder—you are still going forward! But, more often than not, when you feel that way, you are simply enrolled in the class of "get ready." Even when Satan tries to throw obstacles and hardships your way, God promises to bring you through victoriously. What Satan means for evil, God will work for good (Genesis 50:20), if you keep your heart right, if you are distraction-proof, and if you remain focused forward.

God will make sure that your turnaround arrives in His perfect timing, no matter what obstacles you may encounter. In the midst of my writing this book, I have had to walk through several challenging things, including the death of my brother and the injuries I sustained in an automobile accident.

I had planned to dedicate this book to my brother long before he was diagnosed with cancer. And then, I had written the section about David's miracle healing long before he was diagnosed the second time. Does that mean that David didn't receive his miracle? Of course not. David received his miracle the first time, and everyone knew it was the hand of God. When David was later diagnosed again with the cancer that took his life, he still received his miracle turnaround, although it didn't occur in the way that we had hoped. We had hoped that his miracle healing would take place here on earth, just like his first healing had, but God saw fit to heal him in heaven. All healing comes in the presence of the Lord, and both of David's miracles confirmed this truth, even though they occurred in different places.

When I had only a few more chapters to write in order to finish this book, I was stopped at a traffic light when someone rear-ended me going forty miles per hour. I suffered my first concussion, as well as injuries to my neck and back. Although this event delayed the completion of the book, I knew in my heart and in my spirit that God was still working out His awesome plan behind the scenes. Was it God's will for that lady to run into me that day? Of course not. Yet, God always works things out for our good! Even the most challenging of circumstances can be used by God to supernaturally thrust us forward into His purposes for us, as long as we don't drop out of His preparation process during the season of "get ready."

God showed me in more ways than one how He would use that car accident to fully prepare me for the next season that I was about to cross over into. I know I'm going to lead people into their Promised Land more than ever in the years ahead. I now have compassion more than ever for people who suffer from car accidents and families who go through battles with cancer. I have learned to be strong and courageous like never before. At the same time, I've learned how to rest when I need to rest and grieve when I need to grieve. All of this will serve me well as I lead other people into the promises of God for their lives.

Again, Joshua 1:6 says, *"Be strong and courageous, because you will lead these people to inherit the land I swore to their forefathers to give them."* Many people whom I'm called to lead have no idea how to possess the land that God wants to give them. Some of the people God has called me to lead don't even want to be led because they aren't yet saved! Yet, God doesn't allow anything to go to waste. He takes everything—the good and the bad—and works it for the good of those who love Him and who refuse to drop out of the class called "get ready."

Sometimes, we are forced to take classes that we don't really enjoy. These are the classes we ought to pass the first time through because we need to complete every prerequisite before we ascend to the next level, and it's no fun retaking a class we don't enjoy! God will bring our total turn-around if we remain focused forward and keep pressing into Him.

Be Strong and Courageous

Joshua 1:7 says, *"Be strong and very courageous. Be careful to obey all the law my servant Moses gave you; do not turn from it to the right or to the left, that you may be successful wherever you go."* They were to get ready, first and foremost, by being strong and courageous. This was such an important part of their preparation in the season of "get ready" that the Lord repeated it multiple times! When God repeats Himself, He does so for a reason. He's trying to get the point across, loud and clear! God was emphasizing this part of "get ready" more than any other requirement.

In the dictionary, *strong* is defined as "physically powerful;...morally powerful; having strength of character or will; intellectually powerful; able to think vigorously and clearly;...powerfully made, built...tough; firm; durable;...able to resist and endure attack." Part of the process of getting ready is to develop strength of character. Character counts the most! You may have all of the gifts and talents in the world, but if you lack character, you will never be ready for the total turnaround that is necessary to bring you to the next level.

I love the definition "able to resist and endure attack." Yes, we are engaged in spiritual warfare, and we must be able to resist the enemy's attacks and endure his onslaughts as we rely on our strength in the Lord. During the season of "get ready," the Lord is preparing us to cross over. If we can't handle the warfare in the season of "get ready," we won't last long once we have crossed over. The warfare at the new level and new season will be even greater.

The dictionary defines *courage* as "the attitude of facing and deal-ing with anything recognized as dangerous, difficult, or painful, instead of withdrawing from it; quality of being fearless or brave." When faced with difficult situations and challenging circumstances, many of us would rather withdraw. We'd rather retreat. But, when we have the Holy Spirit dwelling within us, we can be powerful and courageous as we face our enemy head-on. We can rely on God's strength, not our own limited abilities, to get us through. Again, this is a vital part of our preparation during the season of "get ready."

When you come into the Promised Land, once you experience your total turnaround and end up at the next level, you have to be distraction-proof and rejection-proof like never before. You can't shrink back; you must stand up and fight!

Don't Be Afraid or Discouraged

It's never wrong to feel afraid, unless we allow our fear to steer us off course. We should always be led by the Holy Spirit rather than by fear and discouragement.

Joshua 1:9 says, *"Have I not commanded you? Be strong and courageous. Do not be terrified; do not be discouraged, for the Lord your God will be with you wherever you go."* If you allow yourself to be terrified or afraid, you won't go forward and possess the land when God says move! You can't afford to fear failure; you can't afford to fear rejection; you can't afford to fear man. You must only fear God if you are going to experience total turnaround in every area of your life and possess all of God's promises for you.

Discourage is defined as "to deprive of courage, hope, or confidence;… to prevent or try to prevent by…raising…obstacles." The enemy doesn't want you to be confident, and he definitely doesn't want you to be confident in the Lord—in what God can do in you and through you. When the enemy succeeds at stealing your confidence, you feel hopeless. When you feel hopeless, you lose your confidence. It's a vicious cycle. When the enemy throws obstacles or distractions your way, it's an attempt to distract and discourage you. When you are distracted from your purpose and place in God, you become easily discouraged. But, when you are right where you are supposed to be, doing what you are supposed to be doing, you are so satisfied.

Get your supplies ready—you are about to cross over into your total turnaround!

> *So Joshua ordered the officers of the people: "Go through the camp and tell the people, 'Get your supplies ready. Three days from now you will cross the Jordan here to go in and take possession of the land the Lord your God is giving you for your own.'"* (Joshua 1:10-11)

In the season of "get ready," you must store up your supplies. You will need a supply of the Word after you have crossed over. Stock up on the Word, supersize your faith, and get an abundant supply of His presence!

Separate and Consecrate Yourself

> *Joshua told the people, "Consecrate yourselves, for tomorrow the Lord will do amazing things among you."* (Joshua 3:5)

The final and most important instruction of the season of "get ready" is to consecrate yourself. To *consecrate* means "to set apart as holy; make or declare sacred for religious use;…dedicate."

God takes holiness very seriously, and you and I need to, as well. Holiness wasn't just for people in the "olden days." Do you remember when you were a child and you referred to the "olden days" as the time when your grandparents were growing up? I do! And now, every now and then, when my daughter is feeling brave, she will refer to the "olden days" as the time when I was growing up. I quickly correct her and remind her how young I am!

No matter if you are three or ninety-three, God wants you to live a holy life—holiness never goes out of style! Young people (including me—because I'm young, remember?) like to dress stylishly. That's great, but let's keep it holy. All body parts must be covered, and God must be glorified through your appearance. Modest is always the hottest! Beauty comes from the inside out, and when you live a holy life, you glow with the glory and presence of the Lord!

Again, Joshua told the people, *"Consecrate yourselves."* In other words, nobody else could do it for them. No one can *make* you live a holy life, separated unto the Lord. The choice is up to you. And I want to encourage you that you will be glad you made the choice. When you consecrate yourself in the things of the Lord, you separate from the things of the world. When you feed your spirit the Word and the presence of the Lord—when you fast from natural food and feed your spirit instead, through worship, prayer, and Bible study—you are growing stronger in your spirit. Whatever appetite is the strongest in your life ends up being the one that leads the way and directs your course. When you are led by the Holy Spirit as a result of being separated from the world and what it has to offer, and when you are consecrated in God, you will discern His voice and then walk in His ways. That's the path to a blessed life of success and fulfillment!

Joshua 3:5 states that *"tomorrow"* the Lord will do amazing things. In other words, your time is approaching. Your time is drawing near. Your total turnaround—your new day, your new level, your new season—is just ahead, so finish your preparations, and finish them quickly. You don't want to be found unready when God says it's your time. If it's your time to graduate, yet you haven't fulfilled every requirement, you'll have to retake the classes and you'll miss the commencement ceremony.

Don't wait—consecrate yourself today! God wants to show up and show off in your life, but you must be ready—you are about to step into the biggest total turnaround that you could ever imagine.

Joshua says, *"The Lord will do amazing things among you."* I love it! The glory of God is going to fall in our midst—it's a corporate thing. God is about to do amazing things *among* us in the body of Christ. I believe we are going to see more miracles than ever before *among* us. The miraculous power of God will be displayed in our worship services, but also at the gas station, in the grocery stores, in the airport, and so forth. God is going to show up and show off like never before! So, get ready and consecrate yourself. The world and the church are both desperate for the healing, the power, and the presence of the Lord.

God wants your life to be a platform for His glory. That's the reason for every turnaround He brings about. As you consecrate yourself in His presence and submit to His planning, He will transform your life into a platform for His glory. The whole world is watching because they need a miracle turnaround, too—they just don't have any idea how to get it until you and I show them the way through our life examples!

DISCIPLINE THAT LEADS TO HOLINESS

We need to discipline our flesh so that we are led by our spirit, submitted to the Holy Spirit. We discipline our flesh through fasting and other practices. When we refuse to give in to the dictates of our flesh, and when we refuse to give it what it wants, when it wants it, we become disciplined and walk in holiness, which paves the way for turnaround in every area.

The Bible says that when our flesh is tempted, God will always give us a way out of that temptation (1 Corinthians 10:13). He will never put on us more than we can bear. And, by the way, God is not the one who tempts our flesh; the devil is the one who does the tempting. But when we take the path out of that temptation by saying no to the temptation and yes to God's best, we become stronger and stronger.

> Therefore, since we are surrounded by such a great cloud of witnesses, let us throw off everything that hinders and the sin that so easily entangles, and let us run with perseverance the race marked out for us. Let us fix our eyes on Jesus, the author and perfecter of our faith, who for the joy set before him endured the cross, scorning its shame, and sat down at the right hand of the throne of God. Consider him who endured such opposition from sinful men, so that you will not grow weary and lose heart. (Hebrews 12:1-3)

If something hinders your walk with the Lord, get rid of it—throw it off! I remember to this day a principle that my first pastor taught me as a new Christian: "When in doubt, do without!" I live by that principle to this very day. If I'm not sure if something is right, I don't even get close. If I don't have total peace, I don't make a decision. Whenever I have doubt, I do without. I would rather have Jesus and His peace and presence than anything else!

As we run with perseverance and ignore all interference, our lives can be a platform for the glory of God. As we fix our eyes on Jesus and continually focus forward, we can enjoy all the covenant benefits that come from living a holy life. Again, holiness never goes out of style! We can fulfill Hebrews 12:14: *"Make every effort to live in peace with all men and to be holy; without holiness no one will see the Lord."*

SPEAK TURNAROUND INTO THE LIVES OF OTHERS

We need to be bold as we live the truth and as we speak truth in love to others (Ephesians 4:15). Real friends don't attend our pity parties; they speak the truth to us in love.

The entire third chapter of Ezekiel talks about this very thing—boldly declaring the truth—and that's real love. I recommend that you read the chapter in its entirety. For now, we'll focus on just a few verses.

> [The Lord said to Ezekiel,] *"But the house of Israel is not willing to listen to you because they are not willing to listen to me, for the whole house of Israel is hardened and obstinate. But I will make you as unyielding and hardened as they are. I will make your forehead like the hardest stone, harder than flint. Do not be afraid of them or terrified by them, though they are a rebellious house." And he said..., "Son of man, listen carefully and take to heart all the words I speak to you. Go now to your countrymen in exile and speak to them. Say to them, 'This is*

what the Sovereign Lord says,' whether they listen or fail to listen." (Ezekiel 3:7-11)

This passage and the entire chapter shook me as the Lord gave me revelation like I have never had before. Bottom line, God was saying it's our responsibility to speak the truth to people. It's our responsibility to give them the "word" of the Lord. And then, if they don't listen to us, we are not to be shaken or surprised. God basically said, "If they are not willing to listen to you, don't worry, because they aren't even willing to listen to Me!" Nevertheless, we must do our part—boldly speak the truth in love and give them the opportunity to respond to the word of the Lord. Their reaction is not our responsibility, but we must obey God in speaking the truth, *"whether they listen or fail to listen."*

Later on in Ezekiel, it says that if we don't speak up and declare truth to people when God tells us to, He will hold us accountable for their very lives (verse 18). The day God shook me with this Scripture, He also showed me a couple of people right around me whose lives I needed to speak into. He went on to say that if I didn't warn them of their sin, their blood would be on my hands! That's strong, but that's the truth!

> [God said,] *"Son of man, I have made you a watchman for the house of Israel; so hear the word I speak and give them warning from me. When I say to a wicked man, 'You will surely die,' and you do not warn him or speak out to dissuade him from his evil ways in order to save his life, that wicked man will die for his sin, and I will hold you accountable for his blood. But if you do warn the wicked man and he does not turn from his wickedness or from his evil ways, he will die for his sin; but you will have saved yourself."* (Ezekiel 3:17-19)

God needs you and me to be His watchmen on the wall like never before! If we are too focused on our own problems and on the areas in our lives where we need a turnaround, we will lose sight of our responsibility to speak the word of the Lord into the lives of others. If we don't speak up, for whatever reason—fear, busyness, laziness, and so forth—their blood will be on our hands. In other words, God will hold us accountable.

When the Lord took me to this passage and showed me a couple of people to whom I needed to speak a word from Him, I was afraid of how they would respond, and I plain didn't feel like doing it. Yet, I knew that I needed to "take captive" all of these feelings and thoughts that threatened to prevent me from walking in obedience to the Lord.

After God showed me who I was supposed to talk to and what I was supposed to tell them, I prayed for God to show me His perfect timing and asked Him to prepare their hearts for my phone call. As I made my first phone call, to a middle-aged man who was living with a beautiful young lady to whom he was not married, I was very nervous. It was the same feeling I had during my early days of preaching—a sort of sick feeling in my stomach, similar to the way it feels when you're standing on a high dive, looking down at the water. Yet, I learned long ago that the best thing to do is just to go ahead and jump—just start preaching, speaking, or whatever it is that God is directing you to do.

So, that's what I did that day on the phone—I just "jumped"; I opened my mouth and "let it rip" (in love, of course). Much to my surprise, the man thanked me for telling him the truth. I even explained how God had told me that if I wasn't obedient, and if he didn't get his life right with the Lord again, his blood would be on my hands. Again, he thanked me!

I wasn't responsible for the choice that man made after our conversation that day, but I was responsible for walking in obedience to the Lord by delivering His word in love. God has called you, also, to take His message from Ezekiel 3 to those all around you. When you do, lives will be saved, and the Lord will be glorified.

Again, when a righteous man turns from his righteousness and does evil, and I put a stumbling block before him, he will die. Since you did not warn him, he will die for his sin. The

righteous things he did will not be remembered, and I will hold
you accountable for his blood. But if you do warn the righteous
man not to sin and he does not sin, he will surely live because
he took warning, and you will have saved yourself. (Ezekiel
3:20-21)

Our greatest purpose is to fellowship with the Lord and to bring Him
glory with our lives. Speaking the truth in love into the lives of others ful-
fills that purpose perfectly, for we glorify God and populate heaven when
we deliver life-saving messages to those around us. As we are faithful to
speak the truth to those around us, we point out the places where turnaround is needed, and we pave the way for that turnaround to occur.

Just because someone has entered into a saving relationship with Jesus
Christ does not exempt us from the responsibility for speaking into his or
her life. We will be held accountable when we fail to deliver the Lord's
messages faithfully. Our salvation will have fruit in our lives that show
where our heart lies with the Lord. If a righteous man turns from his
righteousness and does evil, he must repent and get back on the right track
with the Lord. Often, it's the word of the Lord that God wants to bring
through you or me that will draw the person who has drifted away from
the Lord back into restored relationship with Him. And there's nothing
more rewarding than growing the population of heaven by winning souls!

SPEAK LIFE TO THOSE DEAD THINGS

The hand of the Lord was upon me, and he brought me out by
the Spirit of the Lord and set me in the middle of a valley; it
was full of bones. He led me back and forth among them, and
I saw a great many bones on the floor of the valley, bones that
were very dry. He asked me, "Son of man, can these bones live?"
I said, "O Sovereign Lord, you alone know." Then he said to
me, "Prophesy to these bones and say to them, 'Dry bones, hear
the word of the Lord! This is what the Sovereign Lord says to

these bones: I will make breath enter you, and you will come to life.'" (Ezekiel 37:1-5)

A part of getting ready for total turnaround in every area of your life is speaking to the "valleys of dry bones" we encounter, as the prophet Ezekiel did. God specializes in reviving dead things, but your mouth is often the avenue in which He wants to declare the restoration of life to those dead areas that desperately need His total turnaround!

It says in Romans 4:17 (NKJV) that God *"gives life to the dead and calls those things which do not exist as though they did."* That doesn't mean that we should be in denial about our situations and circumstances; it means that we should appreciate the power God has given to the words of our mouths.

God has creative power in His words. He said, *"Let there be light,"* and there was light (Genesis 1:3). Since we have been created in the very image of God, we have creative power in our words, as well. God calls things according to how they are in the spirit—done, healed, complete, and victorious—and we should do the same. We should never call things as they are in the natural if it's opposite of the way God wants them. That's faith in action! Remember, faith without works is dead (James 2:26 NKJV). We can even speak to our dead faith and resurrect it, as well!

When God asks you a question, He already knows the answer. He simply wants you to know the answer that's in your heart. There are examples of this throughout the Bible, including in the book of Ezekiel.

God wants you to know that no matter how dead a situation or circumstance (or person) may be, God has the power to resurrect the entire thing! And that same resurrection power that raised Christ from the dead lives in you (Romans 8:11)! Don't sit on your power. Don't stifle the power that's available to you. Use that resurrection power and prophesy life to any and all dry bones, as God commands you to! Your total turnaround, and the total turnaround of others, depends on it!

Ezekiel 37:10 says, *"So I prophesied as he commanded me, and breath entered them; they came to life and stood up on their feet—a vast army."* God is breathing life into His "vast army" with His prophetic word, and He wants to use you and me as His mouthpieces. The body of Christ and the world represent valleys of dry bones, and God wants to breathe new life through you and me in order to bring about their total turnaround. Will you prophesy as the Lord commands you? Do you believe that God can breathe new life and make the dry bones you encounter to live again? Or have you just accepted the "dead" things as they are with no hope of fresh new life?

Don't buy the lie. Open your mouth, let faith arise, and prophesy total turnaround! God is just waiting on you!

RIGHTEOUS LIVING: THE GOLDEN KEY IN EVERY TURNAROUND

The devil hasn't created a thing—he has no creative powers. All he can do is destroy. The best he can do is pull off cheap imitations of what God has created. The devil's imitations are to bait people into buying the lie in an attempt to get them to fall for his "false" version that brings death and destruction.

Everything that God created is good and intended to bring life (righteous living). But, when we fail to seek the Lord—when we rush ahead and make decisions based on our natural minds and desires—we can find ourselves in a real mess, just as Abraham's nephew Lot did. Abraham (earlier called Abram) sought the Lord before his every move, while Lot looked in the natural, saw what he thought "looked good," and made his choice. Not everything that "looks good" is good. Not everything that looks like a "God thing" is. That's why we need to rely on the guidance of the Holy Spirit, not the inclinations of our unholy flesh!

Pursue Righteous Living

> *The Lord said to Abram after Lot had parted from him, "Lift up your eyes from where you are and look north and south, east and west. All the land that you see I will give to you and your offspring forever."* (Genesis 13:14-15)

God showed Abram all that He had for him after he separated from Lot, who represents compromise and the mixture that results from it. When we remain connected with those who are living in mixture, our vision is blurred so that we cannot clearly see all that God has for us. God went on to tell Abram that everything he could see would be his. God can never give us something unless we have already seen it, as we discussed in Chapter 2. If we can see it in the spirit, it can be manifested in the natural for us.

The key is to avoid mixture, which opens the door to deception. When there is mixture in your life, you become deceived. You don't think there is anything wrong with what you are doing. You are deceived into thinking you are doing the right thing or hearing from God correctly, when you really aren't.

Sometimes, we make decisions based on our emotions, our fears, our lust for the things of this world, our anger, and other things that are swayed by the presence of mixture in our lives. When we eliminate the mixture, we are able to hear clearly from God, so that we know which course to take.

Pitch Your Tent on Holy Ground

In Genesis 13:12, Lot pitched his tent near Sodom. Sodom was a very wicked city, filled with sin and compromise. We must always be careful where we pitch our tents. Our tent represents the place we live, where we reside or hang out. Lot pitched his tent and took up residence at a place of mixture, and he didn't even see it clearly.

I can imagine that Lot thought, *Well, I'm not going to live in Sodom. I'm just going to live on the outskirts.* Well, only one chapter later to the very verse, the Word tells us that Lot was no longer living near Sodom. He was living *in* Sodom.

Genesis 14:12 says, *"They also carried off Abram's nephew Lot and his possessions, since he was living in Sodom."* You can never "pitch your tent" near sin and think it won't affect you because it surely will. If you hang out or live near sin, it won't be too long before you, too, are living in sin and mixture. When you expose yourself to mixture, you quickly become inoculated and are prone to be deceived.

God wants to give you a Holy Ghost GPS and recalculate you right out of the pit of sin. Mixture got you in the pit, but the power and direction of the Holy Spirit will get you out, if you allow Him to.

We should never "flirt" with the devil's detours. We should be quick to obey the voice of the Holy Spirit. We "flirt" with detours when we know God has said not to do something or not to go somewhere, yet we keep entertaining the thought in our mind. We try to talk ourselves into it. We begin to think, *Maybe that wasn't God telling me not to do that.* You and I should never "flirt" with a detour from God's ordained path for our life. Detours can be very destructive, and they may take us so far off track that it's difficult to regain our focus on God's will for our lives.

Don't ever buy the lie from the enemy when he says, "This little bit won't hurt. You can do it just this once, and no one will ever know." Satan comes to steal, kill, and destroy (John 10:10). And he plays for keeps!

Proverbs 28:13 says, *"He who conceals his sins does not prosper, but whoever confesses and renounces them finds mercy."* If you are concealing your sin today, and you think no one knows, that's a lie. First and foremost, God knows everything, and He's the one who really counts. The only person who is really being fooled is you, so don't be deceived by the enemy any longer. Get things right with God. Through prayer, confess your sin, repent of it, and ask the Holy Spirit to give you the power to stay on God's course for your life. Then, ask God to give you some Christian friends on fire for God and filled with the Holy Spirit who will encourage you and hold you accountable as you pursue holiness, righteousness, and mixture-free living.

Blessed is the man who does not walk in the counsel of the wicked or stand in the way of sinners or sit in the seat of mockers. But his delight is in the law of the Lord, and on his law he meditates day and night. He is like a tree planted by streams of water, which yields its fruit in season and whose leaf does not wither. Whatever he does prospers. (Psalm 1:1-3)

When you live according to the Word, you will be prosperous in everything you do. A life of holiness and righteousness causes you to be firmly planted, while mixture causes you to fall during times of wind and rain.

Those on the rock are the ones who receive the word with joy when they hear it, but they have no root. They believe for a while, but in the time of testing they fall away. The seed that fell among thorns stands for those who hear, but as they go on their way they are choked by life's worries, riches and pleasures, and they do not mature. (Luke 8:13-14)

Make it your goal to grow every day in the Word of God and in righteousness. When you have righteousness in your root system, you won't fall away when the storms of life blow your way.

Don't Live in Mixture; Expose It

God wants us to live a life of righteousness and holiness. Righteousness is simply doing the right thing. We live out righteousness in our relationships with people and we live out holiness in our relationship with the Lord. As we live a life of holiness and righteousness, those around us who are living in mixture, steeped in sin and compromise, will be convicted by our example.

I can usually tell when a close friend or family member is not living right because that person will avoid me. He or she will go out of his or her way not to be around me. When people aren't living right, they may attack you verbally and accuse you of judging them. Meanwhile, the reality is that they are being convicted by the presence of God in your life. I have also known born-again believers who were living in sin and who replied, when confronted about the mixture in their lives, "That's not holiness; that's bondage. Don't condemn me."

Holy, righteous living is hardly living in bondage. It's actually true freedom! And true freedom is to be enjoyed only by those who have been freed from bondage to sin.

> *Have nothing to do with the fruitless deeds of darkness, but rather expose them. For it is shameful even to mention what the disobedient do in secret. But everything exposed by the light becomes visible, for it is light that makes everything visible. This is why it is said: "Wake up, O sleeper, rise from the dead, and Christ will shine on you."* (Ephesians 5:11-14)

God wants your lifestyle to expose the evil deeds of darkness. Sometimes, you don't even have to say a word. Your lifestyle, and the presence of the Lord in you, does all the talking.

A Kingdom Divided

Many churches and ministries today are divided in that they are entertaining righteous and unrighteous leadership. Often, the ministry leader doesn't even know that mixture is represented in some of those in leadership. The book of Esther gives us an example of the divided kingdom.

The king did not even realize that there was mixture in his palace. Esther, representing righteousness, rose to power only a few verses before the rise of Haman, who brought mixture and sin into the government. Even as mixture and Haman were in the kingdom, righteousness through Esther was victorious over it. Esther was called "for such a time as this" (Esther 4:14), to expose mixture in the kingdom and be a voice of righteousness. The same is true of you today. You are called for such a time as this, to be a voice of righteousness for the kingdom of God, to expose mixture for what it is, and to be a catalyst of turnaround in the lives of those around you.

Matthew 10:26b says, *"There is nothing concealed that will not be disclosed, or hidden that will not be made known."* God is exposing mixture today, as part of His plan to bring total turnaround to His body, the church. He is calling for those who will set an example of righteous living and bring a total turnaround in their families, their churches, their communities, their nations, and the world. Once you have experienced turnaround in your life and are walking in the righteousness of God, He can use you to bring turnaround in the lives of others. That's why righteousness is a golden key for every type of turnaround!

THE GOD OF HOPE

What do you do when your turnaround doesn't happen at the time you had hoped? What do you do when your turnaround doesn't happen the way you had hoped? You keep on trusting in the Lord and hanging on to the God of your hope. After all, He *is* your hope.

Romans 15:13 says, *"May the God of hope fill you with all joy and peace as you trust in him, so that you may overflow with hope by the power of the Holy Spirit."* Keep trusting in the Lord. Keep your hope alive. God always works all things together for your good. Don't quit now; your turnaround is closer than ever before! Allow God's joy and peace to fill you. The joy of the Lord is your strength—don't cut yourself off from your strength source!

Keep on expecting. Keep on hoping. Guard your peace and guard your joy, for you are about to step into your total turnaround. Just stay focused forward, and you will possess all of God's promises as you undergo the turnaround He has for you.

#12 | Lead a righteous life.

POINTS TO PONDER

1. Identify your area of greatest challenge or deepest need and then hand it over to the Lord in prayer. As He builds expectation in your heart, trust Him to bring a turnaround in that area.

2. In Joshua's season of "get ready," God commanded him to be strong and courageous and not to be afraid or discouraged. Explain why this was such an important part of his preparation in the season of "get ready." Think about how this preparation applies to your life, as well.

3. We need to discipline our flesh through fasting and other practices. How does this lead to holiness in our lives? What in your life is hindering your walk with the Lord? Are you ready to get rid of it?

4. Are you are still waiting for your turnaround? Or has it already come, just not in the way you imagined it would? How will you stay encouraged to keep on hoping in God?

Meditate on these Scriptures, speak them aloud, and commit them to memory:

> *Be strong and very courageous. Be careful to obey all the law my servant Moses gave you; do not turn from it to the right or*

to the left, that you may be successful wherever you go. (Joshua 1:7)

No temptation has seized you except what is common to man. And God is faithful; he will not let you be tempted beyond what you can bear. But when you are tempted, he will also provide a way out so that you can stand up under it. (1 Corinthians 10:13)

Make every effort to live in peace with all men and to be holy; without holiness no one will see the Lord. (Hebrews 12:14)

May the God of hope fill you with all joy and peace as you trust in him, so that you may overflow with hope by the power of the Holy Spirit. (Romans 15:13)

About Danette Crawford

Danette Crawford is also the acclaimed author of *Don't Quit in the Pit*, which encourages readers of God's power to turn their situations around. Her second release, *Pathway to the Palace*, takes readers on a journey through the lives of Esther and Joseph, telling them how to become the person of influence that God has called them to be. Her internationally known book, *God, You've Got Mail*, is about financial turnaround in the lives of God's people! Danette Crawford is not only a phenomenal author but also a powerful speaker and TV host. She has been featured on ABC, CBS, NBC, The 700 Club, Living the Life, TBN, 100 Huntley Street, and many other networks, as well as in numerous newspapers and magazines. For more information on speaking engagements contact Danette Crawford at:

www.JoyMinistries.tv
Joy@JoyMinistriesOnline.org
P.O. Box 65036
Virginia Beach, VA 23467
(757) 420-2625

OTHER BOOKS BY DANETTE CRAWFORD

Don't Quit in the Pit

Pathway to the Palace

God, You've Got Mail